D1112872

Army Uniforms
of World War 2

Andrew Mollo

Army Uniforms
of World War 2

BLANDFORD PRESS

Poole   Dorset

First published in the U.K. 1973
Reprinted 1974
This edition published 1981
Copyright © 1973 Blandford Press Ltd,
Link House, West Street,
Poole, Dorset BH15 1LL

ISBN 0 7137 1189 2

Printed in Hong Kong
by South China Printing Co.

CONTENTS

ACKNOWLEDGEMENTS

Malcolm McGregor and I, while accepting full responsibility for the accuracy of the text and illustrations, would like to express our gratitude to all the people whose specialised knowledge and co-operation was placed at our disposal, and in particular to the following:

Messrs Laurie Milner and M. J. Willis of the exhibits department, and David Nash of the Library, Imperial War Museum; Thor Brynhildsen of the Haermuseet, Oslo; P. H. Buss, B.A. (Hons); Brian L. Davis; Colonel C. M. Dodkins C.B.E., D.S.O., Retd; Colonel C. Liang; M. Lukich, Captain W. Milewski and K. Barbarski of the Polish Institute and Sikorski Museum, London,; F. Ollenschläger; G. Rosignoli; J. Rowntree; J. Shorne, Government Surplus Specialists, Harrow, London; Major E. Silvo, Finnish Embassy, London; H. Woodend of the Royal Small Arms Factory, Enfield Lock; B. Mollo of the National Army Museum and J. Mollo.

Andrew Mollo
Malcolm McGregor

PREFACE

Malcolm McGregor and I have set out to illustrate and describe the field uniforms of twenty-four nations who fought in World War 2. Each major campaign has been covered chronologically and illustrated by a commander, officer and soldier of the opposing forces in typical clothing and equipment.

It has not been possible to include every country and if we offend national susceptibilities by the omission or slight coverage of any we apologise, for it was not our intention. We have tended also to give preference to the smaller independent armies, each of which had completely different traditions and uniforms, rather than show endless variations on the battle dress theme which was so prevalent in British, colonial and dominion troops. This equally applies to the colonial armies of the other European nations. The Far Eastern theatre has also received less attention because of its complexity. In the 14th Army in Burma 118 different languages and dialects were spoken, and each of those peoples wore their own distinctive dress or badge.

This volume deals specifically with army uniforms; naval, marine and air force uniforms are covered in a companion volume. For this reason we have not included air force or naval units in this work even if they fought on land. One exception has been German parachute troops, who inconveniently transferred from the army to the air force before the war. Germany was the only country to place its airborne forces under air force command, so it would be illogical to exclude them. The same reasoning in reverse lies behind the omission of the Soviet Russian and American air forces which were not independent arms but a branch of the army. Auxiliary and paramilitary forces such as resistance movements, partisans, police and anti-partisan formations have been included although technically they were not part of the armed forces.

A.M.

INTRODUCTION

The end of World War I saw the emergence of many independent states as the vanquished monarchies found themselves in the throes of major social and political upheaval.

The greatest territorial changes had taken place in Eastern Europe, where Russia, defeated and in the midst of civil war, was being stripped of its empire. The republics to emerge from former Russian territory were Poland, Estonia, Latvia, Lithuania and Finland. The republics of Czechoslovakia and Hungary were established in countries formerly part of the Austro-Hungarian Hapsburg empire. The Kingdom of Yugoslavia unified Serbs, Montenegrins, Bosnians, Slovenes and Macedonians under a Serbian monarch. Rumania and Bulgaria retained their dynasties.

While the victors demobilised and tried to convince themselves that the 'great' war had been the war to end all wars, the newly independent nations set about building armies, to ensure their independence. The cadre for these new armies had spent much of their life in the service of the Austrian Emperor or Russian Tsar, and were happy to continue in this tradition. But for nationalistic and political reasons a complete break with the past was called for, and attempts were made to create 'new' armies with new uniforms, which would mirror the political aspirations of the country.

It was natural that it should be to the victorious nations that these emerging armies looked for advice and equipment, and most turned to France. Politically and culturally France had influenced Eastern Europe to such an extent that in some countries French had become a second language. In the 1920s France could claim to have invented military science as it was then known, and her victory over Germany had confirmed the prestige of her arms.

While France provided the model for soldiers' uniforms, and Belgian, Italian, Polish, Rumanian, Soviet and Yugoslav armies wore the French 'Adrian' steel helmet, England set the trend for officers. The English popularised the shirt-and-tie uniform, the long-skirted tunic with huge patch pockets and the flat-topped and horizontal-peaked service cap. So closely did Belgian, Greek and Rumanian officers copy this style of dress that it is often difficult to tell them all apart. The English steel helmet was worn by the armies of Greece, Norway, Portugal and the United States of America.

The Red Army also had reasons to make a break with tradition and, after a determined effort to go French in the 1920s, reverted step by step to its traditional uniforms. Not one of the former Russian territories adopted Russian-style uniforms. Poland developed its own distinctive uniforms and re-introduced many traditional features such as the *czapka* and zigzag lace which were so reminiscent of the Napoleonic wars.

The countries which had formed part of the Austro-Hungarian Empire such as Czechoslovakia dressed their armies in khaki with an English-style peaked cap for officers and a rather Germanic uniform for other ranks. Hungarian uniform continued in the Austrian tradition. By the outbreak of war military uniform can be divided into the following distinct groups. The Anglo-Saxon countries together with their colonies and dominions were developing 'colonial' uniforms which had been developed for unconventional warfare in varied climates. European uniform was more conventional and on the whole followed the French lead, with certain concessions to English fashion. Russia continued its own line of development. In the Far East both Japan and China had adapted European uniform to suit their own industrial capabilities and climatic conditions.

Soon after the beginning of the war many of the smaller armies had been swept from the board, and military uniform polarised around England, Germany, Soviet Russia and Japan. The personnel of the defeated armies who managed to escape to England or the Middle East were issued with British uniforms and equipment. They attempted all the same to preserve their national identity by wearing as much of their old insignia on battle dress as they could, and designing new formation flashes to conform with British practice. Once America entered the war she took some of the strain off England's over-stretched resources by supplying the largest exile force, the Free French, with U.S. clothing and equipment.

In the east, Germany's satellites, unprepared and ill-equipped for a long drawn out war of attrition, came to rely more and more on German *matériel*. This inevitably led to an increased German influence in the appearance of Hungarian, Rumanian and Slovakian troops and even of the 'Tsarist' Bulgarians.

Russia was completely oblivious to new trends in modern military clothing and equipment, partly because of her limited industrial capacity, but partly also because she had found by experience that traditional Russian peasant-style uniform and the most rudimentary equipment was not only the cheapest, but also the most practical, for the climate and conditions in which the army had to fight.

Soviet Russia also equipped exiled Polish, Czech and Yugoslav formations with Soviet uniforms.

To this day the basic Soviet uniform is a greatcoat, shirt, breeches and high leather boots, and any recent departure has been brought about by Russia's new stance as a power capable of mounting airborne and amphibious operations anywhere in the world.

There is no doubt that at the beginning of the war Germany led in the field of uniform technology, and had pioneered a number of special uniforms which were to provide models for other nations. But once war was declared she contributed little to the development of new clothing or manufacturing techniques. Any innovations she did introduce in the field of synthetic textiles were due primarily to her deteriorating raw material situation.

The concept of one basic uniform which was both practical in the field and smart enough to enhance morale and wear as a full dress or for walking out, lasted until the advent of mechanisation. Mechanisation was to start a trend which began with the mechanic's overall, and ended with two distinct types of uniform – combat dress and service dress – neither of which had anything in common. The overall was an absolute necessity for any soldier forced to work with large pieces of oily machinery such as tanks. In fact all the armies who participated in World War 2 introduced either one- or two-piece overalls for their tank crews. Germany designed a special black tank uniform in 1935, but also began to issue overalls during the war for economy reasons. The gap widened with the advent of airborne troops who had to be supplied with special clothing which could hardly be worn off duty. Once again Russia, the first to experiment effectively with parachute troops, turned to the overall. The Germans were quick to realise the importance of this new arm, and tried out a complete dress which could be safely worn during a fall, and in action on the ground. This included a special rimless steel helmet, a smock to wear over the personal equipment during the jump, trousers and special boots with rubber soles. After Germany's successful airborne operations at the beginning of the war, England formed her own parachute troops, and dressed them in a copy of the German uniform. America also at first issued its parachutists with a flying helmet, overall and lace-up ankle boots, but by the time she committed them to action she had modified the normal combat uniform, but unlike the British and Germans, the Americans found that the smock which covered the equipment for the jump was not necessary and even delayed the combat readiness of a paratrooper on landing. Instead every item of equipment which could possibly get entangled with the parachute lines was strapped carefully to the body with lengths of webbing strap.

Both airborne and armoured troops considered themselves an élite and tended to wear their special clothing off duty. In the German army the black tank uniform was issued in addition to the field-grey clothing, for wear when on duty with the vehicle, but was so proudly worn on all occasions that the second set of field-grey clothing was no longer issued during the war.

England's great contribution to world uniform was the development of the colour khaki, and the 'battle dress' which she first introduced in 1937. Few people seem to have anything good to say about 'B.D.', and it was very difficult to look smart in it, and yet it so impressed the Americans that they began to issue it in 1944. In the same year Germany copied it because of its simplicity of manufacture and economic use of cloth. After the war British battle dress was adopted by many countries, and although discarded by the English and Americans, is still in extensive use in other armies.

America was the first to begin to separate the service and field uniforms by introducing a field jacket in 1941. In 1943 after extensive trials, she revolutionised the design of combat clothing with the introduction of a lightweight weatherproof uniform, which could be adapted to varying climatic conditions by the addition of layers of various kinds of undergarments. This layer principle is today utilised throughout the world.

NOMENCLATURE

Although this book would have been much easier to write in French or German, I have tried to be consistent and apply only correct British military usage. The English language is very rich, but it has never been systematically applied to matters of military uniform. The reason is that military dress in England has never been very disciplined but often subject to the whims and fancies of regimental colonels. There is not even a word in English for the study of uniform, such as the German *Uniformenkunde*. The Germans tended to go to the other extreme, but the words they invented or adopted from the French make the study of a precise subject much easier. A useful German word is *Waffenfarben*, which can only be translated into English as 'arm colour'. One cannot use 'arm badge' to describe a badge that identifies the arm of the wearer because it conflicts with a badge worn on the arm, so one is forced to use the three-word compound 'arm-of-service'.

Most countries used colours to identify different arms, and when a further distinction was required, say between two types of artillery, a second colour, usually in the form of a piping, was added to the first. Inevitably a simple system was elaborated to such an extent that it was almost impossible for a soldier to remember them all. The Russians had the word *Pribor* and the Germans *Knopffarbe* to describe the colour (usually gold, silver or bronze) of the buttons, metal fittings, lace and embroidery on a uniform, which in most European armies was consistent. I have used the term 'button colour' for the same purpose.

Throughout I refer to lace as being flat and woven in metallic or silk thread, as opposed to braid which is usually round or oval in section.

For simplicity I have reduced the many different orders of dress (the way in which a uniform should be worn) to three. Service dress refers to the uniform worn everyday when not actually in action. Undress uniform was worn off duty, and field service or combat dress in action. Every army had its own name for the soft cap which was worn when neither the steel helmet nor another more formal head-dress was prescribed. The Americans called it an overseas cap; the British official designation was 'cap, field service' (although it had many more colourful and unrepeatable names). The Italians called it

15

a *bustina* or envelope, and the Germans a *Schiffchen* or little boat. I have decided to call all peakless soft caps (except berets) which were worn on the side of the head, side caps. All other soft caps with peaks or other features are referred to as field caps. Berets are referred to as berets.

Rank badges are very difficult to describe satisfactorily, and should really be illustrated, but space and time would not allow it. I have described badges of rank in four groups: N.C.O.s (sometimes sub-divided into corporals and sergeants), company officers (2nd lieutenant to captain), field officers (major to colonel) and general officers and field-marshals. Normally the three or four ranks within the groups were indicated in sequence. For example in the British army a 2nd lieutenant had one pip, a lieutenant two and a captain three pips. A major had a crown, a lieutenant-colonel a crown and a pip and a colonel a crown and two pips. The crown was common to all field officers and distinguished them from company officers. When I describe company officers as having one to three stars it literally means that the most junior lieutenant had one star and the captain three stars.

UNIFORM NOTES

BELGIUM

In 1940 the Belgian army was dressed in practically the same khaki uniforms as in 1918. While the soldier's uniform was almost identical to the French, officers adopted an English-style service dress in 1935.

The khaki tunic was single-breasted with stand-and-fall collar, five gilt metal buttons in front and plain pointed shoulder straps to which the unit number was affixed. The breast patch pockets had a pleat, flap and button, while the side pockets had flap and button only. The officer's tunic had long skirts and large patch pockets. It was worn with white or light khaki shirt and khaki tie. Unmounted personnel wore matching pantaloons with black ankle boots and front-lacing gaiters, while cyclists and mounted personnel had high leggings. Officers wore either beige cord breeches and brown riding boots or long khaki trousers and brown shoes. The greatcoat was double-breasted with fall collar and two rows of five buttons in front and side pockets with flap and button.

Head-dress included a khaki cloth peaked cap with matching peak, and crimson band for generals and scarlet for the rank of Colonel-Brigadier. Officers had gold chin cords, warrant officers, silver, and other ranks, a brown leather chin strap. On the front all ranks wore their arm-of-service badge in gilt metal surmounted by a circular cockade in the national colours – red, yellow and black. The side cap was made of khaki cloth with piping in the arm colour along the centre seam and edge of the cuff. A tassel in the arm colour hung in front, while the arm-of-service badge was worn on the left front.

The steel helmet was the French model with a stamped metal lion's head, or the regimental number and a crown in paint on the front.

Rifle troops (*Chasseurs Ardennais*) wore a bright green beret with boar's head cap badge and a black leather coat, similar in cut to the tunic, or a short single-breasted version of the greatcoat. They also used the high leather leggings. Motorised troops had a special leather-covered helmet with the lion's head in front and a short brown leather coat. Tank troops wore the French mechanised troops' helmet and a short black leather coat.

Rank was indicated on the peaked cap and on the collar patches, shoulder straps and cuffs as follows:

17

N.C.O.s	One to three diagonal silver lace stripes on cuffs.
Company officers	One to three six-pointed stars on the collar patch and shoulder strap. Piping in arm colour on the side cap.
Field officers	One to three six-pointed stars and a gold bar on the collar patch and shoulder strap, and two vertical gold bars on the front of the peaked cap. Wide khaki lace on the side cap.
Generals	Two or three six-pointed stars and four gold bars on the collar patch and shoulder strap, and one or two vertical gold bars on the front of the peaked cap. Wide gold lace on the side cap.

Arm-of-service colours appeared on the collar patch often in conjunction with a gilt metal arm-of-service badge. The basic colours and badges were as follows:*

Arm/Unit	Collar patch	Piping	Badge
Infantry	Scarlet	Royal blue	Crown
Grenadiers	Scarlet	Royal blue	Grenade
Carabiniers	Dark green	Yellow	Horn
Rifles	Dark green	Yellow	Crown
Ardennes Rifles	Green	Scarlet	Boar's head
Carabinier cyclists	Green	Yellow	Bicycle wheel
Frontier Cyclist Regiment	Scarlet	Royal blue	Bicycle wheel
Guides	Amaranth	Green	Crown and crossed sabre
Lancers	White	Royal blue	Crossed lances
Chasseurs à Cheval	Yellow	Royal blue	Sabre and horn
Light Horse	Royal blue	Scarlet	Flaming grenade

After the capitulation in 1940 Belgian volunteers were formed, together with other nationalities, into an Inter-Allied Commando unit and later into the Special Air Service Brigade.

There was also an Independent Brigade Group which saw service in North Western Europe at the end of the war. Belgian personnel wore battle dress with a khaki flash and Belgium in maroon letters within a maroon border.

* For further details of Belgian badges of rank see Guido Rosignoli, *Army Badges and Insignia of World War 2: Great Britain, Poland, Belgium, Italy, U.S.S.R., U.S.A., Germany*. Plates 33–5 and pp. 143–6.

BULGARIA

Since 1877 Bulgarian uniforms followed closely those of Russia, and at the end of World War 1 she adopted a rather greyish khaki. During World War 2 Bulgaria began to adopt German uniform features. The khaki uniform included a single-breasted tunic with stand-and-fall collar, six buttons in front, and breast and side pockets with Austrian-pattern flaps. Before the war the collar of the officer's tunic was in the arm colour, but during the war officers began to wear an open tunic with dark green collar and shirt and tie. Other ranks had a single-breasted greatcoat with fall collar, seven buttons in front, vertical slash side pockets and turn-back cuffs. The officer's version was made of lighter grey cloth with a darker velvet collar piped in the arm colour, and piped turn-back cuffs. Other ranks wore matching trousers and marching boots, or ankle boots and puttees, while officers wore breeches (generals with red *Lampassen*) and riding boots. The peaked cap was khaki with band and piping in the arm colour, and black peak and chin strap. In front there was an oval cockade in the national colours – white, green and red. The steel helmet was similar in shape to the German model and had a shield in the national colours on the left, and a red shield charged with a gold lion rampant on the right side.

Rank badges were in the form of Tsarist Russian shoulder boards, which were in plain arm-of-service colour for other ranks, and gold or silver lace for officers. Under German influence officers began to wear German *Litzen*, and generals, red collar patches with gold-embroidered oak leaves.

Senior Privates	One narrow yellow lace bar across the base of the shoulder strap.
N.C.O.s	One to three yellow lace (warrant officers one wide silver lace) bars across base of shoulder strap.
Company officers	Gold or silver lace shoulder board with one red or black stripe and one or two contrasting four-pointed stars.
Field officers	Gold or silver lace shoulder board with two red or black stripes and one to three contrasting four-pointed stars.

| Generals | Gold or silver zigzag-pattern lace with one to three contrasting four-pointed stars. |

Arm-of-service colours appeared on the cap band and piping, on the officer's tunic collar and greatcoat piping, on other ranks' shoulder straps and collar patches and as the base and stripe colour of officers' shoulder boards and collar patches.

Arm	Cap band	Piping	Tunic collar	Collar patch
Generals	Black	Red	Arm colour	Red
General staff	Black velvet	Red	Black velvet	Black velvet
Infantry	Red	Red	Red	Red
Cavalry	Red	White	Red	Red
Artillery	Black	Red	Black	Black
Engineers	Black	Red	Black	Black

CHINA

After World War 1 China adopted a grey-green German-style field uniform, but during the war with Japan, between 1937 and 1945, two distinct colours of uniform were worn. In the summer various shades of khaki cotton were worn, while the wadded winter uniforms were made of a bright blue cotton.

The typical single-breasted tunic had a stand-and-fall collar and five buttons in front. Breast and side patch pockets had flap and button. Long or short trousers were worn with tightly-bound puttees which, unlike European ones, were worn right up to the knee, with canvas or leather boots or sandals.

Rank was indicated on the collar in the form of detachable patches made of cloth, plastic or metal, as follows:

N.C.O.s (corporals)	Collar patch with one or two three-pointed gilt stars.
N.C.O.s (sergeants)	Collar patch with yellow stripe and one to three three-pointed stars.
Company officers	Collar patch with two silver stripes and one gold and one to three three-pointed stars.
Field officers	Collar patch with two gold stripes and one silver and one to three three-pointed stars.
Generals	Gold collar patch with one to three three-pointed silver stars.

Arm-of-service colours appeared on the collar patches and as a border to the white cotton identification patch which was worn above the left breast pocket as follows:

Arm	*Colour*
General staff	Golden yellow
Infantry	Red
Cavalry	Yellow
Engineers	White
Train*	Black
Medical	Green
Military police	Pink
Commissariat	Dark red

In April 1940 the Japanese formed a puppet Nationalist Chinese government in Eastern China, and its army of 40,000 men was issued with Japanese uniforms and equipment, while retaining Chinese badges of rank. A Chinese Expeditionary Corps was also uniformed and equipped by Britain and the United States and saw service in Burma.

CZECHOSLOVAKIA

The newly-established Czech Republic under French guidance introduced a khaki uniform in 1920, the officer's version of which bore a remarkable resemblance to that of Britain. The tunic was single-breasted with stand-and-fall collar and fly front with concealed buttons. The patch pockets had a flap with concealed button. Shoulder straps were made of the same material as the tunic. The greatcoat was double-breasted with two rows of six buttons. Soldiers wore pantaloons, puttees and ankle boots, while officers wore breeches and black riding boots. Generals had red *Lampassen* on their breeches and trousers, while officers had a single wide stripe in arm-of-service colour on their trousers.

Head-dress consisted of a side cap with the national emblem on the left front, and the Czech M.1934 steel helmet, which replaced the German model. Officers had an English-model khaki cloth peaked cap with matching peak. The top of the band was piped in branch colour. The national emblem was worn on the band in front,

* Train in this context refers to supply train or transport troops.

and the chin cord was in khaki silk or gold or silver braid, according to rank.

Buttons, rank badges and other metal insignia were in matt bronze for other ranks, silver for N.C.O.s, and gold for officers. The unit number in the form of a small square metal badge was worn on the side of the collar just above the shoulder-strap button. Collar patches and shoulder strap piping were in the arm colour.

Ranks were indicated on the shoulder straps as follows:

Other ranks	One to four silver balls on a strip of cloth in the arm colour across the base of the shoulder strap.
N.C.O.s	One to three silver lace bars across the base of the shoulder strap.
Company officers	One to four five-pointed gilt metal stars on the shoulder strap.
Field officers	One to four five-pointed gilt metal stars and gold-embroidered edging to shoulder strap.
Generals	Three gold-embroidered lime leaves on the collar patch, gold-embroidered edging to shoulder strap, and two to four five-pointed stars on both cuffs. Gold-embroidered lime leaves on the cap peak.

The arm-of-service colour appeared as piping on the peaked cap, trouser stripe and collar patches:

Arm	*Colour*
Generals	Scarlet
General staff	Scarlet
Infantry	Cherry
Militia	Cherry
Mountain troops	Cherry
Frontier guards	Cherry
Tank troops	Cherry
Artillery	Scarlet
Cavalry	Yellow
Train	Yellow
Signals	Light brown
Engineers	Dark brown
Transport	Dark green

This uniform continued to be worn during the war by members of the Slovak Light Division on the eastern front, and with minor alterations by the Government Troops (*Regierungstruppen*) of the German Protectorate of Bohemia and Moravia.

In 1940 an Independent Czech Brigade was formed in England and its personnel were dressed in British battle dress with the Czech flash ('Czechoslovakia' in red within a red border on khaki ground) on the top of the sleeve and Czech rank badges. Czech personnel also served in North Africa and wore British tropical uniform.

DENMARK

Most countries reduced their military spending in peacetime, but none so drastically, it seems, as Denmark. A khaki field uniform was introduced in 1923, but, for economy reasons, it was still in store in 1940 so that during the German invasion the rank and file were still wearing obsolete black greatcoats and light grey trousers, while the regular officers and N.C.O.s, who normally provided their own uniforms, wore khaki.

The M.1923 uniform consisted of a single-breasted tunic with stand-and-fall collar and six brass buttons in front. The pleated breast patch pockets had a flap and button, while the side patch pockets were plain. Generals could also wear an open tunic with shirt and tie. Soldiers wore long matching trousers, which were worn rolled up over the calf-length brown leather lace-up boots. Officers wore breeches and black leather riding boots. The greatcoat was double-breasted with two rows of six buttons in front, stand-and-fall collar and turn-back cuffs.

The peaked cap was made of khaki cloth with brown leather peak and chin strap (generals gold braid). On the front was the army emblem surmounted by a red and white national cockade. There was also a side cap which was plain for other ranks, but decorated with various widths of khaki or silver lace for officers. Finally there was the M.1923 Danish steel helmet.

Rank was indicated as follows:

N.C.O.s	One to three chevrons on both cuffs.
Company officers	One or two small gilt six-pointed stars on shoulder straps and medium-light khaki lace on side cap.

| Field officers | One or two medium-size six-pointed gilt metal stars on the shoulder straps and wide dark khaki lace on the side cap. |
| Generals | One or two large six-pointed gilt metal stars on the shoulder straps and wide silver lace on the side cap. |

There were no arm-of-service colours in the Danish army and each arm had its own circular metal badge which was worn above the right breast pocket.

In 1909 the Danish Royal Guard was issued with a grey-green uniform which during the German occupation was used by the pro-German Danish Schalburg Corps. Danish personnel who escaped to Sweden were formed into a Brigade, which the Swedes clothed in a copy of the British battle dress, but made of a grey material.

FINLAND

In 1936 Finland modernised the clothing of its armed forces and began to replace the old light grey uniform with a darker grey one, which resembled that of Germany. The M.1936 tunic was single-breasted with matching shoulder straps and stand-and-fall collar and six buttons in front. The pleated breast patch pockets had a flap and button, while the side pockets had a flap only. All ranks wore matching breeches (generals with red and general staff officers with crimson *Lampassen*), and black leather boots. In winter the double-breasted greatcoat with two rows of six buttons, slash side pockets with flap, fall collar and turn-back cuffs was worn.

The winter field cap had a matching peak and flap which fastened in front with two buttons, and above the buttons was the Finnish blue and white cockade for other ranks and gilt metal lion for officers. For the summer there was a side cap with brown leather chin strap and the cockade for other ranks and gold lion for officers. The steel helmet was the M.1915 German one which was gradually replaced during the course of the war by the 1935 German model. The Soviet Russian M.1940 helmet was also used behind the front.

Because of the extreme winter climate extensive use had to be made of winter clothing and many different types, mainly white cotton overalls and sheepskin coats, were utilised.

Ranks were indicated as follows:

Corporals	One yellow chevron on the collar patch which was edged with one woven line.
N.C.O.s	Two to four yellow chevrons on the collar patch which was edged with one woven line. Sergeant-major one wide gold chevron.
Company officers	One to three gilt metal rosettes on the collar patch which was edged with one woven line.
Field officers	One to three larger gilt metal rosettes on the collar patch which was edged with two woven or embroidered lines.
Generals	One to three gilt metal lions on the collar patch which was edged with one wide and one narrow gold-embroidered lines.
Marshal	Crossed batons in gold on silver lace collar patch.

Arm-of-service colours appeared on the collar patches as follows:

Arm	*Collar patch*
War Ministry	Light blue
Generals	Red
General staff	Crimson
Infantry	Light grey
Rifles	Green
Artillery	Red
Cavalry	Yellow
Tank troops	Black
Train and Technical	Purple

FRANCE

France entered World War 1 in brightly coloured uniforms and it was not until 1915 that these were replaced by horizon blue. Horizon blue lasted exactly twenty years before it too gave way to the ever more dominant khaki in 1935. *Bleu horizon* continued in use for everyday wear even after the beginning of World War 2.

The khaki tunic or *vareuse* was single-breasted with low fall collar and six drab metal buttons in front. The officer's version had seven buttons and breast patch and large side patch pockets. All ranks had round cuffs. The greatcoat was double-breasted with large fall collar and two rows of seven buttons in front. The side pocket flap was rectangular and fastened with two buttons. On both sides there was a cloth belt loop with button and, as in World War 1, the flaps of the greatcoat could be buttoned back to facilitate movement. Breeches were worn with khaki puttees by unmounted, and leather leggings by mounted, personnel. Officers wore beige cord breeches and brown boots.

There were three basic kinds of head-dress, the most famous being the kepi. The kepi was worn by all ranks and was made of horizon blue or khaki, but for undress there was a kepi in the old pre-World-War-1 colours. The field cap or *bonnet de police* was made of khaki cloth and indicated the N.C.O. rank of the wearer by small chevrons on its front. Later in the war officers began to wear the side cap with their rank badges on the left front. The steel helmet, although identical in shape to the original 1915 model, had undergone certain improvements between the wars. It was now made of manganese steel and stamped in one piece. Each arm of service had its own stamped badge for wear on the front of the helmet. An unofficial but respected custom was to wear a stamped metal plaque on the peak which bore the name of the wearer and the inscription 'a soldier of the Great War' within two laurel branches.

Special uniforms were developed for tank and armoured car crews which included a special helmet with neck guard and padded leather front. Earlier models of this helmet were just modifications of the normal steel helmet and retained the comb, but in 1935 the final khaki model was put into service. In addition they received a three-quarter-length brown leather coat and, instead of the side cap, a dark blue beret. Infantry regiments designated 'mountain type' wore a large dark blue beret and a waterproof cotton duck anorak.

The sombre dress of the French metropolitan army was enlivened by that of her colonial troops which combined features of native dress with French uniform to create splendidly exotic uniforms.

In the French army rank was indicated on the head-dress and sleeve of tunic and greatcoat. On special uniforms such as the leather coat for armoured troops and on tropical and native dress, rank badges were worn on a detachable dark blue cloth tab, which could be buttoned or sewn to the front of the garment. Rank badges were as follows:

N.C.O.s (corporals)   Two diagonal khaki lace bars on both cuffs, and two khaki lace chevrons on the side cap.

N.C.O.s (sergeants)	One to three diagonal gold lace bars on both cuffs, and one or two medium, or three narrow, gold lace chevrons on the side cap.
Company officers	One to three horizontal gold or silver lace bars on the cuff and one to three narrow lace chevrons on the side cap.
Field officers	Four (battalion commanders three gold and two silver) or five horizontal gold lace bars on the cuffs, and four or five braid rings on the kepi and lace chevrons on the side cap.
Generals	Two to five five-pointed silver or bronze stars on the cuffs, front of kepi, left front of side cap or front of steel helmet.
Marshal	Seven five-pointed bronze or silver stars on the head-dress and silver crossed batons on the side cap.

Arm of service was indicated by the colour of the kepi and the collar patches as follows:

Arm	Collar patch	Piping	Unit numbers
Infantry	Khaki	Dark blue	Red
Artillery	Red	Blue	Blue
Tank troops	Khaki	Light grey	Light grey
Engineers	Black	Red	Red
Train	Green	—	Red
Medical	Red	—	Light blue

After the defeat of France and the establishment of the Vichy government, the development of French uniform was split in two. Vichy troops continued to wear the pre-war uniform with only minor changes, while the Free French, cut off from supplies, had to be re-equipped first by Great Britain and then by the United States. The French were proud of their traditions and hung on to as many of the details of French uniform as possible, so that their dress became a very interesting combination of French, British and American uniform. Rank badges began to be worn on the beret and American steel helmet and on dark blue removable shoulder straps, and for the first time units such as the 2nd Armoured Division began to wear formation signs on their uniforms.

GERMANY

World War 2 German army field uniform was basically a development of that introduced in 1915, and included many traditional
Prussian features dating back to the Napoleonic wars which had
been effectively modified over the years to make them suitable for
modern uniform. Modernisation began in 1935 with the introduction of a smaller version of the M.1915 steel helmet, and a field
blouse with pleated patch pockets. A new black uniform for crews
of enclosed armoured vehicles was followed in 1940 with a field-grey
version for crews of self-propelled guns and other types of armoured
vehicles. Other special uniforms were developed for parachute
troops (who were later transferred to the air force) and mountain
troops, who were issued with a mountain cap, special baggy long
trousers and hobnailed boots.

Intervention in North Africa saw German troops parading in the
sort of pseudo-functional tropical uniform favoured by the colonial
empires. British and Germans soon discarded any restrictive gar-
ments and the pith helmet in favour of looser-fitting clothing and
the steel helmet.

The emergence of the *Waffen-SS* as an effective fighting force also
drew attention to many of its advanced innovations in the field of
combat clothing and personal equipment. The *Waffen-SS* could
claim to have invented two items which today form the basis of all
modern combat clothing. The first was a smock-like jacket (and
steel helmet cover) made of a camouflage material which the SS had
patented in 1935, and a three-quarter-length winter anorak, a
garment which today has almost completely replaced the greatcoat.

No radical alteration to the appearance of the German soldier took
place until 1943, by which time the marching boot had been restricted
to certain types of unit, and most soldiers were wearing British-type
anklets and ankle boots. In 1943 a new standard field cap modelled
on the mountain cap began to be issued generally. Modifications to
the field uniform and the introduction of different kinds of overalls
for tank crews and artillerymen were made primarily for economy
reasons. This trend culminated in 1944 with the new 'Field Uniform
44' which, to all intents and purposes, was a copy of the British
battle dress. The deterioration in the appearance of the uniform was
to some extent offset by an increase in distinctive insignia for élite
units and awards for various types of combat – infantry assault, tank

assault and partisan warfare – which could be worn with uniform.

Rank was indicated by a star and chevrons on the sleeve for other ranks, silver (later grey silk) lace on the collar and shoulder straps for N.C.O.s, and silver cords (generals gold) on the peaked cap, and silver piping on the side and field cap, and finally by the shoulder straps.

Other ranks	One or two chevrons and a star on left sleeve.
N.C.O.s	Silver lace, and from none to three white metal stars on the shoulder straps.
Company officers	Four flat silver braids and from none to two gilt metal stars on the shoulder straps.
Field officers	Three interwoven silver braids and from none to two gilt metal stars on the shoulder straps.
Generals	Three (two gold and one silver) interwoven braids and from none to three silver stars on the shoulder straps.
Field-marshal	At first two gold and one silver, and later three gold interwoven, braids and silver crossed batons on the shoulder straps.

Arm-of-service colours or *Waffenfarben* appeared as piping on the peaked cap (and on the side cap until 1942, when it was abolished) and as piping on other ranks', and as a base colour on officers', shoulder straps. Certain formations such as mountain and rifle regiments wore an edelweiss and oakleaf cluster on their head-dress and right sleeve respectively.*

Arm	*Colour*
Generals	Scarlet
General staff	Crimson
Infantry	White
Mountain troops	Bright green
Cavalry	Yellow
Tank troops	Pink
Artillery	Red
Signals	Lemon yellow
Engineers	Black
Medical	Cornflower blue

* For further details of German badges of rank see Guido Rosignoli, *Army Badges and Insignia of World War 2 : Great Britain, Poland, Belgium, Italy, U.S.S.R., U.S.A., Germany.* Plates 74–88 and pp. 207–73.

GREAT BRITAIN

Britain's long succession of colonial wars, particularly those in India and South Africa, brought about the development of a protectively coloured, loose-fitting and thoroughly practical field uniform for wear on active service. A universal khaki service dress was first introduced in 1902, but it was not until 1913 that the service dress, including a very modern tunic with lapels for officers, became obligatory for all ranks on all occasions, except full dress.

The service dress for other ranks consisted of a single-breasted khaki serge tunic with stand-and-fall collar, five metal general service pattern buttons in front, patch breast and side pockets with flap and button, and matching rounded shoulder straps. Pantaloons in khaki and serge for unmounted, and Bedford cord for mounted, personnel were worn with black ankle boots and khaki puttees. The greatcoat was single-breasted with five buttons, fall collar and matching shoulder straps.

Head-dress included the M.1916 helmet (later known as the Mk 1), stiff peaked service cap, and the side cap (Cap, F.S., or 'fore an aft'). Some regiments and corps retained distinctive head-dress. With service dress officers wore an open tunic with light khaki shirt and tie, matching khaki pantaloons, puttees and brown ankle boots, or long khaki trousers with brown shoes. Officers in mounted units, and mounted officers in unmounted units, as well as staff and general officers, could also wear cord breeches and brown leather field boots. In addition to the regulation double-breasted greatcoat, officers could also wear the double-breasted beige 'British warm' or a mackintosh

After extensive trials a new 'battle dress' began to replace the service dress in April 1939, although the changeover was not completed until the end of 1940. The single-breasted blouse was made of a rough serge with stand-and-fall collar, fly front, pleated breast patch pockets with flap and concealed button (the buttons were made of a vegetable compound and were green in colour). At the waist the blouse was gathered into a waistband and fastened with a flat metal buckle on the right of centre. Trousers were straight with, in addition to the normal side and hip pockets, a large patch pocket with flap on the left thigh, and a pleated pocket on the right front just below the waist. At the bottoms the trousers had a tab and button, so they could be fastened around the ankle for wear with black leather ankle boots and web anklets. A new double-breasted greatcoat was issued at the same time, but there were not enough for the Home Guard, who had to make do with a new 'Austrian pattern' cape. In 1940 manufacture was simplified by doing away with the pocket pleats and concealed buttons on the battle dress blouse, so that now five buttons appeared in front, and one on each pocket flap and shoulder strap. For wear as a working dress, there was a set of denims. The denims were in the same cut as the battle dress and were extensively used as a summer battle dress. With shirtsleeve order soldiers wore the collarless drab angola shirt.

Armoured vehicle crews also received the battle dress which was worn under a one-piece black denim overall, and with a khaki or black fibre helmet, gloves and goggles. The black overall and helmet were soon relegated to training units, and armoured corps personnel wore normal clothing and the denims. Practical experience brought about the introduction of a special sand-coloured one-piece overall ('pixie suit') with khaki cloth lining and collar, in time for the last winter of the war.

Parachute troops were hastily organised after Germany's successful airborne operations, and the first hand-picked volunteers were dressed in an almost exact copy of the German parachutist's smock. It was single-breasted with stand-and-fall collar and shoulder straps, and was made of a grey-green cotton duck. It had a fly front with concealed pop-studs and was gathered at the wrist. Like its German counterpart it fastened around the thighs and under the crutch. A number of different types of helmet were tested, and a leather flying helmet was actually worn on the first airborne operation. For training there were various models of canvas helmet padded with foam rubber. By late 1941 paratroopers were being issued with the 'Denison' camouflaged smock and rimless steel helmet with leather chin strap and cup, which was later replaced by webbing straps and rubber cup. For the actual jump a special loose-fitting sleeveless jump jacket with zip fastener was worn over the camouflage smock and personal equipment. Winter clothing was restricted to woollen underwear, pullovers and gloves, and the famous relic of the trenches, the leather jerkin. There was also a sand-coloured 'Tropal' coat which was issued to troops in Norway, and the duffle coat which turned up in Italy in the last two winters of the war. In North-Western Europe extensive use was made of white snow smocks and helmet covers.

Tropical clothing included a pith hat or 'Bombay bowler', khaki drill jacket, shirt and long trousers (cotton cord for mounted personnel), shorts and canvas shoes with rubber soles. It is impossible to list all the regulation and non-regulation items of dress worn by British and Imperial troops who fought in the desert. Personified by Jon's 'two types' they gained a reputation for a total disregard of regulation and affected a scruffiness unsurpassed in any other theatre during the war. At first 'K.D.' was also worn in the Far East, but in 1942 new jungle-green combat clothing consisting of a shirt, long and short trousers, canvas shoes and a 'jungle hat' became standard issue. The slouch hat, at first limited to Australian and New Zealand troops, soon became the most popular form of head-dress. Rank badges in metal on the service dress and worsted embroidery on battle dress appeared on the shoulder strap. Senior officers with the rank of substantive Colonel and above wore red cap bands and gorget patches.

N.C.O.s	One to three white chevrons on both sleeves.
Company officers	One to three pips on both shoulder straps.
Field officers	One crown and from one to three pips.
Generals	Crossed baton and sword and one pip, one crown, and a pip and a crown, respectively.
Field-marshal	Crossed batons within a laurel wreath surmounted by a crown.

Arm-of-service colours were introduced in 1940, and consisted of strips of felt worn above the formation sign as follows:

Arm	*Colour*
Infantry	Scarlet
Rifle regiments	Rifle green
Royal Artillery	Red–blue
Royal Armoured Corps	Red–yellow
Royal Engineers	Blue–red
Pioneer Corps	Red–green
Royal Electrical and Mechanical Engineers	Red–yellow–blue
Royal Signals	Blue–white
Royal Army Medical Corps	Dull cherry
Corps of Military Police	Red

AUSTRALIA

Australian troops entered World War 2 in practically the same uniform as they had worn in World War 1. Instead of battle dress they continued to wear a shirt-like single-breasted tunic with stand-and-fall collar, four bronzed buttons in front, matching shoulder straps and sleeves gathered and fastened at the wrist. Long matching trousers were worn with canvas anklets and ankle boots. The greatcoat was single-breasted with fall collar, five buttons in front, slanting side pockets with flap and turn-back cuffs.

Head-dress consisted of the wide-brimmed khaki felt slouch or 'wide-awake' hat which was worn on most occasions when the steel helmet was not prescribed. For formal occasions the brim was folded up on the left and fastened with a bronze Australian or regimental cap badge.

Officers wore khaki service dress with either the peaked cap or slouch hat.

The Australian khaki service dress was made of a lighter material than the British battle dress, and was also worn in North Africa. Khaki drill clothing was also issued, and officers wore a light khaki service dress with bronzed buttons and badges.

Towards the end of the war in the Far East, Australian troops wore jungle-green clothing and equipment of American manufacture.

Badges of rank were the same as British.

CANADA

Canadian uniform was basically the same as British, although the khaki material used for battle dress was of better quality and a greener shade of khaki than its British counterpart.

Any Canadian peculiarities such as the fur 'Yukon' cap, which was worn by members of the first Canadian contingent to arrive in England in December 1940, were soon withdrawn. As the war proceeded Canadian clothing was increasingly standardised on the British pattern.

Badges of rank were identical to the British.

NEW ZEALAND

At the beginning of the war New Zealand troops were still wearing service dress with long matching trousers, short puttees and ankle boots. The distinctive head-dress was the slouch hat, which differed from the Australian one in that the crown was pointed and indented on four sides, and the brim was never officially folded up. The cap badge was worn in front, and a puggree in regimental or corps colours was worn around the base of the hat.

Officers wore service dress with either the slouch hat or peaked cap. As with other Dominion forces, New Zealand troops received standard British clothing and equipment.

Badges of rank were identical to the British.

GREECE

In 1912 the Greeks adopted an olive-green (khaki) field uniform which, by the outbreak of World War 2, had incorporated many British features, particularly in the uniforms of officers.

The tunic was single-breasted with stand-and-fall collar and five buttons in front. The pleated breast and plain side pockets had buttoning flaps. The shoulder straps were made of the same cloth as the tunic, and bore the cypher of the infantry regiment or unit number. The single-breasted greatcoat had five buttons in front and a large fall collar and side pockets with flaps. The officer's version was double-breasted with six buttons, fall collar and turn-back cuffs. The officer's tunic was either the older closed, or the more modern English-style, tunic with large patch pockets. Soldiers wore matching pantaloons with puttees and ankle boots while officers wore breeches and riding boots, or leather leggings.

The British-model steel helmet was in the process of being replaced by a new Greek model, and both were worn concurrently during the Italian invasion. Officers wore either the kepi or a khaki peaked cap with matching peak (embroidered in gold for generals), and all ranks had a side cap. On the front of the kepi, peaked cap and side cap was the black, light blue and white circular Greek cockade surmounted by a silver crown.

A special uniform was worn by the Royal Guard or *Evzones*, who had originally been the rifle regiments or *Jägers* of the Greek army. The uniform, or national costume, consisted of a white full-sleeved shirt, waistcoat, pleated kilt or *Fustenella* and a red tasselled cap. In wartime the *Evzones* wore a khaki frock coat and breeches, and a khaki cap with black tassel. Officers wore standard army uniform in action.

Summer uniform consisted of a cotton side cap, long-skirted shirt-like tunic with low stand collar and patch breast pockets, and cotton breeches. Rank was indicated on the officer's kepi and shoulder straps, and on the N.C.O.'s chevrons.

N.C.O.s	One to three chevrons on both sleeves. Senior N.C.O.s, diagonal lace stripes on both cuffs.
Company officers	One to three six-pointed white metal stars on the shoulder strap, and three rows of narrow drab lace around the kepi.
Field officers	A silver crown and one to three six-pointed gilt metal stars on the shoulder strap, and three rows of narrow and one of medium drab lace on the kepi.
Generals	Gilt crossed swords and one or two six-pointed gilt metal stars on the shoulder strap, and wide gold lace on the kepi, and gold embroidery on cap peak.

Arm-of-service colours appeared on the pointed collar patches as follows:

Arm	*Colour*
Infantry	Red
Artillery	Black
Cavalry	Green
Engineers	Crimson
Medical	Crimson velvet

A Greek Independent Brigade as well as the 'Sacred Regiment' served in North Africa and the 3rd Greek Mountain Brigade served in Italy. In each case British uniform with Greek insignia and badges of rank was worn.

HUNGARY

Apart from adopting khaki in 1922, Hungary continued the Austro-Hungarian tradition in the design of its uniforms.

The standard khaki tunic was single-breasted with stand-and-fall collar and five dull metal (officers gilt) buttons. The pleated breast and side pockets had a flap and button. The officer's tunic had four buttons and was basically the same as the soldier's, but had a waist seam and three small buttons at the cuff. Shoulder straps were plain for other ranks and made of gold braid for all officers irrespective of rank. Other ranks wore long khaki trousers with marching boots, later replaced by ankle boots and puttees, while officers wore khaki breeches and black boots.

The greatcoat was double-breasted with large full collar and two rows of six buttons in front. It had turn-back cuffs, and side pockets with flaps. Other ranks had plain shoulder straps, while officers had their badges of rank on the cuffs. Generals had red lapels on the greatcoat.

The side cap was cut high in the front and had a flap which fastened in front with two buttons. On the front of the cap officers wore an inverted chevron according to rank with, at its apex, the circular red, white and green Hungarian cockade. On the left side of the cap was a triangular piece of cloth in the arm colour, which was trimmed with three pieces of drab braid. The field cap was identical to the Austrian kepi, and bore the same badges as the side cap. The steel helmet was the M.1915 German one which was gradually replaced during the war by the 1935 model.

Armoured vehicle crews received a brown leather jacket with khaki cloth collar, and matching leather trousers.

Rank was indicated on the collar patches and head-dress as follows:

Senior privates   One six-pointed star on the collar patch.

N.C.O.s   Two to three six-pointed stars and silver lace on the collar patch which was trimmed with silver braid.

Company officers   One to three six-pointed stars on the collar patch which was trimmed with narrow gold braid. One to three narrow lace chevrons on the cap, and one to three narrow lace bars on the greatcoat cuffs.

Field officers	One to three six-pointed stars on gold lace which was mounted on the collar patch and trimmed with narrow gold braid. One or two narrow and one medium lace chevrons on the cap, and one or two narrow and one medium lace bars on the greatcoat cuffs.
Generals	One to three six-pointed silver-embroidered stars on gold lace which was mounted on the red collar patch and trimmed with narrow gold braid and decorated with embroidered oak leaves. One or two medium and one wide gold lace chevrons on the cap, and one or two medium and one wide lace bars, surmounted by a badge consisting of the crown of St Stephen and oak leaves, on the greatcoat cuffs.

Arm-of-service colours appeared on the collar patches and on the triangle on the left side of the side and field cap as follows:

Arm	Collar patch	Piping
Generals	Scarlet	—
General staff	Black velvet	Scarlet
General staff (technical)	Brown velvet	Scarlet
Infantry	Grass green	—
Frontier guards	Green	Red
Cavalry (hussars)	Light blue	—
Artillery	Scarlet	—
Technical troops	Dark grey green	—
Tank troops	Dark blue	—
Train	Brown	—
Medical	Black	—
Musicians	Violet	—

INDIA

Before the war basic Indian army field service dress consisted of a silver-grey collarless flannel shirt, a khaki drill or cellular khaki shirt, or a Mazri grey cotton type shirt, which was worn by certain units on the north-western frontier. In such cases the shirt was worn with khaki drill shorts and a khaki woollen pullover if required. Footwear consisted of knitted woollen socks, woollen hose-tops and short puttees with ankle boots or *chaplis* – a form of sandal usually worn by Frontier Force units.

It was in this simple and practical uniform that the Indian Army went to war in 1939.

There were of course modifications and contradictions. For example, the Service Corps companies which went to France wore the khaki serge *kurta* (three-quarter-length single-breasted tunic with stand collar) with battle dress trousers, webbing anklets and ankle boots. As the war progressed very great variations in uniform existed owing to stocks running out and a system of local purchase having to be introduced, but from about 1942 standardisation was fairly regular throughout the whole army.

Indian officers wore the same uniform as their men whereas British officers usually wore the pith sun helmet. During the war the peaked cap, side cap and beret took the place of the sun helmet. Indian head-dress was normally the khaki *puggree* which varied in shape according to the religion and tribe of the wearer. In general terms all Muslims wore the pointed *kullah* or skull cap inside the *puggree* and one end of the *puggree* was formed into a large comb standing up behind the *kullah*, while the other end of the *puggree* hung down behind to the small of the back, and was used to protect the face from dust and sandstorms. The Sikh wore the well-known type of Sikh *puggree* with his uncut hair in a bun which was normally tied with red cloth. The Jats and other Hindoos wore their *puggree* as appropriate to their particular tribe or clan.

Since the Mutiny all Indian units, with a few notable exceptions, were based on three classes of Indian soldiers. For example there would be a Sikh company, a Muslim company and a Jat company, and all would be mixed in the Headquarters Company.

During the war, apart from the Sikhs, the other religions and tribes tended to replace the *puggree* with the side cap, woollen cap comforter or other more practical forms of the head-dress.

In 1942 those scheduled to fight in the Far Eastern jungles were issued with jungle-green battle dress or jungle-green shirt and trousers; the *puggree* when worn was dyed green.

The Gurkhas and the Royal Garhwal Rifles wore the special double *terai* slouch hat, which was in fact two felt hats one inside the other. The army single slouch hat and the jungle hat were generally adopted by other units and along with the cap comforter became the most common form of head-dress in the Far East.

British and Indian officers holding the King's commission wore British rank badges, while subordinate Indian officers commissioned by the viceroy wore British pips with an additional loop of braid running across the shoulder strap under the pip.

ITALY

The grey-green uniform of World War 1, first introduced in 1909, underwent modernisation in 1925 and 1933 and again in 1935. In keeping with most other countries, uniform was standardised and basically the same for all ranks. Italy was also one of the first countries generally to adopt a 'shirt and tie' uniform.

The grey-green single-breasted tunic was designed to be worn open with matching shirt and tie. It had five buttons in front, pleated patch breast and side pockets with flap and button. The shoulder straps were made of the same cloth and had pointed ends. The cuffs were round and plain for officers and pointed for other ranks.

The officer's tunic was usually made of finer quality material in a much lighter shade, as were the breeches which had two 2-cm.-wide black stripes on either side of a piping in arm colour.

In 1939 a new tunic with matching cloth belt was issued to other ranks in the infantry and unmounted services, while cavalry and artillery retained their traditional tunic with the half-belt at the back. Other ranks wore pantaloons with puttees or woollen socks and ankle boots, while mounted personnel wore breeches with black leather leggings and ankle boots.

The greatcoat for officers, warrant officers and sergeants was double-breasted with fall collar, two rows of three buttons in front and side pockets with flap. It was normally worn open with lapels folded back. There were different patterns of greatcoat for mounted and dismounted other ranks.

From June 1940 the black collar on the issue and officer's tunic was abolished, although those who had such tunics continued to wear them. Head-dress consisted of the side cap or *bustina*, which bore the arm-of-service badge in front and the rank badges on the left front. The peaked cap was worn by all ranks and had a black peak and rows of lace around the band according to rank. The French steel helmet began to be replaced by a new Italian model in 1935 on which it was customary to spray in black paint through a stencil the arm-of-service badge. Special corps wore their own distinctive head-dress. Rifle regiments or *Bersaglieri* wore a black hat with cockerel-feather plume on the right side, which even appeared on the steel helmet as well. Mountain troops wore the traditional felt hat with a crow, eagle or white goose feather for other ranks, officers and generals respectively. Fascist Militia and members of the Young Fascist Division wore a black tasselled fez on the back of their heads. Crews of armoured vehicles received an overall and black leather helmet with padded rim and leather neck guard, as well as a double-breasted black leather coat.

Tropical clothing followed closely the cut of the temperate uniform, but was made of a light khaki drill. In addition there was a semi-official bush jacket or *sahariana*, which must have been very comfortable because it was also worn by the British and Germans. On the front of the tropical helmet the Italians wore a circular cockade in the national colours on which was fixed a brass arm-of-service badge. Italian colonial troops wore Italian uniform combined with many colourful traditional native features such as a red tarbush, turbans of many different colours and sandals instead of boots.

In 1942 a new and very distinctive field uniform was introduced for paratroops, which was a combination of the existing field tunic and the *sahariana*. It was open at the neck and had neither collar nor lapels. The sleeves fastened tightly at the wrist and it was worn with a matching cloth belt. The trousers were baggy and fastened at the ankle. This uniform was first given to the newly-formed *Folgore* (Lightning) Parachute Division, but later became standard issue to all parachute units. Italian parachute uniform closely followed the German pattern, and in many cases German clothing and equipment was actually issued to Italian parachutists. Among the many items specially developed by the Italians were a new steel helmet with forked chin strap and leather nose pad in front, a smock and helmet cover made from both German and Italian camouflage material and a sleeveless waistcoat made of canvas with integral pouches on the front and back for sub-machine-gun magazines.

In September 1943 monarchist Italy declared war on Germany, while Mussolini established his Northern Italian Social Republic in Salò. From that moment on until the end of the war Italian uniform developed along two independent lines. In the north the nucleus of Mussolini's army of four German-trained divisions wore Italian uniform with German equipment and many Roman-inspired badges and emblems. It was intended to Germanise the uniforms further with new dress and clothing regulations which incorporated many German features, but these were only adopted by very few particularly pro-German officers before the war came to an end. In the Southern Kingdom Italian troops were rapidly reformed and thrown into the fighting and, having earned the confidence of the Allies, were soon re-equipped with British uniforms and American heavy equipment and designated the Italian Liberation Corps.

Officers' rank was indicated on the left of the side or field cap, and by the number and width of the lace loops and bars on the cuffs. On tropical uniforms officers wore black pointed shoulder straps with gold-embroidered five-pointed stars. N.C.O.s and men wore chevrons on both sleeves.*

N.C.O.s (corporals)	One wide and one or two narrow black lace chevrons.
N.C.O.s (sergeants)	One wide and one or two narrow yellow lace chevrons.
Company officers	One to three gold lace bars with a loop on the top (or only) bar on both cuffs, and one to three gold-embroidered five-pointed stars on the side cap.
Field officers	One to three narrow and one wide gold lace bars with a loop on the top bar on both cuffs, and one to three gold-embroidered five-pointed stars within a rectangular border on the side cap.
Generals and Marshal of Italy	One row of silver-embroidered *greca*, a narrow silver-embroidered loop and one to four narrow silver-embroidered bars on both cuffs,

* For further details of Italian badges of rank see Guido Rosignoli, *Army Badges and Insignia of World War 2 : Great Britain, Poland, Belgium, Italy, U.S.S.R., U.S.A., Germany.* Plates 39–50 and pp. 153–75.

| | and one to four gold-embroidered five-pointed stars on a silver rectangular lace patch on the side cap. |
| First Marshal of the Empire | Two rows of silver-embroidered *greca* with gold-embroidered eagle on a red ground in the centre of the two rows, and on the side cap. |

Arm-of-service colours appeared on the collar patches and flames, and arm of service was further identified by the cap badge, which also appeared in a reduced form on the shoulder strap. The basic arm-of-service colours were as follows:

Arm	*Colour*
General staff	Turquoise blue
Infantry, Grenadiers	Scarlet
Bersaglieri	Crimson
Alpini	Green
Artillery	Yellow
Motor transport, Admin. and Supply	Blue
Engineers	Crimson
Commissariat	Violet

JAPAN

Japan's first world war began in 1937 with the invasion of China. By the time she attacked Pearl Harbor, her armed forces were well tried and tested, and any impracticalities or superfluities in clothing and equipment had been eradicated, so that there was little change between 1941 and 1945.

The Japanese adopted khaki after World War 1, and modified the uniform in 1930 (M.90). In 1938 the single-breasted tunic with stiff stand collar was replaced by one with a softer stand-and-fall collar (M.98). Both tunics had breast and side pockets with flap and button, matching pantaloons which were worn with puttees criss-crossed with khaki tapes and black canvas boots or *tabi* with separated big toe and rubber soles. The M.90 greatcoat was single-breasted with fall collar and two rows of six buttons in front and slanting side pockets with flap. The M.98 greatcoat was double-breasted, and both models had a matching detachable hood.

Officers' uniforms were basically the same, with the exception of turn-back cuffs and side vents to facilitate the wearing of the sword. Matching breeches were worn with black boots.

Head-dress consisted of a soft field cap with matching peak, brown leather chin strap and detachable neck guard, made of four separate pieces of cloth. On the front was a five-pointed yellow star. Caps were made of many different kinds of materials and some were even plaited out of straw, while others were daubed with paint for camouflage or covered in bits and pieces to break up the outline. This cap was often worn under the circular steel helmet, which was painted a mustard colour and had a yellow metal five-pointed star on the front. The tropical helmet was made of cork and covered with light khaki cotton drill.

In China the woollen temperate uniform was worn together with special winter clothing, such as the three-quarter-length fur-lined khaki canvas sleeveless greatcoat, knitted wollen underwear, wadded trousers and a leather or cloth winter cap with fur ear flaps.

In the Far East and Pacific cotton drill uniforms were worn mostly. The standard lightweight tunic was single-breasted with stand-and-fall collar (usually worn open) and five composition buttons in front, two pleated breast pockets with flap and button and two side pockets with flap. Matching long or short trousers were worn with leather ankle boots or *tabi*, either with or without the separate big toe, and puttees. In jungle warfare the Japanese were masters at improvisation and concealment, and made good chronic shortages by making additional and camouflage clothing from local materials.

As standards deteriorated leather was replaced by equipment made from canvas and rubberised fabrics. In the Pacific all ranks tended to wear shirt and shorts instead of tunic and trousers.

Tank crews were issued with a one-piece khaki drill overall and a brown leather or canvas padded helmet. On the collar of the tunic they wore a small gilt metal tank.

Paratroopers wore a German-type smock and special leather (later canvas-covered steel) helmet and high lace-up leather ankle boots with rubber soles.

Rank badges were worn on red *passants* on the edge of both shoulders of the M.90, and as small rectangular collar patches on the

M.98 tunic, shirt and greatcoat. On the open tunic the collar patches were often moved to the lapels, because the shirt collar would otherwise obscure them. On certain special uniforms one patch was worn on the left sleeve.

Officers wore khaki braid rings on the greatcoat cuffs, and towards the end of the war this was extended to the sleeves of the tunic. Rank was indicated as follows:

N.C.O.s	Red collar patch with yellow stripe and one to three gilt metal five-pointed stars.
Company officers	Red collar patch with three gold stripes and one to three five-pointed stars, and one braid ring on the cuffs.
Field officers	Gold collar patch with three red stripes and one to three five-pointed stars, and two braid rings on the cuffs.
Generals	Gold collar patches with one to three silver five-pointed stars and three braid rings on the cuffs.

Arm colours appeared first on the collar patches of the M.1930 uniform, and then as a zigzag strip of cloth above the right breast pocket. Basic arm colours were:

Arm	*Colour*
Infantry	Red
Tanks	Red
Cavalry	Green
Artillery	Yellow
Engineers	Dark brown
Train	Blue

Note on Japanese army swords

World War 2 Japanese army swords were closely modelled upon the *Seki* style which had been evolved for infantry use during the *Momyama* period (1573–1638).

In 1937 the design of the regulation officers' and warrant officers' swords was changed from a Westernised style to a modification of the archaic *Tachi* mounting (suspended vertically from one scabbard ring rather than horizontally from two rings, as in the original version). The design feature common to the modern (*Shōwa-tō*) sword was the cherry blossom, a traditional symbol of military valour.

The grip of an officer's sword was bound with a khaki or brown braid over ray skin with brass or steel mountings. The warrant officers' version was cast and painted to simulate that of the officers. Scabbards were cast in metal and painted khaki with brass mountings, or made of lacquered wood with leather covering.

The sword was worn on the left side and suspended from a belt worn under the tunic by a short leather strap.

Sword knots were made of brown woven braid ending in two tassels. Different combinations of colours denoted the rank group of the wearer as follows:

Brown with red and gold stripes	General officers
Brown with red and white	Field officers
Brown with blue	Company officers

THE NETHERLANDS

The Dutch Army began to receive a grey-green field uniform in 1912, while the old black uniform continued to be worn almost up to the outbreak of World War 2, as an undress uniform.

The tunic was single-breasted with stand collar and round cuffs piped in the arm colour for all arms, except cavalry, horse artillery, and police troops with seven bronze buttons down the front. The earlier model tunic had two slash breast pockets with pointed flap and button, which were set low on the chest, and no side pockets. Later a new looser pattern tunic was introduced which had pleated patch breast and side pockets with pointed flap and small button. The shoulder straps were made of matching cloth and were finished in a roll which prevented the equipment from slipping off the shoulders. Dismounted other ranks wore matching pantaloons, puttees and black ankle boots, while mounted other ranks and officers had breeches reinforced with black leather, and black riding boots. The outside seam of the breeches for officers were piped in the arm colour, except for those arms listed above. The greatcoat was double-breasted with fall collar and two rows of seven bronze buttons.

Head-dress included a stiff grey-green kepi with matching peak, brown leather chin strap with gilt buckle, and two rows of piping in the arm colour (officers gold or silver). In front was an oval orange cockade joined to a small button by a white or yellow (officers gold or silver) braid loop. Generals had a peaked cap with black peak and chin strap, gold piping and a line of gold-embroidered oak leaves around the bottom of the band. The oval cockade within a wreath of laurel and oak leaves was worn in front. A side cap with gold piping around the flap was worn by officers and a plain one by other ranks. The regimental number in orange metal was worn on the left side. The steel helmet was Dutch and bore a remarkable resemblance to the Rumanian model. On the front was a stamped metal oval coat of arms in bronze finish.

In the Dutch East Indies a similar uniform made of grey-green cotton drill was worn with a wide-brim slouch hat. The brim was folded up on the right side and fastened with a circular metal cockade in the national colours.

Privates 1st class	Red cotton lace chevron on the left cuff.
Corporals	Narrow yellow or white cotton chevron with edging in arm colour on the left cuff.
N.C.O.s	Sergeants one gold or silver lace chevron with edging in arm colour on both cuffs. Sergeants 1st Class as for sergeants but a narrow gold or silver braid chevron with a loop at the top. Sergeant-Majors two gold or silver lace chevrons with edging in arm colour ensigned by a silvered metal crown on both cuffs.
Warrant officers	Silvered metal button on the tunic and greatcoat collar and one row of silver braid on the kepi, and silver piping on the side cap.
Officer adjutants	One silver, one silver and one gold, or two silver and one gold six-pointed stars on the tunic and greatcoat collar. One row of silver braid on the kepi, and silver piping on the side cap.
Company officers	One to three six-pointed gold stars on the tunic and greatcoat collar, and two rows of gold braid on the kepi, and gold piping on the side cap.
Field officers	Vertical bar (horizontal on the greatcoat) and one to three six-pointed stars on the tunic and greatcoat collar and three rows of gold braid on the kepi and gold piping on the side cap.

General officers	Gold-embroidered oak leaves on the front and top of the tunic collar, and two silver and two gold six-pointed stars for Major-Generals, and four six-pointed silver stars for Lieutenant-Generals on the tunic and greatcoat collars.

Arm-of-service colours appeared as piping on the tunic collar and cuffs, and on officers' breeches (as applicable), and on the kepi, and other ranks' side cap. The arm-of-service badge was worn on the tunic collar as follows:

Arm	Colour	Distinctions
Infantry	Blue	Regimental number in orange on side cap
Grenadiers	Red	Flaming grenade on side cap and collar
Rifles	Green	Hunting horn on side cap and collar
Cavalry	—	Officers in 3rd Hussars had red piping on their breeches
Field artillery	Red	Crossed cannons
Coast artillery	Red	Crossed shells
Anti-aircraft artillery	Red	Crossed cannons superimposed on propeller
Corps Horse artillery		Crossed cannons; officers yellow piping on the breeches
Engineers	Blue	Roman (sappers) helmet
Bridging and Mining Corps	Red	Foul anchor
Cyclists	Blue	Bronze wheel
Motor Service	Blue	Red wheel
Medical Troops	Blue	White enamel badge with red cross
Corps Police Troops	—	Plaited white lanyard from collar to left shoulder. Officers black breeches piping
Royal Military Academy	—	Yellow silk bars on the collar for cadets

The Royal Netherlands 'Prinses Irene' Brigade was formed in England and saw service in North Western Europe at the end of the war. Its personnel wore battle dress with Dutch rank badges and a khaki shoulder flash bearing the inscription 'Prinses Irene' in orange letters within an orange border. Under the brigade flash they also wore a khaki patch with a yellow lion rampant and the inscription 'Nederland' within a yellow border.

NORWAY

A grey-green service uniform was first introduced in 1912, as standard clothing for all those undertaking military service, and as a service uniform for regular officers and N.C.O.s.

There were three basic kinds of tunic. The service tunic was single-breasted with stand-and-fall collar piped in red, fly front, breast and side pockets with rounded flaps, round cuffs piped in red and no shoulder straps. The winter service tunic was looser fitting, to enable thick underclothing to be worn. The patch pockets were sewn on the outside. The summer version was made of a lightweight cotton drill with side pockets only. Finally there was a waterproof cotton duck anorak. Matching trousers were long and piped red, and were usually worn tucked into thick woollen socks and ankle boots. The greatcoat, which seems to have been discarded in favour of various kinds of anorak or sheepskin, was either the obsolete dark blue one, or the grey-green double-breasted coat with two rows of five buttons, fall collar, matching shoulder straps and side pockets with flap. One unusual feature was a pocket with flap on the side of the left breast.

The service head-dress was a stiff grey-green kepi with black leather peak and chin strap and red, silver or gold lace or braid according to rank. On the front was a circular cockade in the national colours, white, blue and red, which was joined by a black and silver (generals black and gold) loop to a red-enamelled button charged with a gilt metal rampant lion. The other ranks' button was white metal. The side cap had red piping and a cloth version of the cockade in front. The most common head-dress during the German invasion was the *Finnmarkslue*, a soft field cap with matching peak and ear flaps piped in red, which fastened at the side of the cap with a small button, and cloth cockade. Steel helmets appear rarely to have been worn, although the Norwegian army had both the British and the Swedish M.1921 civil defence helmet which was adopted by the Norwegian army under the designation M.1931. From 1935 an oval stamped badge bearing the Norwegian lion was attached to the front of both the British and Swedish helmets.

Rank was indicated by the number of rows and colour of the lace or braid on the kepi, the lace and the number of stars on the tunic collar and greatcoat shoulder straps, and by the lace on the cuffs of N.C.O.s.

N.C.O.s	One vertical or two horizontal red lace stripes on the cuffs, and one or two vertical lace stripes on the kepi.
Company officers	One to three five-pointed silver stars on the tunic collar and greatcoat shoulder straps, and one to three silver braid stripes on the kepi.
Field officers	One to three five-pointed silver stars and a row of lace on the tunic collar and greatcoat shoulder straps, and one wide lace, and from one to three narrow braid, stripes on the kepi.
Generals	One to three five-pointed silver stars and wide gold lace on the tunic collar, and one narrow and from one to three gold lace stripes on the kepi.

Arm-of-service was identified by the colour and design of the buttons as follows:

Arm	*Colour*	*Design*
Generals	Gold	Crossed batons
General staff	Gold	Crossed batons
Infantry	Silver	Norwegian lion
Cavalry	Silver	Horn
Artillery	Gold	Rosette
Engineers	Silver	Helmet and breast plate
Train	Gold	Wagon wheel

A Norwegian Mountain Brigade was formed in Scotland and its personnel wore battle dress with Norwegian rank badges and a khaki shoulder flash with 'Norge' in white on the right sleeve and the Norwegian flag on the left.

POLAND

Khaki was originally adopted by Poland in 1919, and in 1935 the uniform was extensively modernised so that by the outbreak of war the Polish army was universally dressed in a standard khaki uniform.

49

The tunic was single-breasted with stand-and-fall collar and seven white metal buttons in front. The breast and side patch pockets had a flap and button. The pointed shoulder straps were plain, and the regimental number or cypher was usually painted in yellow on a cloth side, so that it could be removed when desired; on officers' shoulder straps the number or cypher was embroidered in silver. The cuffs were plain with an opening at the back for other ranks, and one button for officers. Trousers were long and worn with short puttees and ankle boots. Officers and mounted personnel wore khaki breeches (Generals with blue *Lampassen*) and black boots. The great-coat was single-breasted with fall collar, six buttons in front, turn-back cuffs with tab and two buttons, and plain pointed shoulder straps.

Head-dress included the *czapka* which was stiff with square khaki top, band in arm or regiment colour and black leather peak and chin straps. On the front all ranks wore the Polish eagle and their badge of rank. A soft version of this cap with ear flap and metal buckle in front was worn as a field cap. The *czapka* was worn by all ranks in all units except *Chevaux Légers* and Frontier Corps, who wore a similar cap but with round top. At the beginning of the war the French helmet was in the process of being replaced by the 1935 Polish model, so that it was still being worn by cavalry and artillery.

Tank troops were dressed very much like their French counter-parts with double-breasted black leather jacket, black beret and the French motorised troop helmet, painted khaki. The arm-of-service colour worn on the collar patches shaped like lance pennants were orange and black cloth. Mountain troops wore the traditional circular khaki felt hat with brim and eagle's feather on the left side and a long khaki cloak which was worn over the left shoulder.

Rank was indicated on the front of the cap and on the shoulder straps as follows:

N.C.O.s (corporals)	One to three silver-embroidered bars on the cap, and lace ones across the middle of the shoulder strap.
N.C.O.s (sergeants)	One or two red-edged silver-embroidered chevrons on the cap, and red-edged silver lace chevrons and edging on the shoulder straps.
Company officers	One to three five-pointed silver-embroidered stars on the shoulder straps and cap with, in

	addition, one row of silver braid around the top of the cap band.
Field officers	One to three five-pointed silver-embroidered stars and two bars on the shoulder straps, and one to three stars and two rows of silver braid on the cap.
Generals	One to three five-pointed silver-embroidered stars and zigzag embroidery across base of shoulder strap (and on collar patches and cuffs) and on the cap band with, in addition, two rows of silver braid on the cap.
Marshals	As generals but with gilt crossed staffs or *bulava*, surmounted by the Polish eagle.

Arm-of-service and regimental colours appeared on the cap and collar patches, as well as on the undress trousers, as follows:*

Arm	Cap band	Collar patch	Piping
Generals	Khaki	Dark blue	Crimson
Infantry	Dark blue	Dark blue	Yellow
Rifle battalions	Dark blue	Dark blue	Green
Field artillery	Dark green	Dark green	Scarlet
Heavy artillery	Dark green	Dark green	Crimson
Anti-aircraft artillery	Dark green	Dark green	Yellow
Engineers	Black	Black	Scarlet
Signals	Black	Black	Cornflower blue
Tank troops	Orange	Black/Orange	—

After Poland's defeat her soldiers were scattered all over Europe with large groups in France, Russia and the Middle East. Those in France were at first issued with obsolete horizon-blue uniforms, but by the time the Polish Mountain Brigade was sent to Norway in 1940 it had been issued with French mountain troop uniforms, while the distinctive khaki cape was retained and worn with French uniform. After the Norwegian fiasco Polish troops changed their uniforms for the second time since the beginning of the war. British battle dress was not immediately available, and Polish units forming in Scotland

* For further details of Polish badges of rank see Guido Rosignoli, *Army Badges and Insignia of World War 2: Great Britain, Poland, Belgium, Italy, U.S.S.R., U.S.A., Germany.* Plates 17–32 and pp. 125–42.

wore a mixture of Polish, French and British uniform. By the end of 1940 battle dress had been generally issued and some semblance of uniformity began to prevail. Polish personnel were identified by a red shoulder flash with 'Poland' in white, Polish rank badges and the Polish eagle on the head-dress.

RUMANIA

Rumania changed the basic colour of its field uniform from horizon-blue to khaki in 1916, and in 1931 adopted a British-style service dress for its officers.

The tunic was single-breasted with stand-and-fall collar, matching pointed shoulder straps and cuffs, and a fly front. The breast pockets had a pleat, flap and button, while side pockets had a flap and button only. The cuffs were gathered and fastened tightly around the wrist with two buttons. The tunic was worn with matching pantaloons puttees and leather ankle boots. Officers also wore the closed tunic in action. The service dress tunic for officers was open with four gilt buttons in front, pleated breast patch pockets with flap and button, and large side pockets with flap and button. The cuffs were pointed with two buttons at the back. The tunic was worn with white or khaki shirt and khaki tie, long khaki trousers or light khaki breeches and black leather lace-up field boots. The greatcoat was double-breasted with large collar, turn-back cuffs and side pockets with straight flaps.

In 1931 an English-style khaki peaked cap with large flat crown and khaki band (red for generals). The peak was black leather with gold-embroidered oak leaves for generals. The chin strap was black leather edged in gold wire. The cap badge was a gold-embroidered oak leaf wreath surmounted by a crown with, in the centre, the arm-of-service badge.

Officers and other ranks wore either a side cap or field cap with matching cloth peak. Various widths of lace in the form of inverted chevrons on the front of officers' side and field caps indicated rank. The steel helmet was a Rumanian model introduced in the mid-thirties. Tank troops wore a large black beret, and mountain troops a khaki one.

Rank was indicated on the shoulder straps and side cap as follows:

N.C.O.s	One or two wide and one narrow lace bars across the shoulder strap.
Company officers	One to three gold braid bars across the shoulder strap, and three narrow lace chevrons on the side cap.
Field officers	A medium gold lace stripe down the centre of the shoulder strap with one to three narrow gold braid bars across the shoulder strap. One medium and one or two narrow lace chevrons on the side cap.
Generals	Gold lace shoulder straps with one to four braid bars across the shoulder strap. One wide and one to three narrow lace chevrons on the side cap.
Marshals	As generals but with crossed batons on shoulder straps.

Arm-of-service colours appeared on the band of the peaked cap and on the pointed collar patches as follows:

Arm	*Collar patch*	*Piping*
Generals	Dark red velvet	—
General staff	Black velvet	—
Infantry	Dark blue	—
Rifles	Dark green	—
Cavalry	Crimson	—
Artillery	Black	—
Tanks and armoured cars	Grey	—
Engineers	Black	Red
Intendance	Lilac	—

UNION OF SOVIET SOCIALIST REPUBLICS

In 1939 Russian uniform was passing through the last stages of Sovietisation, which had begun during the Civil War in an attempt to break with Tsarist tradition, and ended in 1945 with a complete revival of Tsarist uniforms.

The basic uniform in 1939 was a khaki cotton shirt or *rubaha* with stand-and-fall collar (piped in arm colour for officers) and breast patch pockets with flap and button. The sleeves were gathered at the wrist and the cuff, which were piped in arm colour for officers, fastened with two small buttons. It was worn with matching khaki breeches by all ranks in unmounted units, while all ranks in mounted units wore royal blue (officers, with piping in arm colour) breeches. In December 1935 new, rather Germanic uniforms were introduced to distinguish further those in position of command, i.e. officers, which included a single-breasted tunic or *French* with stand-and-fall collar, six buttons, pleated breast patch pockets with flap and button, and slash side pockets with flap. The collar and round cuffs were piped in arm colour. The tunic could be worn with either khaki or blue trousers, piped in arm colour, and black shoes, or royal blue piped breeches and black boots.

The greatcoat or *kaftan* was made of dark grey cloth, turning in some cases to brown, and was double-breasted with fall collar and fly front. The turn-back cuffs were cut at an angle with the highest point at the back; the side pockets were slashed. From December 1935 officers were to wear a new double-breasted greatcoat with fall collar and two rows of four buttons and turn-back cuffs. The collar and cuffs were to be piped in arm-of-service colour. In addition to the greatcoat officers were permitted to wear, from 1932 on, a khaki *bekesha*. This double-breasted coat with fly front and lambswool collar had been very popular during World War 1. In very cold weather all ranks made extensive use of wadded coats or *telogreika* and trousers.

The head-dress most immediately associated with the early Red Army was the pointed grey cloth helmet, known officially as the *shlem*, and more popularly as the *budionovka*, after the legendary cavalry commander Budjenny. The peaked cap or *furashka* had a khaki top and band and piping in arm colour. Peak and chin strap were black, and a five-pointed red star was worn in front of the band. During the bitter winter battles in Finland, the *shlem* was found to be useless and in 1940 was replaced by a grey cloth cap, or *ushanka*, with fur flaps (officers real, soldiers artificial) which covered the ears and back of the neck.

In the late thirties the French helmet began to be replaced by a new Russian model, which still retained the metal comb of its predecessor. This helmet did not last long and was replaced by the 1940 model, which is still worn today.

In 1935 a khaki cloth side cap or *pilotka* was authorised for all ranks. The officer's version was piped in arm colour around the crown and top of the flap.

In January 1943 there was a complete revival of Tsarist uniforms which coincided with the re-introduction of shoulder boards. The *French* was replaced by a single-breasted *kitel*, with piped stand collar, shoulder boards, five brass buttons in front, breast pockets with flap, and piped round cuffs. The stand-and-fall shirt collar and fly front were changed and the shirt now reverted to its traditional cut, with stand collar and two buttons and three exposed buttons on the front of the shirt. The patch pockets were removed and officers now had slash breast pockets with flap, while other ranks had no pocket at all. The greatcoat was replaced by the Tsarist officer's double-breasted one with fall collar shoulder boards, two rows of five buttons in front and turn-back cuffs. The other ranks' version was basically the same, with round turn-back cuffs and fly front. All ranks wore rectangular khaki collar patches with button and piping in arm colour. Generals had a light grey greatcoat with red piping down the front and around the collar, cuffs and pocket flaps. Collar patches were red with gold piping. At the same time a light grey full dress for generals, and a khaki full dress tunic with stand collar for both officers and men, was introduced. Finally in 1945 Marshals and generals were given a special full dress uniform in which to participate in the great victory parade in Moscow. The double-breasted tunic with stand collar was made of 'sea wave green' material which in fact was identical to the pre-revolutionary uniform colour 'Tsar's green'.

In 1935 tank troops were authorised to wear steel-grey instead of khaki service dress. On duty with their vehicles tank crews wore a one-piece black or dark blue overall. During the war crews wore a brown leather (later black canvas) padded helmet with special ear flaps to hold microphones. The wartime overall had a fall collar on which collar patches were sometimes worn, zip-fastener in front, and matching cloth belt with metal buckle. There was a patch pocket with flap on the left breast and right thigh, as well as slash side pockets which gave access to the breeches pockets. Later in the war two-piece suits were introduced. In winter crews were issued with three-quarter-length sheepskin coats.

In 1936 traditional uniforms were revived for Don, Terek and Kuban Cossacks. In action they tended to wear standard army clothing with a black or grey astrakhan cap with red, light blue and red top for Don, Terek and Kuban Cossacks respectively. Other ranks had black, and officers gold, braid in the shape of a cross on the top of the cap, and all ranks wore the red star in front.

Cossacks wore baggy blue trousers when available with light blue or red piping for Terek and Kuban, and a wide red stripe for Don, Cossacks. In winter they wore a stiff black felt cape or *bourka*, which was suspended from the shoulders by a wooden yoke.

In 1938 a wide-brimmed khaki drill sun hat was introduced for wear in very hot regions. In winter the greatcoat was supplemented by full- or three-quarter-length sheepskin or wadded jacket, wadded trousers and felt boots. One-piece camouflaged overalls were issued to assault troops and snipers, while in winter extensive use was made of various kinds of white smocks and camouflage suits.

In no other army did rank titles and badges prove such a sensitive question. Since the revolution shoulder boards and the old titles of general, colonel, lieutenant and sergeant, symbolised Tsarism and the class struggle. Soviet officers were known as commanders (Army down to section), and it was only in very gradual stages that the titles colonel to lieutenant were re-introduced in 1935. In July 1940 the title of general, followed a few days later by non-commissioned officer titles, were once again established. During this period ranks were indicated by small red enamelled triangles, squares, rectangles and rhomboids on the collar patch, and red and gold chevrons on both sleeves. At the beginning of 1943, Stalin appealed for the re-introduction of traditional Russian military titles and distinguishing marks of rank. So the Soviet army won the greatest war that Russia had ever fought, dressed not as Soviet, but as Russian, soldiers.

From 1940 to 1943 ranks were indicated as follows:

N.C.O.s	Two to four triangles on the collar patch.
Company officers	One to three squares on the collar patches and a narrow red chevron with one to three gold lines on both cuffs.
Field officers	One to four rectangles on the collar patches and a medium red chevron with two medium or one medium, and one or two slightly wider, gold lines on both cuffs.
Generals	Two to five five-pointed gold stars on the collar patches, and a gold star and wide gold chevron with red edging on both cuffs.

Marshal of the Soviet Union	Large gold-embroidered five-pointed star and laurel leaves on the collar patch and large gold star and two chevrons and laurel leaves on both cuffs.

From January 1943 until the end of the war, ranks were indicated as follows:

N.C.O.s	One to three lace bars across the khaki shoulder board. Senior sergeant (*starshi* sergeant) one wide lace bar, and *starshina* one wide, with below it one medium-wide, vertical lace bar.
Company officers	One red stripe and one to four small five-pointed stars on the khaki shoulder board.
Field officers	Two red stripes and one to three medium five-pointed stars on the khaki shoulder board.
Generals	Gold zigzag pattern-lace shoulder board with one to four large five-pointed silver stars.
Marshal of the Soviet Union	Gold zigzag-pattern lace shoulder board with one very large five-pointed silver star.

Arm-of-service colours appeared on the cap band and piping, on the tunic, shirt and greatcoat piping, on the collar patches and, after January 1943, on the shoulder boards. In addition to the colours there were small metal badges which determined the function within the arm, and were first worn on the collar patch, and then on the shoulder board.

Arm	*Collar patch and cap band*	*Piping*
Generals	Red (and arm colour)	Red
Infantry (rifles)	Raspberry red	Raspberry red
Cavalry	Royal blue	Black
Artillery	Black	Red
Tank troops	Black	Red
Engineers	Black	Blue
Chemical warfare	Black	Black
Intendance	Green	Red

On the field service (khaki) shoulder boards and greatcoat collar patches the following simplified system was utilised:*

* For further details of Russian badges of rank see Guido Rosignoli, *Army Badges and Insignia of World War 2: Great Britain, Poland, Belgium, Italy, U.S.S.R., U.S.A., Germany*. Plates 51–62 and pp. 176–90.

57

Arm	Collar patch
Generals	Gold
Infantry	Raspberry red
Cavalry	Royal blue
Artillery	Red
Tank troops	Red
Engineers	Black
Intendance	Raspberry red
Medical, veterinary and legal	Red

UNITED STATES OF AMERICA

The American army first began to wear khaki as a tropical dress in 1903, and the uniform worn at the beginning of World War 2 was a development of that introduced in 1926.

The standard soldier's uniform in 1941 consisted of an olive-drab (khaki) single-breasted tunic with open collar, matching shoulder straps, four gilt (later bronzed metal) buttons in front, breast and side patch pockets with flap and button, and matching cloth belt. It was worn with olive-drab shirt and black tie, until February 1942, when the tie was changed to olive-drab. Long trousers were made of matching cloth, and were worn with brown shoes or ankle boots and canvas leggings. In 1941 a short sand-coloured weatherproofed field jacket with zip fastener and six (or seven depending on length) buttons in front and diagonal slash side pockets was introduced. With the introduction of the field jacket, the service dress tunic was reserved as a walking-out and dress uniform, and in 1942 it underwent modifications to improve its appearance. The olive-drab melton greatcoat was double-breasted with open collar, matching shoulder straps, two rows of three buttons in front, and vertical side slash pockets. In addition to the greatcoat there were a number of different patterns of raincoat and three-quarter-length reefer coats (Mackinaws M.41 and M.43).

Officers' service dress consisted of an olive-drab tunic in the same cut as that issued to the men but with slash side pockets with flap and button and khaki lace around the cuff according to rank. The tunic was worn with light khaki shirt and tie and matching long trousers, although officers could also provide themselves with beige cavalry twill trousers known as 'pinks'. Officers had both a long double-breasted greatcoat and a short one with roll collar, two rows of three buttons, side patch pockets with flap, matching cloth belt and rank lace on the cuffs.

Head-dress consisted of the peaked or 'garrison' cap in olive-drab with artificial mohair band and brown peak and chin strap. Officers wore the American eagle on the front, while other ranks wore a smaller eagle mounted on a gold disc on the front above the band. The felt 'campaign' hat was still in limited use at the beginning of the war. In 1941 the English-model steel helmet was shipped off to China and replaced by the new two-piece American Mk 1 helmet which comprised a lightweight fibre liner and a steel shell for wear when in action. The side or 'overseas' cap was made of olive-drab material with piping in the arm colour. In 1941 a knitted woollen cap designed for wear under the helmet was introduced.

In 1943 a new combat uniform, the first to employ the layer principle, began to be introduced after extensive trials. The jacket was made of an olive-drab sateen lined with poplin, and had matching shoulder straps, breast patch pockets with flaps and diagonal slash side pockets, and the sleeves were gathered at the wrist and fastened with a tab and button. The waist could be adjusted by means of a drawstring. Various kinds of knitted and pile linings were designed to make the basic jacket suitable for most climatic conditions. In addition to the jacket there were matching trousers, field cap and russet leather lace-up boots with integral leather anklets. In 1944 a hood, sufficiently large to fit over the helmet, was added to the uniform.

Special clothing for crews of armoured fighting vehicles consisted of a one-piece herringbone twill overall with patch pockets on the breast and thighs and matching cloth belt, and a short jacket with zip-fastener in front, knitted woollen collar, cuffs and waistband and vertical slash breast pockets. To protect the head and hold the earphones, there was a lightweight fibre helmet.

Paratroopers wore a special combat dress consisting of steel helmet with forked chin strap and rubber chin cup, combat jacket with fly front and large diagonal patch breast and side pockets, and trousers with a large patch pocket on the outside of the thigh. They also received high lace-up brown leather ankle boots with rubber soles which later became standard army issue.

In the Pacific and Far Eastern campaigns American army clothing developed along lines dictated by climate and the very special combat conditions that prevailed. In 1941 the standard tropical uniform consisted of a light khaki cotton shirt, which could be worn open or with a light khaki tie and matching trousers. Additional head-dress included the campaign hat, a cotton version of the overseas cap and the fibre sun helmet. Officers wore a lightweight tunic. This basic uniform with additional clothing originally intended as working or 'fatigue' dress, formed the basis of U.S. uniform in the Pacific until the introduction of specially designed combat clothing in 1942. The first item was a one-piece reversible twill overall with large breast and thigh pockets. It was light khaki with a printed green camouflage pattern on one side. This was replaced by a more practical two-piece camouflage suit. Finally a two-piece jungle-green suit was introduced in March 1944.

Ranks were indicated by a system of gold or silver badges which were worn on the shoulder straps (or shoulders of clothing without straps), or on the right side (generals both sides) of the shirt collar. Officers wore their rank badges on the left front of the overseas cap and painted in white on the front, and sometimes on the back, of the steel helmet. N.C.O.s and men wore olive-drab chevrons on a blue ground on both sleeves.

N.C.O.s (corporals)	One to three inverted chevrons.
N.C.O.s (sergeants)	Three inverted chevrons and one to three 'rockers'. First Sergeant Grade 1 had a rhomboid between the chevrons and rockers.
Company officers	One gilt and one or two silver bars.
Field officers	Gold maple leaf and silver maple leaf and silver eagle.
Generals	One to four five-pointed silver stars.

Arm-of-service was indicated by metal badges worn on both lapels by officers, or on the left side of the collar by other ranks. Other ranks also wore their arm-of-service badges on the left front of the overseas cap. All ranks wore coloured cords on their campaign hats, and coloured piping on the overseas cap as follows:*

* For further details of United States badges of rank see Guido Rosignoli, *Army Badges and Insignia of World War 2: Great Britain, Poland, Belgium, Italy, U.S.S.R., U.S.A., Germany.* Plates 64–73 and pp. 191–206.

Arm	*Colour*
General staff corps	Gold interwoven black
Generals	Gold
Infantry	Light blue
Artillery	Red
Armour	Yellow (from 1943 green interwoven yellow)
Cavalry	Yellow
Engineers	Red interwoven white
Signals	Orange interwoven white
Quartermasters' corps	Buff

YUGOSLAVIA

The uniform of the newly-formed Yugoslav army followed closely the Serbian pattern, which itself was a cross between Austro-Hungarian and Imperial Russian uniform. By the outbreak of war there was a marked lack of standardisation, with at least three different models of steel helmet in use concurrently. The colour of the uniform also varied, and whereas officers wore field-grey, other ranks' uniforms ranged from the light grey of World War 1 Serbian uniforms to a khaki brown.

The standard tunic was single-breasted with stand collar, fly front, matching shoulder straps with square ends (the right one of which usually ended in a roll or *parolli*), slanting breast and side slash pockets with Austrian-pattern flaps, and turn-back cuffs. The obsolete double-breasted tunic with coloured collar was also still in use. The tunic was worn with matching pantaloons, puttees and ankle boots. The greatcoat was double-breasted with fall collar and two rows of six buttons converging towards the waist, turn-back cuffs and side pockets with straight flaps.

Officers' uniforms were generally of superior quality, and the tunic had a stand collar in the arm colour. The turn-back cuffs were also piped as were the matching breeches. Generals had red *Lampassen*. The three helmets in concurrent use in 1941 were the French model with or without the Yugoslav coat of arms on the front, the German M.1915, and the Czech model. Officers wore a stiff kepi with black leather peak and chin strap and an oval cockade in white, blue and red with the royal cypher in gilt metal in the centre. All ranks also wore a side cap with flat top and curved flap.

Rank was indicated on the shoulder straps, and on the kepi by officers, and on the lower left sleeve of the mountain jacket by those authorised to wear it as follows:

Corporals	One four-pointed yellow metal star on the shoulder straps, and one narrow lace chevron on the mountain jacket.
N.C.O.s	Two or three yellow metal stars on the shoulder straps which were piped in the arm colour. Two or three yellow lace bars on the mountain jacket.
	Sergeant-majors had shoulder straps in the arm colour with four yellow metal stars arranged to form a lozenge with above one (3rd Class) to three (1st Class) narrow gold lace bars according to class of sergeant-major. One to three gold lace bars on a patch in the arm colour on the mountain jacket.
Company officers	Gold lace shoulder straps with longitudinal line in arm colour and one (2nd Lieut.) to four (1st Capt.) four-pointed silver stars. One to four gold lace bars on patch piped in the arm colour on the mountain jacket. Piping in arm colour around the crown of the kepi.
Field officers	Gold lace shoulder straps with one to three four-pointed silver stars. One wide with one to three narrow gold lace bars above on a patch piped in the arm colour on the mountain jacket. Gold piping around the crown of the kepi.
Generals	Twisted gold braid shoulder straps with silver coat of arms and Royal cypher for Field-Marshals. One to three six-pointed stars on both forearms. Generals of Brigade had piping and shoulder strap underlay in arm colour, whereas Generals of Army and Division and Field-Marshals had light blue. General officers had a peaked cap.

Arm-of-service was indicated by the colour of the collar, piping, and stripe and underlay of the shoulder straps, as well as by the badge on the shoulder straps, greatcoat collar patches, and trouser piping for officers. Other ranks had coloured collar patches on the tunic and greatcoat, and N.C.O.s coloured shoulder straps, or shoulder strap piping. Badges were either worn on the collar patches or shoulder straps as follows:

Arm	Colour	Badge
Generals	Light blue	
General staff	Red velvet	
Infantry	Dark red	
Mountain infantry		Triangular mountain landscape framed by skis and ski sticks
Cavalry	Blue	
Cyclists		Bicycle wheel superimposed on crossed swords
Armoured troops		Tank
Artillery	Black velvet	Crossed cannons ensigned by exploding shell
Anti-aircraft artillery	Black velvet	Crossed cannons ensigned by winged bird
Fortress artillery	Black velvet	Crossed cannons superimposed on castle
Mountain artillery	Black velvet	Hunting horn
Engineers	Violet velvet	
Signals		Two intertwined lightning bolts
Signals (wireless)		Three lightning bolts emanating from the centre
Motor transport		Winged wheel and steering wheel
Gendarmerie	Scarlet	
Administration	Green	
Medical Service	Brown velvet	Aesculapius rod
Veterinary Service	Brown velvet	Horse's head superimposed on a Caduceus
Reserve Officers School		Crossed swords

Some of these badges have indicated special qualifications and were worn in conjunction with the colour of the arm in which the wearer was serving.

In May 1941 Croatia became an independent state under German hegemony. The first alteration to the uniform was to replace the Yugoslav coat of arms on the helmet with a white painted letter U which stood for *Ustacha* or uprising, the symbol of Dr Ante Pavelich's Fascist Independence Movement. Many senior Croatian officers equipped themselves with Germanified field-grey uniforms, while the bulk of the army continued to wear the Yugoslav uniform. Moslem Bosnian regiments wore a red fez with black tassel instead of the side cap. For the rest of the war Yugoslavia was a battleground for pro-communist partisans under Tito, and pro-monarchists under Mihailovitch, who simultaneously fought each other and the occupiers.

Tito's and Mihailovitch's men were irregulars who wore whatever they could find – old Yugoslav uniforms and captured German and Italian clothing – but there was a marked difference in the appearance of the two sides. Tito adopted the red star and tried to standardise the uniform of his followers, while Mihailovitch's men dressed like brigands with beards and astrakhan caps adorned with the double-headed eagle.

An independent Yugoslav Army Group fought on the eastern front with the Red Army, and its personnel wore Soviet uniform.

1. Polish infantryman

2. Polish tank officer

3. Polish general

The Invasion of Poland, 1939

4. Polish lancer officer

German infantryman

7. German infantry officer

6. Slovak infantryman

The Finnish Campaign, 1939

8. Finnish general

9. Russian infantryman

10. Finnish rifleman

The Western Front, 1939—40

11. British general

12. French general

13. French infantryman

The Invasion of Norway and Denmark, 1940

14. German mountain trooper

15. German general

16. German infantryman

17. Norwegian general

18. Norwegian infantryman

19. Danish infantryman

The Invasion of Norway and Denmark, 1940

20. Polish mountain trooper

22. British infantryman

21. French mountain trooper

23. German tank officer

24. German general

25. German infantryman

The Invasion of the Low Countries and France, 1940

26. German artilleryman

28. German engineer

27. German paratrooper

The Invasion of the Low Countries and France, 1940

29. Dutch artillery officer

31. Dutch infantryman

30. Dutch officer

The Invasion of the Low Countries and France 1940

32. Belgian mountain trooper

34. Belgian motorcyclist

33. Belgian general

35. French infantryman

37. French artilleryman

36. French infantry officer

The Invasion of the Low Countries and France, 1940

38. Scottish highlander

39. British infantryman

40. French infantryman

The Libyan Campaign, 1940—41

41. British guards officer

42. British general

43. British guardsman

44. Italian tank officer

45. Italian marshal

46. Italian infantry officer

47. British officer cadet

49. Polish rifleman

48. British home guardsman

The British Home Front

50. Czech infantry officer

51. French légionaire

52. British infantryman

53. German mountain trooper

55. German paratroop officer

54. German SS infantryman

The Invasion of the Balkans, Greece and Crete, 1941

56. Italian infantryman

57. Hungarian officer

58. Bulgarian infantryman

59. Australian infantryman

61. Yugoslav infantryman

60. Greek rifleman

The North African Campaign, 1941

62. British tank man

63. French légionaire

64. Indian infantryman

The North African Campaign, 1941

65. German infantryman

66. German general

67. German tank man

The North African Campaign, 1941

68. Italian infantryman

70. Italian colonial infantryma

69. Italian general

71. German staff officer

72. German military policeman

73. Finnish infantryman

The Invasion of Russia, 1941

74. German SS infantryman

75. Italian cavalry officer

76. German infantry officer

77. German cavalry trooper

The Invasion of Russia, 1941

78. Slovak infantryman

79. Rumanian infantryman

80. Hungarian infantryman

81. Russian political commissar

82. Russian general

83. Russian artillery officer

The Invasion of Russia, 1941

84. Russian tank man

85. Russian infantryman

86. Russian NKVD officer

87. Japanese general

89. Japanese infantry officer

88. Japanese infantryman

The Far East, 1942

90. British officer

91. Dutch infantryman

92. Indian infantry officer

93. French general

95. British staff officer

94. British general

The North African Campaign, 1942

96. German engineer officer

97. German general

98. German infantryman

99. Russian infantryman

101. Russian infantryman

100. Russian tank officer

102. German infantry officer

104. Italian mountain troop

103. German infantryman

105. US general

107. Australian infantryman

106. US infantryman

The Far East, 1942

108. Japanese tank man

109. Japanese artilleryman

110. Japanese paratrooper

111. Chinese infantryman

113. Chinese infantryman

112. Chinese general

114. Japanese tank officer

115. Japanese staff officer

116. Japanese infantryman

117. French infantryman

119. US tank man

118. British infantryman

The Tunisian Campaign, 1943

120. German artillery officer

122. Italian general

121. German cavalry officer

123. Russian engineer

125. Russian infantryman

124. Russian general

The Russian Campaign, 1943

126. German tank man

127. German SS grenadier

128. German infantryman

129. Italian paratrooper

131. German paratrooper

130. German mountain troop officer

132. New Zealand officer

134. Polish infantryman

133. US artilleryman

135. French infantry officer

The Resistance, Western Europe, 1943—45

136. Danish resistance man

138. Italian partisan

137. French resistance man

139. French militiaman

141. Russian Cossack

140. German policeman

The Resistance, Eastern Europe, 1943—45

142. Russian partisan

144. Yugoslav partisan

143. Polish partisan

145. Russian Cossack officer

147. Russian auxiliary policeman

146. German security policeman

The Far East, 1944

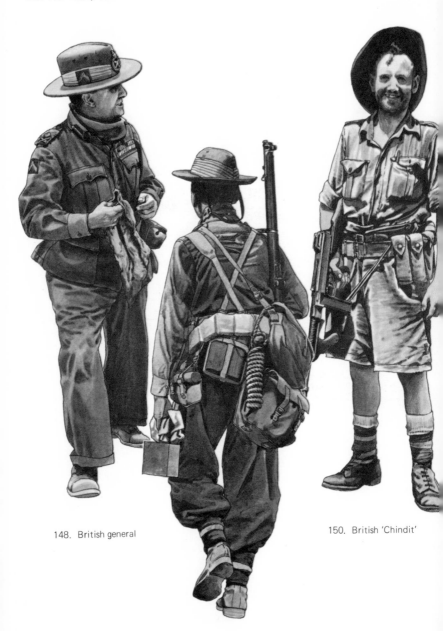

148. British general

149. Indian Gurkha rifleman

150. British 'Chindit'

1. Australian infantryman

153. US marauder

152. US tank man

154. Japanese general

156. Japanese infantryman

155. Japanese infantryman

British military policeman

159. British infantryman

158. British infantryman

160. US infantryman

162. British commando

161. US paratroop officer

163. German SS general

165. German SS tank officer

164. German field-marshal

166. German grenadier

167. German assault artillery office

168. British paratrooper

169. US general

170. British tank man

The Eastern Front, 1944

171. German grenadier officer

172. German general

173. German infantryman

174. Polish infantryman

176. Russian Cossack

175. Russian traffic controller

The Italian Campaign, 1944—45

177. German infantryman

178. German general

179. German SS officer

180. Russian Cossack security policeman

The Italian Campaign, 1944—45

181. Italian rifles officer

182. US infantryman

183. British military polic

184. German infantryman

186. German SS grenadier

185. German infantryman

The Western Front, 1945

187. US infantryman

188. US military policeman

189. Canadian infantryman

190. Russian tank officer

191. Russian engineer

192. Russian infantryman

The Eastern Front, 1945

193. German people's grenadier

194. German leader

195. German home guardsr

196. US infantryman

197. West African rifleman

198. British infantryman

199. Japanese officer

201. Japanese soldier

200. Japanese general

202. French infantry officer

204. US military policeman

203. Scottish drummer

205. Russian infantryman

207. Russian infantry c

206. Russian marshal

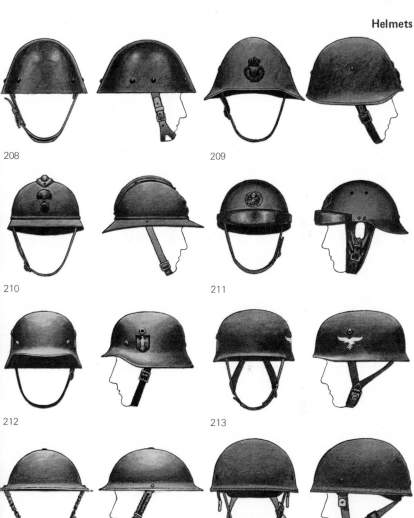

208

209

210

211

212

213

214

215

216

217

Helmets

218

219

220

221

222

223

224

225

226

227

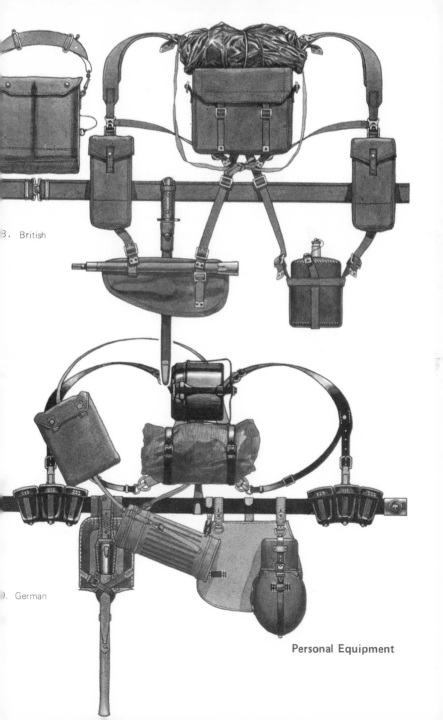

B. British

9. German

Personal Equipment

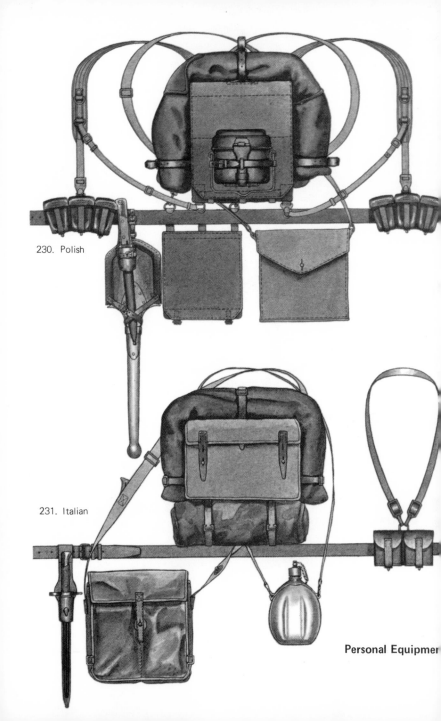

230. Polish

231. Italian

Personal Equipmen

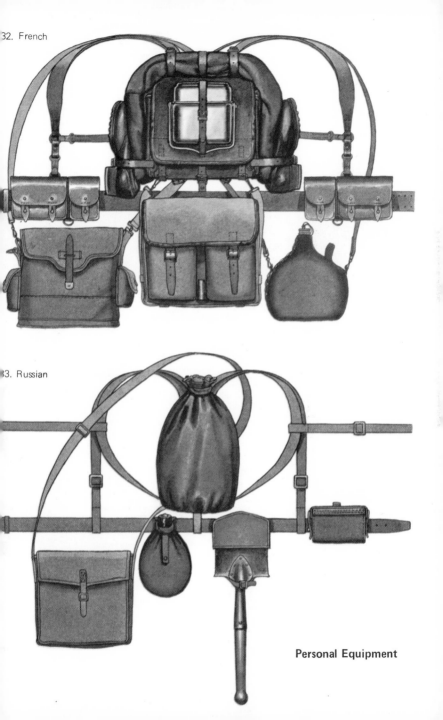

32. French

33. Russian

Personal Equipment

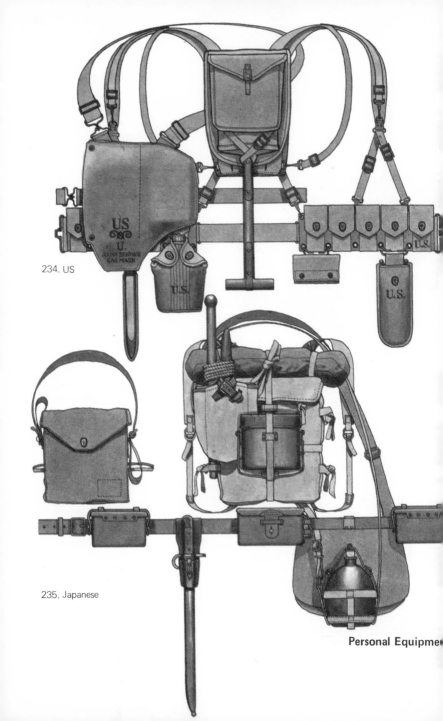

234. US

235. Japanese

Personal Equipme

236

237

238

239

240

241

242

243

244

245

246

Small Arms

247

248

249

250

251

252

253

254

255

256

257

NOTES TO PLATES

1. Poland: Infantryman, 1939

This soldier wears the standard M.1935 field service uniform with the M.1935 steel helmet. The regimental number was painted in yellow on a cloth slide on the shoulder strap, which could be removed when in action. Ankle boots were worn with either long or short puttees or, in summer, short canvas anklets which fastened with two buttons on the outside.

Equipment: Standard Polish M.1935 infantry equipment.

Weapons: Polish Mauser 7·92 mm. 98 service rifle.

2. Poland: Captain 8th Tank Battalion, Poland 1939

The black leather coat was worn by officers and sergeants while other ranks wore a light khaki overall. The tradition of the black uniform was continued on British battle dress in the form of a single black shoulder strap by members of the 10th Motorised Cavalry Brigade.

Equipment: Regulation officer's waistbelt and cross-strap.

3. Poland: Marshal Śmigly-Rydz, Warsaw 1939

The C.-in-C. of the Polish army wears standard officer's service dress with the order of Virtuti Militari 5th Class on his left breast.

Equipment: Regulation officer's waistbelt and cross-strap.

4. Poland: Colonel 11th Lancers, Poland 1939

This regimental commander wears the officer's version of the *czapka* and the regulation greatcoat on which medal ribbons could be worn. While the infantry had received the M.1935 steel helmet the cavalry continued to wear the French model. There were no less than twenty-seven regiments of lancers, each distinguished by the colour of the cap band, collar patch and lance pennant as well as by the regimental cypher on the shoulder strap and badge which was worn on the right breast.

Equipment: Basically the same as that of the infantry, but with leather instead of canvas straps supporting.

Weapons: M. 1921 officer's sabre.

5. Germany: Senior Private 164th Infantry Regiment, Poland September 1939

The standard field service uniform of the German army began to be introduced in 1936, and underwent no changes until the outbreak of war. Trousers were still stone-grey, and all insignia were machine-embroidered in silver-grey artificial silk thread. Arm of service was identified by the white inverted chevron on the side cap and white stripes on the collar patch *Litzen*.

Equipment: Standard infantry equipment, in black leather, with the exception of the rifle sling which was brown.

Weapons: German Mauser Gew. 98k service rifle.

6. Slovakia: Corporal of infantry, Southern Poland 1939
This uniform, the standard field service dress of the former Czech army, continued to form the basis of Slovak uniform until the end of the war.

Equipment: Made of brown leather and khaki canvas, Czech equipment combined features of World War 1 Austrian and more recent German equipment.

Weapons: Czech VZ (short) M.1924 Mauser service rifle.

7. Germany: 2nd Lieutenant 2nd Infantry Regiment, Poland September 1939
Most German officers continued to wear tailor-made uniforms in the field at the beginning of the war. The first official alteration to the peacetime uniform was the discontinuation of the brown leather cross-strap for the duration of the war.

Equipment: Regulation officer's belt, map case and pistol holster.

Weapons: German M.1908 Parabellum automatic service pistol.

8. Finland: Major-General Wallenius, Salla December 1939
Under a typical sheepskin coat he wears the M.1936 grey-green service uniform of the Finnish army.

Equipment: Regulation officer's waistbelt and cross-strap, flashlight and pistol holster.

Weapons: Finnish 9 mm. Lahti M.L.-35 service pistol.

9. U.S.S.R.: Private of infantry, 1939
The pointed cap or *shlem* first appeared in 1919, but was withdrawn after the winter campaign of 1939–40 because it was found to be impractical.

Equipment: Basic Soviet infantry equipment was simple in the extreme and usually consisted of narrow leather belt with single-pronged steel buckle, World War 1 pattern ammunition pouch, gas mask and haversack.

Weapons: Russian Moisin 7·62 mm. rifle and bayonet, which was usually carried on the rifle, either in the fixed or reversed position.

10. Finland: Private of rifles, Soumussalmi 1939
The white snow suit was intended as camouflage and many different types were used. The steel helmet at this period of the war was the German M.1916 version.

Equipment: Ammunition pouches, pack, haversack, water bottle and entrenching tool were basically the German model, while the narrow belt was made of natural-coloured hide with a plain single-pronged steel buckle.

Weapons: Russian Moisin 7·62 mm. rifle and bayonet.

11. Great Britain: General Lord Gort, V.C., France 1940
As C.-in-C. British Expeditionary Force in France Gort wears a 'mac'

over his khaki service dress. His rank badges were a gilt metal crown, pip and crossed sword and baton on his shoulder straps, red gorget patches with gold-embroidered oak leaves and a red cap band.

12. France: Brigadier (Général de Brigade), 1939–40

This very personal uniform was typical of many during the bitter winter of 1939–40. The original caption to the photograph from which this drawing was made stated that 'all French generals on active service are typified by this Brigadier, his neck wrapped in a long scarf and his moustache still damp with soup'.

13. France: Private of infantry, 1939–40

There was little activity during the 'sitzkrieg' on the western front, so soldiers of both sides were kept busy and warm by clearing snow. The greatcoat and side cap are regulation whereas the clogs (although common) were not standard issue.

14. Germany: Private 138th Mountain Rifle Regiment, Trondheim 1940

Personnel in mountain units wore standard infantry field uniform with ski cap, baggy climbing trousers, climbing boots with studded soles, and short elasticated puttees. The arm colour was bright green while a further distinguishing mark was the edelweiss in white metal on the left side of the ski cap, and in white

on a dark green oval ground on the upper right sleeve.

Equipment: Standard infantry equipment with rucksack instead of the pack and a larger-capacity water bottle.

Weapons: German Mauser Gew. 98k with an additional butt plate to prevent the wooden butt from being damaged by the cleats on the sides of the soles of mountain boots.

15. Germany: Infantry General Eduard Dietl, Narvik 1940

The popular commander of the 3rd Mountain Division and Narvik Group won his Knight's Cross in May 1940, and Oak Leaves two months later. He wears the ski cap and old-style piped field blouse. On his right breast is the enamelled badge for Army Mountain Guides.

16. Germany: Private 159th Infantry Regiment, Norway 1940

Both the Germans and the Allies suffered severely from exposure and were forced to improvise winter clothing from whatever was available – even captured enemy uniforms.

Equipment: Machine-gunners wore standard infantry equipment, but instead of two ammunition pouches they carried a pistol and a leather case containing machine-gun stripping and cleaning tools and an anti-aircraft sight.

Weapons: German MG.34 light machine-gun, 08 or P.38 service pistols and stick grenade 24.

17. Norway: King Haakon VII, Norway 1940

The King wears the uniform of a Norwegian general, which was basically the same for all officers. On the greatcoat the rank badges appeared on the shoulder straps.

Equipment: Regulation officer's waistbelt and cross-strap.

Weapons: Norwegian M.1914 service pistol.

18. Norway: Sergeant of infantry, Norway 1940

During the winter this uniform was usually worn under the obsolete dark blue double-breasted greatcoat. Steel helmets appear rarely to have been worn.

Equipment: Standard infantry equipment with (not shown) green canvas rucksack and gas mask in natural-coloured canvas bag on the left side.

Weapons: Norwegian Krag-Jorgensen M.1894 or M.1894/10 service rifles.

19. Denmark: Infantryman, Copenhagen 1940

Apparently the M.1923 khaki uniform had not been generally issued to the rank and file, although regular officers and N.C.O.s had equipped themselves with it. Typical is the method of wearing the trousers.

Equipment: Brown leather equipment was intended to have been worn with khaki, but existing stocks of black equipment were still being used up.

Weapons: Danish 8 mm. Krag-Jorgensen M.1894/10 service rifle.

20. Poland: Lance-corporal 1st Battalion 3rd Light-Brigade of the Polish Independent Highland Brigade, Narvik 1940

On the beret is the eagle, originally worn by General Haller's Polish army in France during World War 1, and revived in 1940. The anorak is that issued to French Alpine troops.

Equipment: Standard French infantry equipment with gas mask on left hip.

21. France: Private Alpine troops (Chasseurs Alpins), Narvik 1940

Sheepskin coats of various types were worn over standard uniform as an expedient to improve the totally inadequate winter clothing which was provided.

Equipment: Old-style French infantry equipment with haversack on left hip.

22. Great Britain: Private King's Own Yorkshire Light Infantry, Norway 1940

One of the few items of special winter clothing available to British troops was the stiff and heavy 'Tropal' coat, which was never intended to be worn in action, but as a guard coat for sentries. The white sheepskin cap came from Norwegian stocks.

23. Germany: 2nd Lieutenant 1st Tank Regiment, France 1940

The black uniform was originally introduced for wear when actually on duty with the vehicle, and with all other orders of dress the field-grey uniform with pink *Waffenfarbe* was worn. The beret incorporated a padded crash helmet.

Equipment: Normally only a waistbelt and pistol holster were worn on the person, while all other kit was stowed away in the tank.

Weapons: German M.08 Parabellum (Luger) or Walther P.38 service pistols.

24. Germany: General of infantry, 1940

Generals were distinguished by gold cords and piping on the cap, gold-embroidered red collar patches, gold and silver braid shoulder straps and red *Lampassen* on the breeches or trousers. Cap badges remained silver until January 1943, when they too became gold.

Equipment: Regulation waistbelt with gilt metal two-pronged belt buckle.

Weapons: General officers normally wore a small-calibre automatic pistol.

25. Germany: Lance-corporal 10th Panzer Grenadier Regiment, France 1940

Panzer Grenadiers tended to fight lighter-equipped than infantry because their kit was carried in armoured personnel carriers or lorries.

Equipment: Standard infantry equipment with the anti-gas cape in the pouch on the chest.

Weapons: German Gew. 98k service rifle and stick grenade 24.

26. Germany: Private of artillery, France 1940

Mounted personnel were issued with breeches and riding boots in place of long trousers and marching boots. Arm-of-service colour was red.

Equipment: Mounted personnel were not issued with packs because they carried their kit in saddle bags. The straps supporting are the cavalry pattern.

Weapons: German Mauser 98k rifle.

27. Germany: Lance-corporal Assault Company Koch, Eben Emael 1940

The olive-green cotton duck one-piece jump smock was worn over the equipment; on landing it was removed and replaced under the equipment.

Equipment: Standard infantry equipment was modified so as not to cause injury to the wearer on landing. Ammunition and flare cartridges were carried in cloth bandoliers, and the gas mask was removed from its metal cannister and carried in a soft cloth bag.

Weapons: German Mauser 98k rifle.

28. Germany: Private 18th Motorised Engineer Battalion, Northern France 1940

Engineers wore standard field service uniform with black *Waffenfarbe*. This engineer wears stone-grey trousers, which began to be replaced by field-grey ones in 1940.

Equipment: Special technical equipment and apparatus was issued for a particular operation, and could include heavy-duty wire cutters and smoke cannisters.

Weapons: German Mauser 98k service rifle.

29. The Netherlands: Captain Field Artillery, 1940
On the standard officer's service dress, arm of service was indicated by the colour of the piping and collar badge, while rank badges were worn on the stiff stand-up collar.

Equipment: Regulation officer's waistbelt and pistol magazine pouch.

30. The Netherlands: Colonel of rifles, 1940
The gold braid on the stiff kepi indicated the rank group of the wearer, who here wears the regulation officer's greatcoat.

Equipment: Regulation officer's waistbelt and cross-strap.

31. The Netherlands: Corporal of infantry, 1940
The basic grey-green field uniform of the Dutch army was virtually the same as that worn during World War 1. N.C.O.s' rank badges took the form of sleeve chevrons.

Equipment: Regulation Dutch infantry equipment with German-pattern ammunition pouches.

32. Belgium: Corporal 2nd Regiment of Ardennes Rifles, Belgium 1940
The shortened greatcoat and leather leggings were worn instead of standard infantry greatcoat and puttees. Regimental distinctions were the green beret and boar's head badge.

Equipment: Standard Belgian infantry equipment with German-pattern ammunition pouches.

Weapons: Belgian M.1889 7·65 mm. service rifle.

33. Belgium: Leopold III King of the Belgians, Belgium 1940
As C.-in-C. Belgian Army he wears the uniform of a general. This English-style service dress was common to all army officers.

Equipment: Regulation officer's waistbelt and cross-strap.

34. Belgium: Motorcyclist, Belgium 1940
This brown leather uniform was also worn by crews of armoured vehicles, who also wore the French armoured troop helmet. Motorcyclists and motorised troops wore the special leather-covered helmet illustrated.

35. France: Corporal 2nd Infantry Regiment, France 1940
The famous *capote* with its buttoned-back flaps was so typical of World War 1 *poilus* that it gave rise to the belief that French soldiers were not issued with tunics, which in fact they were.

Equipment: Combination of the old and new (M.1935) infantry equipments.

Weapons: French MAS 1936 rifle.

36. France: Infantry battalion commander, France 1940

The regulation officer's service dress tunic is here being worn with non-regulation matching breeches and leather leggings.

Equipment: Regulation officer's waistbelt and cross-strap.

Weapons: French Ruby or Star 7·65 mm. automatic pistol.

37. France: Private of artillery, France 1940

The tunic is made of lightweight khaki drill and is worn with khaki pantaloons.

Equipment: Gas mask in canvas bag on left hip.

38. Great Britain: Private 2nd Battalion Seaforth Highlanders, France 1940

This highlander wears the 1937-pattern battle dress with fly front and concealed buttons under the pocket flaps. The Camerons formed part of the 51st Highland Division whose formation sign is shown.

Equipment: Pattern 1937 web equipment with gas mask worn on the chest (229).

Weapons: British rifle No. 4 Mark I* (better known as the SMLE or ·303).

39. Great Britain: Lance-corporal infantry, 1940

This was the standard uniform of the British army at the beginning of the war, and it remained virtually unchanged throughout.

Equipment: Pattern 1937 web equipment with gas mask slung over the shoulder. The basic pouches were designed to carry two Bren magazines, a number of grenades or small arms ammunition.

Weapons: British rifle No. 3 Mark I*.

40. France: Motorcyclist of Motorised Dragoons (Dragons portés), 1940

Motorised Dragoon regiments included squadrons of motorcyclists and infantry transported in half-tracks. The regulation uniform for motorcyclists was the helmet shown and either a brown leather single-breasted coat, or a rubberised coat with matching trousers.

Equipment: Regulation French infantry equipment.

Weapons: French rifle (Fusil) 1907–15.

41. Great Britain: Captain Willie Forbes 3rd Battalion Coldstream Guards, Libya December 1940

Even during the battle of Sidi Barani guards officers managed to establish and maintain their own distinctive style of dress. This battalion was also responsible for popularising full-length Hebron sheepskin coats. The helmet is covered with sacking to soften its outline and blend it with its surroundings.

Equipment: Pattern 1937 web equipment basic set for officers, with binocular case on the right. In his hand he carries the officer's haversack.

Weapons: British Webley ·455 Mark VI Pistol No. 1.

42. Great Britain: General Sir Archibald Wavell, Libya 1940

By desert standards Wavell was very correctly dressed with British warm, breeches and field boots. He makes an interesting comparison with Monty (94).

43. Great Britain: Guardsman, Libya 1940

Guardsmen continued to wear the stiff service dress cap in the desert. The rest of the uniform consisting of khaki drill shirt, shorts and khaki woollen pullover was standard issue.

Equipment: Pattern 1937 web equipment with gas mask on the chest, and small pack on the back and water bottle on the right hip.

Weapons: British rifle No. 1 Mark III.

44. Italy: Lieutenant Scalise, Commander Assault Gun Battery 132nd Ariete Armoured Division, North Africa 1940–1

The three-quarter-length double-breasted leather coat and blocked leather helmet with padded rim and neck flap were standard issue for crews of armoured vehicles. Rank badges were normally worn on the left breast.

Equipment: Regulation officer's waistbelt and binoculars.

Weapons: Italian Beretta 1934 9 mm. automatic pistol.

45. Italy: Marshal of Italy Badoglio, Libya 1940

This lightweight service dress was standard for all officers and was usually made of gaberdine. The five-pointed star on the collar was the former emblem of the Italian army, and was common to all ranks in all arms.

Equipment: Regulation officer's waistbelt and cross-strap.

46. Italy: Captain 70th Infantry Regiment (Sirte Division), Libya 1940

Normally each division had two infantry regiments and an artillery regiment, each of which was identified by coloured collar patches. The divisional sign in the form of a metal or cloth shield was worn on the upper left sleeve.

Equipment: Regulation officer's waistbelt and cross-strap.

Weapons: Italian Beretta 1934 9 mm. automatic pistol.

47. Great Britain: Officer Cadet Royal Tank Regiment, England 1940

Cadets were distinguished by white gorget patches and a white cap band or backing to the regimental cap badge. The greatcoat is the newly-introduced double-breasted 1937 pattern.

48. Great Britain: Local Defence Volunteer, England May 1940

Before the issue of uniforms a khaki armlet bearing the letters L.D.V. was worn with civilian clothes. Soon after its formation the L.D.V. became the Home Guard.

Equipment: Mainly obsolete equipment of World War 1 vintage or earlier; was gradually replaced by a special brown leather Home Guard pattern. Each man received a gas mask and steel helmet.

Weapons: Broom handles and farm implements were rapidly replaced by weapons of all types and calibres, many of which had been confiscated by American police departments and shipped to England for Home Guard use.

49. Poland: Lance-corporal 1st Armoured Regiment 16th Armoured Brigade, Scotland 1941

British uniform was worn with Polish insignia and badges of rank.

The 10th Motorised Cavalry Brigade became later the 1st Polish Armoured Division whose personnel were to wear one black shoulder strap on battle dress.

Weapons: British Rifle No. 1 Mark 3.

50. Czechoslovakia: Lieutenant Independent Czech Brigade, England 1941

After evacuation from France, Czechs were issued with battle dress with a khaki shoulder title bearing the inscription 'Czechoslovakia' in red letters.

Equipment: Czech officer's waistbelt and British gas mask.

51. France: Légionaire 13th Light Brigade (Demi-Brigade) French Foreign Legion, England 1940

This transitional dress combining French and British uniform was worn for a short time in England after the Brigade had been evacuated from Norway, and before it was sent to North Africa. The white scarf or *chèche* and blue cotton sash were typical features of Foreign Legion uniform.

Equipment: Regulation French infantry equipment.

Weapons: French MAS 1936 rifle.

52. Great Britain: Private of infantry, England 1940

Although rendered obsolete by battle dress the service dress continued to be worn throughout the war, particularly by the Corps of Military Police.

Equipment: Pattern 1908 waistbelt and bayonet frog.

Weapons: British rifle No. 1 Mark I.

53. Germany: Corporal 143 Mountain Rifle Regiment, Greece April 1941

Arm-of-service colour was grassgreen, and mountain troops were further distinguished by a white metal edelweiss on the left side of the cap, and an oval dark green cloth badge with the edelweiss in white, which was worn on the upper right sleeve.

Equipment: Standard mountain troop equipment.

Weapons: German MP.40 sub-machine-gun.

54. Germany: Lance-corporal SS Motorised Bodyguard Regiment Adolf Hitler, Greece 1941

The collar of the field blouse, which was worn under the camouflage smock, was left exposed to display rank badges.

Equipment: Standard infantry equipment with map case.

Weapons: German Mauser 98k rifle.

55. Germany: Air-force 2nd Lieutenant 1st Parachute Rifle Regiment, Crete 1941

Parachute troops were distinguished by yellow *Waffenfarbe*, which appeared on the collar patches and shoulder straps. Members of the 1st and 2nd Parachute Rifle Regiments and the Parachute Division wore a green cuff-band on the right cuff. The German parachutist's landing position necessitated the use of knee pads.

Equipment: Air-force officer's belt, holster and map case, and issue straps supporting.

56. Italy: Private of infantry, Greece 1941

Both Italians and Greeks suffered severely from exposure caused by insufficient winter clothing. The arm-of-service badge was often sprayed in black through a stencil on the front of the helmet.

Equipment: Standard Italian infantry equipment with two ammunition pouches worn in the centre of the body and suspended by a strap around the neck. A feature of Italian equipment was the grey-green leather from which it was made.

Weapons: Italian Mannlicher-Carcano 6·5 mm. rifle.

57. Hungary: Colonel of infantry, 1941

Rank was indicated on the collar patches and by inverted chevrons on the front of the side cap. Arm-of-service colour appeared on the collar patches and triangular badge on the left side of the side cap.

Equipment: Regulation officer's waistbelt.

Weapons: Frommer Lilliput ·25 automatic pistol.

58. Bulgaria: Private of infantry, 1941

The red cap band, collar patches and shoulder straps identified this soldier as an infantryman. The number of most infantry regiments appeared on the shoulder straps, while the 1st and 6th regiments had a Cyrillic cypher, as did the Military Academy and King Boris's Own Regiment.

Equipment: Bulgarian or Russian pattern made of brown leather.

Weapons: Bulgarian M.1895/24 7·92 mm. rifle.

59. Australia: Corporal 6th Infantry Division, Greece 1941
The Australian battle dress still included the tunic of World War 1 vintage. The slouch hat was worn with the flap down or folded up in which case it was fastened with either the regimental or Australian badge.

Equipment: Pattern 1908 web equipment.

Weapons: British rifle No. 1 Mark III*.

60. Greece: Corporal of rifles (Evzones), Greece 1941
This shows the *Evzone* version of the Greek army field uniform. The standard version consisted of a tunic and pantaloons, which were worn with ankle boots and puttees.

Equipment: Natural-coloured leather equipment, with olive-green canvas haversack and pack.

Weapons: French rifle (*fusil*) 1907–15.

61. Yugoslavia: Private of infantry, Yugoslavia 1941
Although the standard uniform of the Yugoslav army was this greyish khaki, World War 1 Serbian uniforms were also in general use. The steel helmet was the French model with the Yugoslav coat of arms on the front.

Equipment: Standard brown leather Yugoslav infantry equipment.

Weapons: Yugoslav M.1924 7·92 mm. service rifle.

62. Great Britain: Corporal Royal Tank Regiment, North Africa 1941
The black beret with its silver badge distinguished men of the Royal Tank Regiment from other personnel. Goggles were an absolute necessity in the desert.

Equipment: Pattern 1937 web equipment set for Royal Armoured Corps and Royal Signals personnel employed with those units.

Weapons: British 0·38 in. service revolver.

63. France: Private French Foreign Legion in the 1st Free French Brigade, Bir Hakiem 1941
This bearded pioneer wears British K.D. shirt and shorts and webbing anklets together with the famous white kepi.

Equipment: Regulation French infantry equipment.

Weapons: French MAS 1936 rifle.

64. India: Private of infantry 4th Indian Division, North Africa 1941
The Indian army pioneered the use of knitted pullovers, while the rest of the uniform followed closely the British pattern. The very long and wide shorts, known to the British as 'Bombay bloomers', were also typical of Indian uniform. The hessian helmet cover was gathered and hung down at the back of the

neck as on a *puggree* and was used to cover the face in dust and sand storms.

Equipment: Pattern 1908 web equipment.

Weapons: British rifle No. 1 Mark I.

65. Germany: Private 2nd Machine-gun Battalion (15th Pz. Div.), North Africa 1941

This rather Anglified tropical uniform was worn by German troops on arrival in North Africa, but after practical experience a more practical and comfortable uniform was evolved.

Equipment: Standard German infantry equipment made of olive-green webbing and light brown leatherwork.

Weapons: German Mauser 98k rifle.

66. Germany: Major-General von Ravenstein, Commander 21st Armoured Division, North Africa November 1941

There was no special tropical dress for general officers, and they normally wore issue uniforms with their appropriate badges of rank.

Equipment: Regulation general officer's waistbelt.

Weapons: German Walther 7·65 mm. automatic pistol.

67. Germany: Corporal 5th Tank Regiment in the 5th Light Division (later 21st Armoured Division), North Africa 1941

Tank troops retained, out of pride on their arm, the death's heads from their black tunics, and wore them on the lapels of their tropical tunics. Crews of armoured vehicles received the side cap instead of the field cap, because the large peak of the latter was inconvenient inside an armoured vehicle.

Equipment: Regulation tropical version of the other ranks' waistbelt.

Weapons: German 08 or P.38 service pistol.

68. Italy: Corporal Young Fascist Armoured Division, North Africa 1942

This army division was recruited from young fascists and wore army tropical clothing with black tasselled fez and rank chevrons.

Equipment: Standard Italian infantry equipment.

Weapons: Mannlicher-Carcano M.1938 7·35 mm. rifle.

69. Italy: Brigadier Bignani, Second-in-Command Trento Division, North Africa September 1942

He wears the tropical bush jacket or *sahariana* and the tropical version of the field cap with matching peak and flap. German officers found the *sahariana* a comfortable garment and wore it on a number of occasions.

Equipment: Regulation officer's waistbelt and cross-strap.

Weapons: Italian 1934 9 mm. Beretta automatic pistol.

70. Italy: Lance-corporal (Muntaz) 3rd Libyan Battalion, North Africa 1942

Like the colonial troops of England and France, Italian *Askaris* wore a combination of Italian uniform and native dress. Each battalion was identified by a different colour tarbush and sash. The chevron denoted his rank, and the two white stars, six years' service.

Equipment: Standard Italian infantry equipment.

Weapons: Italian Mannlicher-Carcano M.91 TS carbine.

71. Germany: General Staff Major, northern sector Russian front 1941

General staff officers wore specially-embroidered *Litzen* on their collar patches and crimson stripes on their breeches.

Equipment: Regulation officer's waistbelt, service binoculars and issue pocket lamp.

72. Germany: Corporal Military Police (Feldgendarmerie), northern sector Russian front 1941

Apart from the gorget with luminous inscription, military policemen were further identified by the orange police badge on the upper left sleeve of the tunic and a brown cuff-band with grey inscription 'Feldgendarmerie' on the lower left sleeve of both the tunic and greatcoat. The coat was made of a rubberised fabric and was issued to motorcyclists and pillion passengers.

73. Finland: Private of infantry, northern sector 1941

This infantryman wears the lightweight summer version of the M.1936 field service uniform. The steel helmet was the 1935 German model.

Equipment: Finnish equipment closely followed the German pattern.

Weapons: Finnish 7·62 mm. M.39 service rifle.

74. Germany: Private 2nd Battalion SS Infantry Regiment Deutschland, centre sector Russian front 1941

This machine-gunner wears the standard SS camouflaged 'tiger jacket' and steel helmet cover with summer pattern exposed.

Equipment: Machine-gunner's version of the standard German infantry equipment.

Weapons: German Walther P.38 service pistol and German MG.34 light machine-gun.

75. Italy: Major 3rd Savoy Cavalry Regiment, southern sector Russian front 1941

This is the regulation officer's service dress with the M.1935 steel helmet. The first four cavalry regiments all had the black cross on the steel helmet. The red tie was worn in commemoration of the battle of Madonna di Campana in 1706.

Equipment: Regulation officer's waistbelt and cross-strap.

Weapons: Cavalry officer's sabre and Italian Beretta 9 mm. 1934 automatic pistol.

76. Germany: Captain of infantry, centre sector Russian front 1941
As the war progressed it was more typical for officers to wear issue uniforms in the field.

Equipment: Regulation officer's waistbelt.

Weapons: German 08 automatic pistol.

77. Germany: Sergeant of cavalry, centre sector Russian front 1941
Mounted personnel were issued with standard field-grey uniform with breeches and riding boots instead of trousers and marching boots.

Equipment: Cavalrymen were not issued with a pack and carried all their personal equipment in the M.1934 saddle-bags. The right bag contained the trooper's extra clothing and cleaning kit, while the left bag contained grooming brush and curry comb as well as spare horseshoes. The baggage case or valise contained the groundsheet, corn sack, canvas bucket and greatcoat, among other things.

Weapons: German Mauser Gew. 98k service rifle.

78. Slovakia: Corporal of infantry Slovakian Light Division, southern sector Russian front 1941
Members of the Light Division were identified by the Slovak emblem painted in white on the sides of the helmet and the blue painted rim.

Equipment: Standard Czech infantry equipment with Austrian-pattern ammunition pouches.

Weapons: Czech VZ 24 service rifle.

79. Rumania: Corporal of infantry Rumanian Army Corps, southern sector Russian front 1941
This soldier wears the standard Rumanian field uniform with the arm-of-service colour appearing on the collar patches.

Equipment: Standard waistbelt and ammunition pouches.

Weapons: Mauser M.1924 service rifle.

80. Hungary: Private of infantry, southern sector Russian front 1941
The standard khaki field uniform was worn with at first the M.1915 German steel helmet and then the M.1935.

Equipment: Hungarian equipment followed the Austrian pattern with later German features.

Weapons: Hungarian M.19/35 service rifle.

81. U.S.S.R.: Junior Politruk (Lieutenant) of infantry, 1941
Political commissars (*Komissars* or *Politruks*) wore the same uniform as their active counterparts, but were not entitled to gold edging to the collar patches or sleeve chevrons. A further badge of distinction was a red cloth five-pointed star on the lower left sleeve.

Equipment: Regulation officer's waistbelt and cross-strap.

82. U.S.S.R.: Army general, 1941
The single-breasted 'French' was introduced in 1935, and generals' rank titles in 1940. The three lowest general officer ranks did not wear red collar patches but those in the colour of their arm-of-service.

83. U.S.S.R.: Lieutenant of artillery, 1941
The side cap or *pilotka* was generally authorised for all ranks in 1935. The officer's side cap and shirt was piped in the arm-of-service colour whereas those of their men were not.

Equipment: Regulation officer's waistbelt.

84. U.S.S.R.: Corporal of tank troops, 1941
A khaki one-piece overall replaced the black one at the beginning of the war and remained in use until the end. It was usually worn over the shirt and left unbuttoned at the throat so that the collar patches on the shirt collar were visible. Sometimes collar patches, and later shoulder boards, were worn on the overall.

85. U.S.S.R.: Sergeant of infantry, 1941
N.C.O.s' ranks and badges were re-introduced in 1940, and in this particular case the striped collar patch and brass triangle indicated the rank, while the colour of the stripes and the brass collar badge identified the man as an infantry-man. The steel helmet still retains the comb of its French predecessor from which it was evolved. In 1940 it began to be replaced by a simpler new model.

Equipment: Brown leather ammunition pouch and waistbelt. The gas mask was carried in a canvas bag on the left hip.

Weapons: Russian Moisin M.1891-30 7·62 mm. rifle. The bayonet was normally carried on the rifle, either in a fixed or 're-versed' position, when not actually in use, but in this particular case the soldier wears a leather scabbard.

86. U.S.S.R.: Captain Internal Security Troops (N.K.V.D.), 1941
Internal Security Troops were organised along military lines with their own armour and artillery. N.K.V.D. personnel wore army uniform with their own distinguishing colours – strawberry and light blue – which appeared on the cap and collar patches and later on the shoulder boards.

Equipment: Regulation officer's waistbelt.

87. Japan: Lieutenant-General Yamashita, Commander 25th Army, Singapore February 1942
Although the Japanese had a reputation for formality the tropical uniform of its officers was remarkably comfortable and practical.

The wearing of the shirt collar outside the tunic collar meant the lowering of the rank badges to the lapels.

88. Japan: Private of infantry 5th Division, Malaya 1942
The circular steel helmet was fastened to the head by a long cotton tape which was first passed through a ring at the back of the helmet, under the chin, then up to two rings on either side of the helmet, and finally back under the chin where it was knotted, often very elaborately.

Equipment: This infantryman is carrying his gas mask on the left and water bottle on the right side. The large ammunition pouch carried a reserve supply of sixty rounds while the two front pouches carried thirty rounds each.

Weapons: Japanese M.38 6·5 mm. rifle.

89. Japan: 2nd Lieutenant of infantry 18th Division, Malaya 1942
This officer wears an issue tropical uniform (note typical variation in the colour of the uniforms in 87 and 89) with rank badges on the tunic lapels.

Equipment: Regulation officer's waistbelt and cross-strap.

Weapons: Standard pattern officer's sword.

90. Great Britain: Brigadier New-Biggin, Chief Administrative officer, Singapore 1942
The khaki drill shirt and shorts were the normal everyday wear for British troops in the tropics. Officers also had a lightweight service dress consisting of single-breasted tunic and long trousers.

Equipment: Regulation officer's 'Sam Browne' belt.

91. The Netherlands: Private, Royal Dutch Indian Legion, Dutch East Indies, 1942
The lightweight version of the grey-green field service uniform was worn in the tropics by both soldiers and marines.

Equipment: Knil-model equipment with gas mask on the chest.

Weapons: Dutch 6·5 mm. Hembrug M.1895 rifle.

92. India: Lieutenant 19th Hyderabad Regiment, Singapore February 1942
Again the K.D. shirt and shorts with khaki stockings and short puttees forming the basic field service order for English officers in Indian infantry regiments.

Equipment: Pattern 1937 web equipment, basic set for officers with map case.

Weapons: British Webley ·455 Mark VI Pistol No. 1.

93. France: Brigadier Philipe de Haute-Clocque (better known as Leclerc), Commander L. Force, North Africa 1942
Leclerc wears a *pelisse coloniale*, which was very popular with French colonial officers. The anchor badge on the collar was common to all French colonial troops.

94. Great Britain: General Sir Bernard Law Montgomery K.C.B., D.S.O., Commander British 8th Army, North Africa 1942

Monty's individual style of dress had nothing to do with regulations and makes an interesting comparison with the rather more martial-looking Wavell and Rommel (97).

95. Great Britain: Captain, North Africa 1942

This staff officer wears the K.D. shirt and shorts with long woollen stockings and his service dress peaked cap. His rank badges are attached to a detachable slide on the shoulder straps.

Equipment: Pattern 1937 web equipment set for personnel armed with pistol only.

Weapons: British Webley ·455 Mark VI pistol No. 1.

96. Germany: Lieutenant-Colonel 33rd Engineer Battalion 15th Armoured Division, North Africa 1942

The steel helmet, although heavy and hot and in short supply, was usually worn in action, and any available goggles were used to protect the eyes from sun and sand.

Equipment: Officer's waistbelt, folding entrenching tool and binoculars.

97. Germany: Colonel-General Erwin Rommel, Commander Panzer Army Africa, North Africa 1942

Rommel's eccentricities of dress were not as extreme as Monty's, and were limited to a tartan scarf and British anti-gas goggles, which he wore on his cap. Many German officers wore bits and pieces of their temperate uniform in the desert, as did the Allies.

Equipment: 10×50 service binoculars.

98. Germany: Acting corporal 200th Panzer Grenadier Regiment (15th Pz. Div.), North Africa 1942

The greatcoat was very necessary in the bitter cold nights, and apart from the olive-green pullover and socks, it was the only woollen item of tropical clothing. The two grenadier regiments of the 15th Pz. Div. identified themselves by a strip of red or green cloth across the shoulder strap.

Equipment: Web waistbelt and straps supporting, brown leather ammunition pouches and water bottle on the right hip.

Weapons: German Mauser Gew. 98k service rifle.

99. U.S.S.R.: Private of infantry, Stalingrad 1942

It is a common misconception that all Russian troops were perfectly equipped for winter warfare, and only the Germans and her allies froze. In fact, although more accustomed to the vagaries of the Russian climate, Soviet troops also suffered from exposure.

Shortage of shoe leather already made it necessary to wear ankle boots (imported from England or

America) with puttees instead of the boot.

Equipment: Standard waistbelt and pack suspended from webbing straps. The German-style ammunition pouch had only two compartments.

Weapons: Russian Moisin-Nagant M.1938 7·62 mm. carbine.

100. U.S.S.R.: Tank officer, Russia 1942
The three-quarter-length sheepskin coat was issued to tank crews as winter clothing.

Equipment: Officer's waistbelt and cross-strap.

101. U.S.S.R.: Private of infantry, Russia 1942
The steel helmet was often worn over the fur cap or *ushanka*, while many different kinds of white snow camouflage were worn over the basic field uniform.

Weapons: Russian PPSh 1941 7·62 mm. submachine-gun.

102. Germany: Captain of infantry, Cholm 1942
Typical of improvised winter uniforms during the first Russian winter of the war were the whitewashed helmet and one or more greatcoats over which some kind of white cotton smock or sheet was worn as camouflage. The boots are Russian felt *valenki*.

Equipment: Other ranks' waistbelt and dispatch case, with MP 38 or 40 magazine pouches and infantry straps supporting.

103. Germany: Private 386th Infantry Regiment, Russia 1942
Standard field-grey field service uniform with matching trousers.

Equipment: The battle pack was made up of a webbing frame to which were strapped an iron ration pack, groundsheet and mess-tin, with a greatcoat strapped on the outside. On the left hip is carried the entrenching tool and bayonet. The gas mask is suspended over the right shoulder by a webbing strap, and on the right hip is the canvas haversack.

Weapon: German Mauser 98k rifle.

104. Italy: Lieutenant-Colonel 8th Alpine Regiment 3rd Julia Alpine Division, Russia 1942
Mountain troops wore the felt hat with a different feather according to rank. The greatcoat and trousers are the special winter model introduced for use on the eastern front.

Equipment: Service binoculars.

105. U.S.A.: Major-General A. M. Patch, Commander U.S. forces, Guadalcanal 1942–3
Patch wears the basic khaki drill tropical uniform of the U.S. army with his service dress peaked cap.

Equipment: Basic webbing belt and leather automatic pistol holster.

Weapons: U.S. ·45 1911 or 1911A1 automatic pistol.

106. U.S.A.: Private 23rd Infantry Division, Guadacanal 1942–3
The one-piece olive-drab herring-bone-twill overall was originally intended for fatigues, but was found to be the most practical stop-gap combat dress available at the beginning of the war.

Equipment: Standard woven waistbelt with ammunition pouches and cotton bandoliers for additional ammunition.

Weapons: 1903 Springfield.

107. Australia: Infantryman 17th Australian Brigade, Wau New Guinea 1942
This basically British uniform with the Australian 'wide awake' hat was later in the war to become the most popular form of head-dress in the far east.

Equipment: Pattern 1937 web equipment with gas mask (rarely worn in the jungle), enamel cup and small pack.

Weapons: British rifle No. 1 SMLE Mark III*.

108. Japan: Sergeant of tank troops, 1942
The padded helmet was covered with canvas and like most head-dress it bore the yellow five-pointed star in front. The bright pea-green one-piece overall was fastened with tapes at the waist and ankles.

109. Japan: Private 1st class artillery, 1942
The typical everyday dress of the Japanese army in the tropics consisted of a shirt, long or short trousers and the field cap, the colour of which varied considerably.

110. Japan: Private 1st Special Parachute Group Yokosuka, Koepang Dutch East Indies 21 February 1942
Japanese paratroop uniform was based on the German model. The padded leather helmet was later replaced by a steel one, although photographs suggest that the German helmet was actually issued to Japanese parachute troops.

Equipment: Standard infantry equipment with additional ammunition bandoliers.

111. China: Private Nationalist infantry, China 1939
Germany had been responsible for the training of the Chinese army, which accounts for the rather Germanic appearance of this infantryman.

Equipment: Normally made of natural-coloured leather, although much was made from canvas. The pack usually consisted of a canvas bundle with bedding roll strapped on three sides, metal mess tin and a cloth tube containing rice, which was either tied to the pack or worn over the shoulder or round the neck.

Weapons: German or Chinese-made Mauser 7 mm. rifles or other types imported from all over the world.

112. China: Generalissimo Chiang Kai Shek, China 1941
This was the regulation officer's service dress throughout the war, although it was made in many variations and different colours and types of cloth according to local conditions.

Equipment: Brown leather officer's waistbelt and cross-strap.

113. China: Private Communist infantry, Shensi Province China 1938
In winter both communists and nationalists wore grey or blue cotton wadded uniforms, while badges of rank remained the same on both sides. In place of the nationalist sun emblem, communists used the five-pointed red star.

Equipment: Ammunition was carried in cloth cartridge bandoliers.

Weapons: Communist forces received weapons from Russia or used captured Japanese ones.

114. Japan: Lieutenant tank troops, China 1938
This officer wears the old-style M.90 other ranks' greatcoat over a woollen pullover. The tank helmet was made of brown canvas and was designed to protect the head from inside the vehicle.

Equipment: Regulation officer's waistbelt and cross-strap, with pistol holster suspended from a strap over the left shoulder.

Weapons: Japanese Nambu Type 1904 8 mm. automatic pistol and sword (not showing).

115. Japan: Major, Mukden 1938
This is the standard M.98 (1938) Japanese officer's service dress with the duty officer's sash.

Weapons: Regulation officer's sword in the *Seki* style.

116. Japan: Private of infantry, Manchuria 1938
The old-style sleeveless winter coat was made of cotton or sometimes sheepskin.

Equipment: Standard infantry belt and ammunition pouches.

117. France: Private colonial infantry, Tunisia 1943
The steel helmet bears the anchor badge of French colonial infantry. The rest of the uniform consists of the 1940-pattern British battle dress with exposed buttons.

Equipment: British-pattern 1937 web equipment.

Weapons: British rifle No. 1 Mark III.

118. Great Britain: Private Queen's Royal Regiment (8th Army), Tunis May 1943
The cap G.S., although similar in shape to a beret, was not as popular, due to its stiffness. The rest of the uniform is standard British khaki drill tropical dress.

Equipment: Pattern 1937 web equipment with binocular case on the left hip.

Weapons: British rifle No. 1 Mark III*.

119. U.S.A.: Sergeant (Grade 4) Armoured Forces, Tunisia 1943
The composition helmet was intended as a lightweight protection for the head from possible injury inside the tank. The zip-fronted field jacket has the early style of pockets, which were later replaced by vertical slash pockets.

Equipment: Basic web belt and cartridge case and brown leather pistol holster.

Weapons: U.S. ·45 1911A1 (Colt 45) automatic pistol.

120. Germany: Captain 334th Artillery Regiment, Tunis May 1943
This is basically the olive-green tropical field service dress which had been worn in North Africa since the German arrival. By the end of the campaign the steel helmet had completely replaced the sun helmet.

Equipment: Regulation officer's waistbelt and standard issue dispatch case.

121. Germany: Major von Meyer, A.D.C. to General Cramer, last Commander of the German African Corps, May 1943
Major von Meyer wears the traditional cap badge which was worn by regimental staff and 2nd and 4th Squadrons of the 6th Cavalry Regiment, and by the 3rd Motorcycle Battalion. He also wears the black armoured troop tie.

Equipment: Regulation officer's waistbelt.

122. Italy: Marshal of Italy Ettore Bastico, C.-in-C. Axis Forces in North Africa, 1943
Bastico wears the leather armoured vehicle crew coat over standard officer's tropical uniform.

123. U.S.S.R.: Corporal of engineers, Russia 1943
In 1943 the shirt in traditional Russian cut (stand collar and no breast pockets) was re-introduced for wear with shoulder boards. When issued it was olive-green in colour but after fading due to sun and washing it ended up a sand colour.

Equipment: Standard other ranks' waistbelt.

Weapons: Russian PPsH-41 sub-machine-gun.

124. U.S.S.R.: Army General N. Vatutin, Charkov 1943
The newly-introduced tunic or *kitel* was almost identical to the Tsarist pattern. His peaked cap is slightly unusual in that the peak is covered with khaki cloth.

125. U.S.S.R.: Private of infantry, 1943
The Russians made use of captured German camouflage uniforms until a one-piece camouflage overall was introduced in 1943. It was loose-fitting with an attached hood and was normally issued to snipers and assault personnel.

Equipment: Standard waistbelt and canvas pouch for submachine-gun drum magazine.

Weapons: Russian PPsH-41 sub-machine-gun.

126. Germany: Private Panzer Regiment 'Grossdeutschland', Russia 1943

One- and two-piece reed-green drill overalls began to be issued in 1942 to improve the protective colouring of armoured personnel outside their vehicles. It also served as a summer uniform and overall to protect the black uniform.

Equipment: Regulation other ranks' waistbelt and binoculars.

Weapons: German MP.40 sub-machine-gun.

127. Germany: Acting corporal SS 'Totenkopf' Division, Charkov 1943

The fur-lined parka with matching overalls was independently developed by the SS as its winter combat uniform. It was expensive to produce and was replaced by the reversible army winter combat uniform by the last winter of the war.

Equipment: Standard German infantry equipment.

Weapons: German Mauser 98k rifle.

128. Germany: Acting corporal 691st Grenadier Regiment, southern sector Russian front 1943

At the end of 1943 the appearance of the German soldier began radically to change, with the introduction of the peaked standard field cap. All insignia were now woven in mouse-grey artificial silk, and dark green collars and badge cloth were getting much rarer.

Equipment: Standard infantry equipment, entrenching tool, gas mask and ammunition box.

Weapon: German Mauser Gew. 98k rifle.

129. Italy: Private II battalion 184th Parachute Regiment, Nembo

Although German-influenced, this uniform was of Italian manufacture. The parachute badge on the left breast is that of the Libyan Parachute Battalion which was disbanded in 1941.

Equipment: German air-force waistbelt and buckle.

Weapons: German stick grenade 24 and egg grenade 39, and Italian MVSN (Black-Shirt) dagger.

130. Germany: 2nd lieutenant mountain rifle regiment, Italy 1943

Contrary to popular belief tropical clothing was worn by German troops not only in Africa, but in all tropical and sub-tropical countries.

Equipment: Regulation officer's waistbelt.

131. Germany: Corporal 1st Company Parachute Demonstration Battalion, Gran Sasso September 1943

The paratroop smock, known as the 'bone sack', was made in a number of different colours and versions – olive-green with and without pockets, light khaki for tropical use, and later in geometric, and finally blurred, camouflage patterns. All pockets and openings were closed either with zip-fasteners or press-studs. The side cap and trousers were part of the standard air-force tropical clothing.

Equipment: Regulation brown leather air-force other ranks' belt and buckle, straps supporting and entrenching tool.

Weapons: German paratroop rifle (*Fallschirmgewehr* – FG–42) 7·92 mm. automatic rifle.

132. New Zealand: Lieutenant of infantry, Italy 1944
The unusual aspect of this uniform, which appears to have been typical of all ranks in this unit, is the dark khaki shirt being worn with khaki drill shorts. This officer is also wearing his service dress peaked cap.

Equipment: Web waistbelt, pistol holster and haversack and water bottle carried on straps over the shoulders.

Weapons: Webley Mark VI ·455 service pistol.

133. U.S.A.: Private 3rd Infantry Division, Italy 1943–4
Here the greatcoat is being worn over the field jacket and together with winter trousers and rubber boots. Under the helmet the soldier wears the knitted woollen cap.

Weapons: U.S. 300 in. M1 carbine.

134. Poland: Private and Polish Corps, Italy 1943–4
The snow suit with hood and white duffle coat was issued to Allied troops in Italy as snow camouflage.

Weapons: U.S. M1 carbine.

135. France: Battalion commander Moroccan Rifles, Italy 1944
The combination of French kepi and native *djellabah* was typical of French colonial officers. On this type of garment, as well as on the greatcoat and leather or jeep coat, rank badges were worn in the form of a tab which was buttoned on the chest. A half moon emblem appeared on the front of the steel helmet.

Equipment: Officer's waistbelt, German pistol holster, water bottle and map case suspended from straps over the shoulders.

Horse furniture: Typical French officer's saddle, bridle and saddle-bags.

Weapons: German 08 automatic pistol.

136. Denmark: Member of the Danish Resistance Movement, 1945
As long as resisters had to blend with the civilian population they could not wear uniform, and it was only for a very short period between the German capitulation and the Allied arrival that members of the resistance donned helmets and armlets.

Weapons: Swedish Model 37–99 9 mm. submachine-gun.

137. France: Franc-Tireur French Forces of the Interior (F.F.I.), France 1944

In the more remote regions of France resistance groups became full-time partisan units while some adopted the Cross of Lorraine as their emblem.

Weapons: British Bren ·303 Light machine-gun.

138. Italy: Communist partisan of the 47th Garibaldi Brigade, Parma Apennines, 1944

Communist partisans were well organised along military lines with their own system of rank badges (red stars and horizontal bars) which were worn on the left breast.

Equipment: Submachine-gun magazines were carried either in the pocket or in pouches made of canvas or leather.

Weapons: British Sten Mark II submachine-gun and British Mills hand grenade.

139. France: Militiaman Franc-Gardes of the French Milice, France April 1944

The *Milice* was a political organisation and the *Franc-Garde*, its executive arm, was organised on a territorial basis. This shows the new uniform introduced in April 1944.

Equipment: M.1935 French army equipment stained black.

Weapons: French MAS 1936 rifle and German 08 or P.38 automatic pistol.

140. Germany: Corporal Police Battalion, 1942

The service uniform illustrated here was in the process of being replaced by a simpler army style field blouse. Rank was indicated on the shoulder straps, which for commissioned ranks were identical to those of the army.

Equipment: Standard German infantry equipment, but usually of obsolete pattern.

Weapons: German Mauser 98k rifle.

141. Russia: Corporal of Siberian Cossacks attached to Security Police, 1944

The traditional blue peaked caps with coloured band and piping were worn with German uniform. This particular Cossack wears the SS national emblem on the upper left sleeve.

Equipment: Standard Russian other ranks' waistbelt.

Weapons: Soviet Russian M.1935 Cossack sabre.

142. U.S.S.R.: Partisan known as 'grandfather' with the 1st Ukrainian Partisan Division Kovpak, Ukraine 1943

Typical winter clothing consisted of *ushanka*, *telogreika* or wadded coat, and wadded trousers. The felt boots or *velenki* were ideal for crisp dry snow, but tended to become waterlogged as soon as the thaw set in.

Weapons: Russian PPsH-41 submachine-gun and 'Molotov cocktail'.

143. Poland: Insurgent Polish Home Army, Warsaw Uprising autumn 1944

Insurgents wore civilian clothing or Polish military uniform, while whole units of Poles wore captured SS camouflage clothing. On the beret he wears the Polish eagle and on the left sleeve an armlet in the national colours. Boots are German.

Weapons: German MP.40 9 mm. submachine-gun.

144. Yugoslavia: Private Slovenian Partisan Army, Litija 1944

This partisan wears a Serbian army tunic, German breeches and a five-pointed red star on his cap.

Equipment: Captured German waistbelt and ammunition pouch.

Weapons: German 7·65 mm. automatic pistol and Yugoslav M.1924 7·92 mm. rifle.

145. Russia: Lieutenant-Colonel Kononov, Commander 5th Don Cossack Cavalry Regiment, Yugoslavia 1944

Kononov wears German badges of rank which, although permitted after 1943, were rarely worn by Cossack officers, who preferred the Tsarist Russian pattern.

Weapons: Either Tsarist or Soviet Russian M.1935-pattern Cossack sabre or *shashka* which was worn on the left hip suspended from a narrow leather belt over the right shoulder.

146. Germany: Lance-corporal Security Police, Warsaw 1943

Initially security policemen wore *Waffen-SS* badges of rank with N.C.O.'s lace on the collar and shoulder straps, but following complaints by the *Waffen-SS*, these were replaced by police shoulder straps.

Equipment: Standard SS other ranks' waistbelt.

Weapons: German Schmeisser MP.28 II submachine-gun.

147. Russia: Corporal auxiliary police, Russia 1943

At first *Schutzmänner* were issued with modified black SS uniforms but gradually German police uniforms began to be issued and worn with special insignia on which the motto 'loyal, valiant and obedient' appeared.

Equipment: Soviet or obsolete German or captured equipment.

Weapons: Russian Moisin Nagant 7·62 mm. rifle.

148. Great Britain: Major-General 'Pete' Rees, Commander 19th Indian Division, Burma 1944

The jungle-green service dress with bush jacket and slouch hat with divisional sign on the *puggree* was the most common form of dress for British officers in the Far East when not actually in action.

149. India: Private 7th Ghurka Rifles, Burma 1942
The cellular shirt and either long or short trousers in jungle-green drill became the standard battle-dress in the Far East.

Equipment: Pattern 1937 web equipment was often painted dark green or even black for use in the jungle. Extra ammunition was carried in cotton bandoliers.

Weapons: British rifle No. 1 Mark III*.

150. Great Britain: Chindit, 1942
The Chindits, named after the griffins that stood guard outside Burmese temples, were a multi-national long range penetration group for operations behind enemy lines. Their clothing was originally pretty standard but after months in the jungle uniforms were reduced to rags.

Equipment: Webbing waistbelt with special pouch for Thompson magazines.

Weapons: U.S. Thompson 1928 ·45 submachine-gun.

151. Australia: Commando 8th Australian Infantry Battalion, Solomon Islands 1944
By this stage in the war Australian uniform in the Far East included much American clothing such as the trousers and gaiters.

Equipment: Pattern 1937 web equipment, although U.S. equipment was also widely used.

Weapons: Australian ·303 rifle No. 1 Mark III*.

152. U.S.A.: Staff Sergeant (Grade 3) Armoured forces, Solomon Islands 1943
In the Far East the most common tank outfit was the one-piece herringbone twill overall, and the lightweight fibre helmet.

Equipment: Standard woven belt with leather pistol holster.

Weapons: U.S. ·45 M.1928 A1 Thompson submachine-gun.

153. U.S.A.: Merrill's Marauders, Northern Burma March 1944
The U.S. answer to Wingate's Chindits was the 530th Composite Unit (Prov.), better known under its more romantic name of Merrill's Marauders. Every soldier found by a process of elimination his ideal combat dress.

Equipment: Standard woven belt, ammunition pouches and water bottle.

Weapons: U.S. M.1 carbine and M.4 knife bayonet, and native *kukri*.

154. Japan: General Kuribayashi, Commander Japanese forces on Iwo Jima, December 1944
Kuribayashi wears shirtsleeve order with his badges of rank on the shirt lapels, riding breeches and boots. In his right hand he carries a stick.

155. Japan: Private of infantry, 1944
This soldier also wears shirtsleeve order, this time with a collarless shirt. Instead of normal leather

ankle boots he wears black canvas *tabi* with rubber soles.

Equipment: Standard Japanese infantry equipment with water bottle, ammunition pouch and canvas grenade pouch.

Weapons: Japanese M.38 (1905) 6·5 mm carbine and bayonet.

156. Japan: Private of infantry, 1944
The Japanese were masters of camouflage and made use of different kinds of fibrous materials to make camouflage smocks. Even field caps were made of platted rushes and daubed with paint or mud to blend with the surroundings.

157. Great Britain, Lance-corporal Royal Military Police, Normandy June 1944
The inflatable 'Mae West' was worn by all troops during the invasion crossing and disembarkation. The paratroop helmet was produced in a crash helmet version for motorcyclists and armoured vehicle crews. Other special clothing for motorcyclists were the Bedford cord breeches, yellow leather drivers' gauntlets and lace-up boots.

158–9. Great Britain: Private 2nd East Yorks, 3rd Infantry Division, Normandy 1944
In this particular case the 1937 battle dress is still being worn. The helmet is covered with a camouflage net to which are attached strips of green and brown hessian.

Equipment: Pattern 1937 web equipment (228). A shovel is carried behind the small pack, under which is the pick *cum* entrenching tool. Inside the pack were carried (among other things) a mess tin and cover, emergency rations, knife, fork and spoon, cardigan, socks, cap comforter and washing kit. The groundsheet is fastened beneath the pack flap. On his left hip he carries a gas mask and on the right a water bottle.

Weapons: British rifle No. 4 Mark I*, bayonet and jack-knife.

160. U.S.A.: Private of Infantry 30th Infantry Division, Normandy June 1944
Camouflage uniforms were worn by certain units in Normandy but were immediately withdrawn when it was found that personnel wearing them were being mistaken for *Waffen-SS* men.

Equipment: Standard U.S. infantry equipment.

161. U.S.A.: Major 82nd Airborne Division, Normandy June 1944
The standard parachutist's uniform was similar to the M.1943 combat dress but with different pocket arrangement. Helmets were often camouflaged in this way as well as having rank badges painted on the back.

Equipment: Woven waistbelt, pistol ammunition pouch, water bottle and field glasses.

162. Great Britain: Private No. 4 Commando, No. 1 Special Service Brigade, Normandy 1944

The green beret was normally worn without a cap badge in action. On his shoulder he wears the 4 Commando shoulder title in red and white on black and the combined operations flash.

Equipment: In addition to the normal pattern 1937 web equipment he carries additional rifle ammunition in a cotton bandolier and extra Bren gun magazines in a special quick-release and expendable canvas harness.

Weapons: British rifle No. 4 Mark I.

163. Germany: SS General 'Sepp' Dietrich, Commander 1 SS Panzer Corps 'Leibstandarte SS Adolf Hitler', Normandy June 1944

Dietrich wears another of his non-regulation uniforms – this time a lightweight service dress. Dietrich was the only SS officer of general rank to wear gold SS insignia.

Equipment: Non-regulation SS officer's belt.

164. Germany: Field-Marshal Gert von Rundstedt, Commander-in-Chief West, 1944

Rundstedt wears a regulation general's greatcoat, with underneath the uniform of an infantry regimental colonel-in-chief (*Chef*) with the badges of rank of a *Generalfeldmarschall*. In his right hand he holds an *Interimstab*, which was in fact the everyday version of the marshal's baton.

165. Germany: Lieutenant Wittmann, Commander I SS Heavy Tank Battalion 501, Normandy 1944

Wittmann wears the special black uniform for tank crews with the tank arm-of-service colour appearing as piping on the cap and jacket collar and as an underlay to the shoulder straps.

Equipment: The regulation SS officer's belt buckle was circular, but the army belt with two-pronged buckle was found more practical.

166. Germany: Private 26th Grenadier Regiment, Normandy June 1944

The triangular camouflage groundsheet was designed for use as a shelter quarter (four making a four-man tent) or as a poncho as shown.

Weapons: Faustpatrone 30 slung on a cord, and box containing the same weapon on the shoulder. German Mauser 98k service rifle and stick grenade 24.

167. Germany: 2nd lieutenant Panzer Artillery Battalion, Normandy June 1944

The special field-grey uniform for crews of self-propelled guns was originally introduced in 1940, and was worn with a number of different collar patches depending on the type of unit and formation. The camouflage helmet cover was introduced in 1942.

Equipment: Officer's waistbelt, map case and pouch for MP.40 magazines.

168. Great Britain: Private 1st Airborne Division, Arnhem September 1944
The camouflage Denison smock was first introduced in 1941 and was worn either over or instead of battle dress blouse, but always under the equipment. Another, sleeveless, smock was worn over the equipment for the jump and discarded on landing.

Equipment: Pattern 1937 web equipment.

Weapons: British Sten Mark V submachine-gun.

169. U.S.A.: Lieutenant-General Patton, Commander 3rd U.S. Army, Normandy 1944
Patton wears the M.1944 U.S. version of the British battle dress with his rank badges appearing on the helmet, shirt collar, and shoulder straps.

Equipment: Non-regulation brown leather officer's belt.

Weapons: A silver-plated Colt ·45 'Peacemaker' with 4½ in. barrels and ivory grips, and a ·357 Smith and Wesson Magnum with blued finish.

170. Great Britain: Trooper 3/4 County of London Yeomanry, North West Europe 1944–5
The one-piece tank overall or 'pixie suit' was a welcome intro-

duction in time for the last winter of the war. Two zip-fasteners ran the full length of the front to facilitate entry and exit, and to enable the suit to be converted into a sleeping bag.

Equipment: 1937 pattern web belt and pistol holster.

Weapons: British Smith & Wesson ·38 service pistol (revolver).

171. Germany: Captain Panzer Grenadier Regiment, 1944
Only late in the war did the army begin to make extensive use of camouflage clothing, and much of this was improvised at divisional or lower level and made use of any available materials. In this particular case the trousers are made of reed-green drill.

Equipment: Regulation officer's belt.

172. Germany: Lieutenant-General Hasso von Manteuffel, Commander Panzer Grenadier Division 'Grossdeutschland', 1944
General officers also took to wearing issue uniforms when on active service. Here divisional insignia consist of white metal 'GD' cyphers on the shoulder straps, and black and silver cuff-band on the right cuff.

Equipment: General officer's belt, pistol holster and binoculars.

173. Germany: Corporal Panzer Grenadier Regiment, Lithuania 1944
A collar-attached shirt was generally introduced in 1943, and from

this date shirtsleeve order was officially recognised in the German army.

Equipment: Standard German infantry equipment with MP.40 pouches.

174. Poland: Lance-sergeant 1st Tadeucz Kościuszko Infantry Division, Warsaw January 1945

This is still basically the pre-September 1939 uniform and shows the regulation greatcoat and soft field cap version of the *czapka*.

Equipment: Standard Polish other ranks' waistbelt.

Weapons: Polish M.29 7·92 mm. service rifle.

175. U.S.S.R.: Traffic controller, Poland 1944

The only concession to femininity in the Soviet army was the issue of a knee-length blue or khaki skirt. The greatcoat with exposed buttons was most unusual.

176. U.S.S.R.: Sergeant Don Cossacks in a Cossack Cavalry Corps 1st Ukrainian Front, River Elbe 1945

Certain modified features of traditional Cossack dress were re-introduced in 1936. During the war standard Soviet uniform was worn with a black astrakhan *papacha* and blue breeches with a 4-cm.-wide red stripe.

Equipment: Captured German other ranks' waistbelt.

Weapons: M.1935 Cossack-pattern sabre or *shashka*.

177. Germany: Private of Panzer Grenadiers, Italy 1945

This uniform, which also included a steel helmet cover, was made from Italian camouflage material.

178. Germany: Colonel-General von Vietinghoff-Scheel, Commander Army Group C, Italy May 1945

Many general officers, the first being Rommel, had themselves made tropical service uniforms, which they wore with shirt and tie. Here such a tunic is worn with issue air force tropical trousers and field-grey service dress peaked cap with gold insignia.

Equipment: Regulation general officer's belt with gilt buckle.

179. Germany: Lieutenant 4th SS Panzer Grenadier Regiment 'Der Führer', Tarvisio May 1945

This grenadier officer wears a combination of SS tropical and temperate uniforms which was quite typical in Southern Europe and the Adriatic. On his left breast pocket are the partisan combat, infantry combat, wound and sports badges as well as the Iron Cross 1st Class.

Equipment: Other ranks' waistbelt and P.38 pistol holster.

Weapons: German P.38 automatic pistol.

180. Russia: Auxiliary Policeman (Schutzmann) attached to Security Police, Carnia Italy 1944-5

This Caucasian wears field-grey *Waffen-SS* uniform with astrakhan *papacha*, plain SS collar patches and the national emblem on the left sleeve (not shown).

Equipment: Cossacks did not traditionally wear spurs and used instead a whip or *nagaika*.

Horse furniture: Typical Cossack saddle which consisted of a wooden frame to which was strapped a leather cushion. This gave the rider his characteristic high seat.

Weapons: British Sten 9 mm. Mark II submachine-gun, destined for Italian partisans but captured and used by Axis security forces.

181. Italy: Captain of rifles 1st Division Italian Liberation Corps, Bologna April 1945
This is basically British uniform and steel helmet to which the cockerel feathers of the *Bersaglieri* have been attached. Although not shown here badges of rank were Italian and the collar patches were in the Italian colours and bore the silver five-pointed star.

Equipment: British web belt and Italian officer's brown leather pistol holster and cross-strap.

Weapons: Italian Beretta 9 mm. submachine-gun.

182. U.S.A.: Private 34th Infantry Division, Italy 1945
This rear view shows the M.1943 combat dress.

Equipment: The equipment shown was a direct development of the first fully-integrated infantry equipment issued in 1910. With only minor modifications it re-mained in use until the mid-1950s. The pack shown is the 1928 model which was made up of short blanket roll, meat pack and entrenching tool. The bayonet could either be worn on the left hip or attached to the left side of the pack. On his left hip he wears the smaller, more compact gas mask, and on the right the water bottle.

Weapons: U.S. ·300 in. M1 (Garand) rifle.

183. Great Britain: Lance-corporal Corps of Military Police, 8th Army Italy 1945
M.P.s were distinguished by red cap covers, which were usually removed close to the front line. White sleeves were worn on traffic duty. Apart from his C.M.P. shoulder flash and 8th Army formation sign, he also wears the Africa Star ribbon on his left breast.

Equipment: Pattern 1937 web equipment.

Weapons: British Sten Mark 2 9 mm. submachine-gun.

184. Germany: Private Panzer Grenadier Regiment, Germany 1945
The M.1944 field uniform only began to appear in any numbers at the end of 1944, and by the end of the war had not been generally issued. It is here being worn with polo-necked pullover, webbing anklets and ankle boots.

185. Germany: Private Grenadier Regiment, Germany 1945
The reversible (camouflage to

white) special winter combat uniform of the German army was introduced in time for the second Russian winter of the war, and consisted of special underwear, coat, trousers, hood and mittens. The first pattern was field-grey on one side and white on the other, the second geometric camouflage, and the third mottled camouflage. Boots were made of felt with leather soles and binding.

Equipment: Standard German infantry equipment with entrenching tool.

Weapons: Czech VZ (short rifle) 24 service rifle.

186. Germany: Acting corporal 1st SS Panzer Grenadier Regiment, Ardennes 1944-5

The camouflage drill uniform was introduced in March 1944 as a combined camouflage and working uniform, and was to be worn with national emblem and rank badges for uniforms without shoulder straps.

Equipment: Standard German infantry web equipment with pouch for MP.40 magazines.

Weapons: German MP.40 submachine-gun.

187. U.S.A.: Private 2nd Infantry Division, Ardennes 1944

This soldier is wearing the M.1943 combat dress with the special rubber winter boots.

Equipment: Standard U.S. army equipment.

Weapons: U.S. Caliber ·30 M1 carbine.

188. U.S.A.: Private William C. Mullins, 50th Armoured Infantry Regiment, Germany 1945

Personnel in armoured divisions tended to wear the field jacket over the one-piece overall as shown here.

Equipment: Basic woven waistbelt and ammunition pouches.

Weapons: U.S. ·30 M1 rifle (Garand semi-auto) with M1 bayonet.

189. Canada: Private of infantry Canadian 1st Army, Reichswald Forest February 1945

The leather jerkin was the World War 1 innovation which enjoyed long life as a popular and comfortable winter garment. This soldier is carrying a German rocket launcher projectile (280 mm.).

190. U.S.S.R.: Guards Lieutenant N. N. Orlov, commander self-propelled gun, 3rd Baltic Front 1944

The peaked cap is still the 1936 steel-grey pattern, which is here being worn with the post-1943 shirt and captured German trousers. The star on his right breast is the Order of the Patriotic War, 1st degree, and beneath it is the Guards badge which was instituted in March 1942.

191. U.S.S.R.: Corporal Engineer Battalion, Budapest February 1945

The one-piece camouflage overall was worn over the field uniform, and was deliberately made as loose fitting as possible to break up the silhouette of the wearer.

Equipment: Combination of captured German and Russian equipment. In his right hand the engineer carries demolition charge detonators.

Weapons: Russian PPsH-41 submachine-gun.

192. U.S.S.R.: Private 3rd Battalion 756th Infantry Regiment, Berlin April 1945

The greatcoat now has traditional collar patches and shoulder straps which were piped in the arm of service colour. The colour of greatcoats varied considerably and ranged from pale grey to red-brown.

Equipment: Standard waistbelt and pouch for six clips of ammunition.

193. Germany: Private People's Grenadier Regiment, Germany 1945

Volksgrenadier personnel did not wear any distinctive uniform or insignia, but because they were formed at the end of the war their uniforms tended to be of the final standard pattern.

Equipment: Standard infantry equipment with blanket strapped to the pack, and water bottle with plastic cup.

Weapons: German Mauser 98k rifle of late manufacture with laminated wooden stock. On his shoulder he carries a disposable anti-tank projectile (Panzerfaust 60).

194. Germany: Leader of the NSDAP, Reich Chancellor, and Commander-in-Chief of the German Armed Forces, Adolf Hitler, Berlin April 1945

Hitler's wartime uniform mirrored his dual position as political leader and military commander, and combined features of NSDAP and army uniform.

195. Germany: Home Guardsman (Volkssturmmann), Germany 1945

Instituted in 1944, the German Home Guard called upon every able-bodied male between the ages of 16 and 60. There was no uniform as such but all existing military, para-military and party uniforms were worn in conjunction with an armlet bearing the inscription 'Deutsche Volkssturm Wehrmacht' (German Armed Forces Home Guard).

Equipment: Whatever was available.

Weapons: Austrian Mannlicher M.88 8 mm. rifle.

196. U.S.A.: Private 77th Infantry Division, Okinawa April 1945

The two-piece camouflage jungle suit introduced in 1944 was worn until gradually replaced by a new two-piece jungle-green combat dress.

Equipment: Basic woven waist belt and ammunition pouches with additional rounds carried in cotton bandolier.

Weapons: U.S. ·30 M1 (Garand) semi-automatic rifle.

197. West Africa: Private Nigerian Regiment, 82nd West African Division

Typical of both sides in the jungle war was this kind of camouflage which rendered a man practically invisible. It is worn over standard British jungle-green uniform, but with slouch hat which was worn by many African units.

Equipment: British pattern 1937 web equipment.

Weapons: British rifle No. 4 Mark I and bayonet No. 4 Mark II.

198. Great Britain: Private Royal Welsh Fusiliers 36th Infantry Division, Burma 1944–5

Again basic British jungle-green uniform with no distinguishing badges whatsoever.

Weapons: U.S. ·45 Model 1928 A1 Thompson submachine-gun and British No. 36 hand grenades.

199. Japan: Captain of Infantry, 1945

The field cap is here being worn with ear flaps. The rest of the uniform is the standard tropical service dress.

Equipment: Map case, binocular case, sword and cane.

200. Japan: General Yoshijiro Umezu, Chief of the Imperial General Staff, U.S.S. Missouri, Tokyo Bay 2 September 1945

General Umezu wears the M.98 (1938) service dress with full-dress aiguillette. From October 1943 commissioned ranks began to wear gold stars and khaki stripes on the cuffs (2nd Lieutenant having one stripe and one star up to General with three stripes and three stars) in addition to the collar patches.

201. Japan: Private of infantry, 1945

This fatigue dress consists of issue sun helmet and pantaloons which could be fastened under the knee with draw-strings.

202. France: Lieutenant of infantry, French sector Berlin 1945

This is basically American uniform with French side cap, rank badges and Legion of Honour lanyard.

Equipment: Standard U.S. army woven belt and leather holster.

Weapons: U.S. ·45 1911 A1 automatic pistol.

203. Great Britain: Corporal Willie Simm, Gordon Highlanders, Munich June 1945

At the American ceremony to hand back the regiment's drums, lost to the Germans in France in 1940, bandsmen wore the Glengarry and doublet version of the pre-war service dress.

204. U.S.A.: Corporal (Grade 5) Corps of Military Police, London 1945

M.P.s or 'snow drops' were immediately recognisable by their build, bearing and profusion of white.

205. U.S.S.R.: Private of infantry, Moscow 1945
Full-dress uniform was introduced in January 1943, and was worn with a peaked cap as a walking-out dress. The standard is that of Adolf Hitler's Bodyguard Regiment which was captured by the Russians in Berlin.

206. U.S.S.R.: Marshal of the Soviet Union M. Malinovsky, Moscow 1945
The sea-green (the colour was formerly known as Tsar's green), full-dress uniform for marshals and generals was introduced in 1945, specially for the victory celebrations and parades. The uniform included many pre-1914 Imperial Russian uniform features.

Weapons: Soviet version of the last pattern Tsarist officer's sabre.

207. U.S.S.R.: Lieutenant of infantry, Berlin 1945
The officer's full-dress tunic was basically identical with the other ranks' version, except that field officers had two spools on the cuffs and two gold lace bars on the collar patches, whereas company officers had only one.

Equipment: Regulation M.1935 officer's waistbelt and buckle.

Helmets
208. Czech M.1934
209. Danish M.1923
210. French M.1915
211. French motorised unit helmet M.1935
212. German M.1935
213. German paratroop helmet
214. British Mk 1

215. British paratroop helmet
216. British M.1944
217. Dutch M.1927 and Rumanian M.1934
218. Italian M.1935 (933)
219. Italian paratroop helmet M.1941
220. Japanese
221. Japanese tank helmet
222. Polish M.1935
223. U.S. Mk 1
224. U.S. tank helmet
225. U.S.S.R. M.1936
226. U.S.S.R. M.1940
227. U.S.S.R. tank helmet

Equipment
228. British Pattern 1937 web equipment
229. German infantry equipment
230. Polish M.1935 infantry equipment
231. Italian infantry equipment
232. French M.1935 infantry equipment
233. U.S.S.R. infantry equipment
234. U.S. infantry equipment
235. Japanese infantry equipment

Weapons
236. British Lee Enfield ·303 in. rifle No. 1 Mk III*
237. British Lee Enfield ·303 in. rifle No. 4 Mk I
238. British Lee Enfield ·303 in. rifle No. 5 Mk I*
239. British Bren light machine-gun Mk I
240. British Sten 9 mm. carbine
241. Italian Mannlicher Carcano 7·35 (6·5) mm. M.1891 rifle
242. Italian Beretta 9 mm. Model 3A submachine-gun

243. France MAS 1936 7·5 mm. rifle
244. U.S. ·30 in. M1 (Garand semi-automatic) rifle
245. U.S. Thompson M1 sub-machine-gun
246. U.S. ·45 in. M3 submachine-gun
247. German Mauser 7·9 mm. 98k rifle
248. German 7·92 mm. MP.44 assault rifle
249. German 9 mm. MP.40 (Schmeisser) submachine-gun
250. U.S.S.R. Moisin Nagant 7·62 mm. M.1891/30 rifle
251. U.S.S.R. Moisin Nagant 7.62 mm. M.1944 carbine
252. U.S.S.R. PPsH M.1941 sub-machine-gun
253. Japanese 7.7 mm. type 99 long rifle
254. Japanese 6·5 mm. type 38 rifle
255. U.S. 2·36 in. Rocket Launcher anti-tank M1
256. British PIAT (Projectile Infantry Anti-Tank)
257. German Panzerfaust (Faust-patrone 60) anti-tank pro-jector

ERRATA

Malcolm McGregor and Andrew Mollo would like to point out the following errors in the colour plates which have come to light since the original publication in 1973:

Fig. 24   Collar and cap band should be dark green and not blue (printing error).

25   Collar should be dark green and not blue (printing error).

29   Stars should be silver, buttons bronze, boots should have spurs.

30   Buttons bronze, no piping around cuffs of greatcoat.

31   No button or breast pocket flap; shoulder strap should have roll.

86   Collar patches should be a little darker.

164   Cap band, tunic and greatcoat collars should be dark green.

205   Standard box with name 'Adolf Hitler' should be gold.

SELECTED BIBLIOGRAPHY

COMMANDANT E. L. BUCQUOY *Les Uniformes de L'Armée Française (Terre-Mer-Air)* illustrated by M. Toussaint, Les Editions Militaires Illustrées, Paris 1935

HEINZ DENCKLER *Abzeichen und Uniformen des Heeres* Heinz Denckler-Verlag, Berlin 1943

Den Norske Haer Moritz Ruhls Forlag, Leipzig 1932

ELIO and VITTORIO DES GUIDICE *Uniformi Militari Italiane dal 1861 ai Giorni Nostri (Vol. II dal 1934 oggi)* Bramante Editrice, Milan 1964

GILBERT GROSVENOR et al., *Insignia and Decorations of the U.S. Armed Forces* (revised edn 1 Dec. 1944) National Geographic Society, Washington, D.C. 1945

O. V. HARITONOV *Uniforms and Marks of Distinction (Insignia) of the Soviet Army 1918–1958* Artillery Historical Museum, Leningrad 1958

EBERHARD HETTLER *Uniformen der Deutschen Wehrmacht – Heer, Kriegsmarine und Luftwaffe* Uniformen-Markt Verlag, Berlin 1939; *Nachtrag (supplement) 1939–40* Uniformen-Markt Verlag, Berlin 1940

Identification (The World's Military, Naval and Air Uniforms, Insignia and Flags) Military Service Publishing Company, Harrisburg, Pennsylvania 1943

PREBEN KANNIK *Military Uniforms of the World in Colour* illustrated by the author, English edition edited by W. Y. Carman, Blandford Press, London 1968

HERBERT KNÖTEL JNR and HERBERT SIEG *Handbuch der Uniformkunde (3rd edn) Stand vom Jahre 1937* Helmut Gerhard Schulz, Hamburg 1937 (reprinted 1956)

DR T. KRYSKA-KARSKI *Piechota (infantry) 1939–1945* privately published by the author, London 1973

A. A. LETHERN, O.B.E. and W. P. WISE *The Development of the Mills Woven Cartridge Belt 1877–1956* The Mills Equipment Company Ltd, London 1956

KAROL LINDER et al., *Zolnierz Polski Ubiór Uzbrojenie I Oporzadzenie od 1939 do 1965 roku* Woydawnicto Ministerstwa Obrony Narodowej, Warsaw 1965

K. J. MIKOLA et al., *Itsenäisen Suomen Puolustusvoimat* Werner Söderström Osakeyhtiö, Helsinki 1969

The Officer's Guide 9th edn, Military Service Publishing Company, Harrisburg, Pennsylvania 1942

KURT PASSOW *Taschenbuch der Heere Ausgabe 1939* J. F. Lehmans Verlag, Munich/Berlin 1939

GUIDO ROSIGNOLI *Army Badges and Insignia of World War 2: Great Britain,*

Poland, Belgium, Italy, U.S.S.R., U.S.A., Germany Blandford Press, London 1972

W. H. B. SMITH *Small Arms of the World (a basic manual of military small arms)* 8th edn , Military Service Publishing Company, Harrisburg, Pennsylvania 1966

Uniformes de L'Armée Française 1937 L'Uniforme Officiel, Paris 1937

UNITED STATES OF AMERICA WAR OFFICE *Handbook on Japanese Military Forces 15 September 1944* (War Dept Technical Manual TM-E 30-480), Washington 1944

VYDALO MINISTERSTVO NÁRODNI OBRANY Česko-Slovenská Armada, Prague

INDEX TO ILLUSTRATIONS

*Army Uniforms
Since 1945*

Digby Smith

Army Uniforms
Since 1945

BLANDFORD PRESS

Poole   Dorset

First published in the U.K. 1980
This edition published 1981
Copyright © 1980 Blandford Press Ltd,
Link House, West Street,
Poole, Dorset BH15 1LL

British Library Cataloguing in Publication Data
Smith, Digby
  Army uniform since 1945. – (Blandford colour series).
  1. Uniforms, Military – History – 20th century
  I. Title
  355.1'4'0904   UC480

ISBN 0 7137 1189 2

Phototypeset in Monophoto Apollo
by Oliver Burridge and Co. Ltd.
Printed in Hong Kong
by South China Printing Co.

Contents

Introduction

In this book an effort has been made to show the uniforms of the armies and irregular forces engaged in actual fighting throughout the world and also the uniforms of the forces of N.A.T.O. and Warsaw Pact countries which are constantly engaged in the 'Cold War'.

Considerable detail has also been given on equipment and weapons as well as 'buttons and bows' so that a broader and deeper impression can be gained of the forces covered.

The campaign histories included are necessarily exceedingly brief but should provide a factual basis so that those who wish to research further will at least have the correct date of the operations involved and the locations over which they were conducted.

I am most grateful for the help given to me in the preparation of this book by Mike Chappell, who has provided many of the most interesting colour plates based on his own collection of references and his personal experiences serving as a professional soldier in various parts of the globe. Similarly, Martin Windrow has been very generous in allowing me to draw on his extensive library of reference material particularly in the areas of French involvement in Algeria and Indo-China.

Without their help, this book would have been much less well balanced and interesting.

Digby Smith, July 1979

The Cold War

Since 1945 there has been armed peace in Europe with the forces of East and West glaring at each other over the Iron Curtain. The West formed the military side of the North Atlantic Treaty Organisation (N.A.T.O.) on 4 April 1949 and it now includes Belgium, Canada, Holland, Luxemburg, West Germany, Denmark, Iceland, Italy, Norway, Portugal, Greece, Turkey, the United Kingdom and U.S.A.

In response to this the Warsaw Pact (WARPAC) was formed in eastern Europe in 1955 and includes Russia, East Germany, Czechoslovakia, Bulgaria, Hungary, Rumania and Poland. The Warsaw Pact has been active in earnest twice—once in 1956 to crush the Hungarian uprising and again in 1968 to suppress Czechoslovakia's bid for freedom.

Over the last six or seven years the balance of power between these groups has swung steadily in favour of the East as far as conventional weapons is concerned and the recent signing of S.A.L.T. 2 in Vienna will scarcely have affected this situation. Western experts are agreed that Russia has far more conventional forces than she needs for pure defence and despite her differences with China, the bulk of these remain firmly either in Eastern Europe or in Western Russia.

Approximate relative strengths (1978/9) are:

	N.A.T.O.	WARPAC
Armoured Divisions	14 (11,000 tanks)	38 (27,200 tanks)
Mechanized Divisions	20	57
Infantry and Airborne Divisions	30	8
Totals	64	103
Light Bombers	150	175
Fighters (ground attack)	2,125	1,675
Interceptors	600	3,050

The Malayan Emergency

During World War II the Malayan People's Anti-Japanese Army (M.P.A.J.A.) had been formed in Malaya mainly recruited from Chinese ex-patriots. It was headed by Lai Teck and was an ineffective force. By the end of the war it had eight regiments with 6,000 men in all. In March 1947 Lai Teck absconded with all the Malayan Communist Party (M.C.P.) funds (the M.C.P. was the political force behind the M.P.A.J.A.) and Lau Yew took over; in February 1948 the M.P.A.J.A. became the anti British M.P.A.B.A. but strength had now dropped to 1,000. By June 1948 they had 3,000 men and operated in the rural areas intimidating peasants and attacking rubber planters and isolated police posts. The Malayan government declared a state of emergency in parts of Johore and Perak states on 16 June 1948 and one month later Lau Yew was killed by security forces near Kajang. He was replaced by Chea Ping and on 1 February 1949 the M.P.A.B.A. became the Malayan Races' Liberation Army with a strength of 4,000 men and women, mainly Chinese. The security forces soon realised that the only way to root out these terrorists (who had set up camps in the jungle where they lived in safety) was to form small, specialist teams to penetrate the jungle and use it to their advantage to track down and destroy the M.R.L.A. The other major government breakthrough was the process of removing villagers from exposed locations in the jungle and re-settling them in defended sites so that the terrorists were denied access to food, shelter and information. Chinese suspected of co-operating with terrorists were punished by being repatriated to mainland China.

Aboriginal tribesmen were recruited by the government as scouts and trackers and formed their own fighting unit, the 'Senoi Praak'.

Gradually the security forces gained the upper hand and in July 1960 the emergency was ended. Casualties during the 12-year war were:

	Killed	Wounded	Captured	Surrendered*
M.R.L.A.	6,710	—	1,287	2,702
Malayan Police	1,246	1,601	—	—
British Army	519	959	—	—
Civilians	2,473	1,385	810 (missing)	

* Terrorists who surrendered were rehabilitated and rewarded with sums of money.

The Korean War

From 1910 to 1945 Korea was occupied by Japan; at the peace negotiations in 1945 it was decided that the country would be placed under

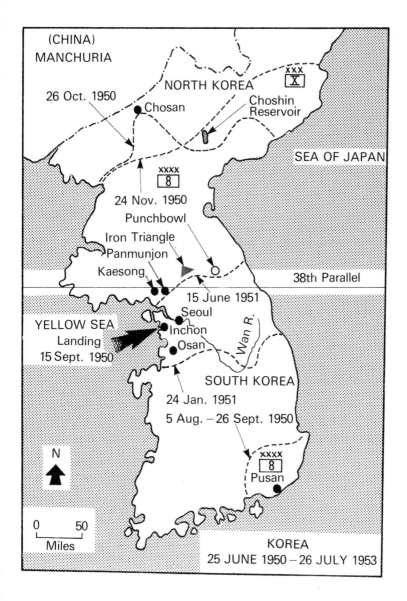

(CHINA)
MANCHURIA

NORTH KOREA

26 Oct. 1950
Chosan

Choshin
Reservoir

SEA OF JAPAN

24 Nov. 1950

Punchbowl
Iron Triangle
Panmunjon
Kaesong

38th Parallel

15 June 1951
Seoul
Inchon

YELLOW SEA
Landing
15 Sept. 1950

Osan

Wan R.

24 Jan. 1951

SOUTH KOREA

5 Aug. – 26 Sept. 1950

N

Pusan

0   50
Miles

KOREA
25 JUNE 1950 – 26 JULY 1953

joint Allied administration, the South being under American control, the north (from the 38th Parallel) being under Soviet control. (Soviet Russia declared war on Japan a few weeks before the end of the war.) The United Nations (U.N.) decided that elections should be held in Korea in 1948 to form a government to take over from the allied administration. This was done in South Korea but the Soviets refused to permit the elections to take place in the north. On 15 August 1948 the Republic of Korea was proclaimed in the south with Syngman Rhee as president and this was followed on 9 September 1948 by the declaration in North Korea of a Democratic People's Republic with authority over the whole of the Korean peninsula. In December 1948 Russia assured the world that she had withdrawn all her forces from North Korea but refused to allow U.N. verification. By June 1949 all but a few U.S. troops had left South Korea—those remaining being small training advisory teams.

The balance of forces was now as follows:

	North Korea	South Korea
Army	127,000 men	98,000 men in 8 divisions
Border Guards	19,000	nil
Tanks	150	nil
Aircraft	200	nil
Ships	nil	small coastal force

Many North Koreans had served with the Chinese Communist army from 1939-45, the army was well equipped with Soviet weapons and had been trained by Soviet instructors. Four of the eight South Korean divisions were equipped with American light weapons and light artillery but they had no anti-tank weapons or heavy artillery. The other four divisions had only light infantry weapons of Japanese manufacture. On 25 June 1950 North Korea invaded the south and advanced on Seoul. In the pandemonium at UN headquarters the Soviet delegation boycotted Security Council meetings and on 27 June (in their absence) the council adopted the American resolution 'to furnish such assistance to the Republic of Korea as may be necessary to repel the armed attack'. That same day President Harry S. Truman authorized use of the U.S. Air Force and Navy and followed this on 30 June 1950 with promise of U.S. Army help. General Douglas MacArthur was appointed U.N. commander and the land forces allied with the Americans included The Commonwealth Division consisting of three infantry brigades with artillery and armour (one British brigade, one Canadian and one partly British, Australian and New Zealander); one Turkish infantry brigade; infantry elements also being drawn from Thailand, Philippines, France, Greece, Netherlands, Belgium, Luxemburg, Columbia and Ethiopia. South Africa, Denmark, Italy, Norway, Sweden and India each contributed a field ambulance team.

By 5 August 1950 a U.S. army detachment had been overrun at Osan and the U.N. forces were confined around the southern port of Pusan where the U.S. Eighth Army (Lt-Gen. W. H. Walker) conducted a successful defence.

The Korean Peninsula lends itself to amphibious warfare and the Americans made use of this; on 15 September 1950 the U.S. Navy landed the U.S. X Army Corps (Maj.-Gen. E. M. Almond) in the enemy rear at Inchon while the Eighth Army broke out of the Pusan perimeter to meet them. The North Korean army broke under these attacks and fled north. By 26 October 1950 advance elements of the Eighth Army were at the Yalu River at Chosan (the Chinese border) and the chase was stopped. The North Koreans lost 100,000 prisoners alone and were crushed as a fighting force. The pendulum swung rapidly back however when 300,000 Chinese army 'volunteers' poured into North Korea on 25 November 1950 and by the 15 December the Eighth Army was back at the 38th Parallel; X Corps was cut off but withdrew to Hungnam where it was successfully evacuated by the U.S. navy. General Walker was killed in a car crash on 23 December and General Matthew B. Ridgway took over command of the Eighth Army. By now combined R.O.K., U.S. and U.N. strength was 365,000 men but on 1 January 1951 they were attacked by half a million Chinese; three days later the Chinese occupied Seoul but the offensive died out by 24 January due to heavy U.S. air attacks on the Chinese logistic supply lines.

A U.N. counter-attack was launched on 25 January and by 23 April they had pushed the Chinese back 20 miles north of the 38th Parallel. International politics had now taken a hand and the U.S. government forbade General MacArthur to attack any targets on the far side of the Yalu River. MacArthur strongly resented this limitation of his powers and on 11 April 1951 he was sacked by President Truman and General Ridgway took over as U.N. commander. General James A. Van Fleet assumed command of the Eighth Army. A Chinese counter-offensive forced ground to be given up again and by 15 June 1951 the line had stabilised across the 38th Parallel.

On 23 June 1951 the Soviets proposed a ceasefire in Korea, this was agreed to and truce talks began at Panmunjon. They lasted for over two years before an armistice was finally achieved and much bloody fighting took place during this time, much of it in the 'Iron Triangle' and the 'Punchbowl'. The truce was finally signed on 26 July 1953 (U.S. date), 27 July (Korean date). Since then there have been repeated armed clashes along the ceasefire line and no true peace yet exists.

Casualties in this war were: Americans—33,629 killed, 103,284 wounded, 4,753 wounded and missing; Chinese—900,000 killed and wounded; North Koreans—520,000 killed and wounded; other U.N. forces (including South Koreans)—74,000 killed, 250,000 wounded, 83,000 missing and prisoners; Civilians—400,000 killed and wounded.

The Vietnam Wars

In 1946 the natives in French Indo-China (Vietnam, Laos and Cambodia) began to agitate for independence from France and this campaign soon became the First Indo-China War, a military struggle which culminated with the crushing French defeat at Dien Bien Phu where 50,000 Viet Minh guerrillas surrounded and overran 10,000 French troops in a fifty-five day battle lasting from 13 March to 7 May 1954. On 21 June of that year a cease-fire was agreed to by both sides at the Geneva conference and French Indo-China became independent. Since 1949 the four states (North and South Vietnam, Laos and Cambodia) had been quasi-independent parts of the French empire but there was considerable friction between the aggressive Vietnamese and their placid neighbours. In 1953 Viet Minh forces invaded Cambodia and in 1954 regular North Vietnamese troops repeated the violation. Following French withdrawal from the area in 1954 most of the rebel Khmer Issarak guerrillas in Cambodia had surrendered to the royalist government there and the International Control Commission (sent to the area following Geneva) was withdrawn in December 1969 at the request of Prince Sihanouk (Cambodian premier). Three months later he was deposed and on 9 October 1970 the Khmer Republic was proclaimed. It enjoyed U.S. support.

In South Vietnam a republic was proclaimed on 26 October 1955 with Madame Ngo Dinh-Diem as president and prime minister and in the Democratic Republic of North Vietnam Ho Chi Minh was president.

The Second Indo-China War began in 1957 when North Vietnamese terrorists (masquerading as South Vietnamese rebel Viet Cong) attacked

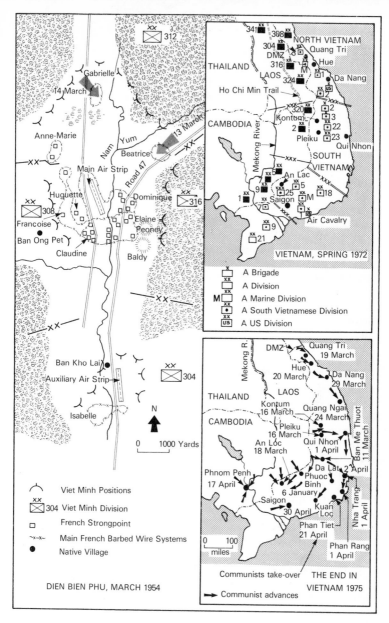

DIEN BIEN PHU, MARCH 1954

Dien Bien Phu map labels:

312

Gabrielle
14 March

Anne-Marie

Nam Yum

Beatrice
13 March

Road 47

Main Air Strip

Huguette

Dominique

316

308

Francoise

Elaine

Peoney

Ban Ong Pet

Claudine

Baldy

Ban Kho Lai

Auxiliary Air Strip

304

Isabelle

N

0   1000 Yards

⌒ Viet Minh Positions

☒ 304 Viet Minh Division

▢ French Strongpoint

~x~x~ Main French Barbed Wire Systems

● Native Village

Vietnam, Spring 1972 map labels:

341 308 NORTH VIETNAM

304 Quang Tri

DMZ

THAILAND 316 Hue

LAOS 324 Da Nang

Ho Chi Min Trail

320

Kontum

CAMBODIA

2

Pleiku 22

23 Qui Nhon

SOUTH
VIETNAM

An Lac

9 5

1 25

Saigon M 18

Air Cavalry

9

21

VIETNAM, SPRING 1972

☐ A Brigade

☐ A Division

M ☐ A Marine Division

☐● A South Vietnamese Division

US A US Division

The End in Vietnam 1975 map labels:

Mekong R.

DMZ Quang Tri
19 March

Hue
20 March Da Nang
29 March

THAILAND LAOS

Kontum
16 March Quang Ngai
24 March

CAMBODIA Pleiku
16 March

An Lôc Qui Nhon Ban Me Thuot
18 March 1 April 11 March

Phnom Penh
17 April Da Lat 2 April

Phuoc
Binh
6 January Nha Trang
1 April

Saigon Kuan
Loc Phan Rang
1 April

Phan Tiet
21 April

Phan Rang
1 April

Communists take-over THE END IN
VIETNAM 1975

➤ Communist advances

15

South Vietnam.

The first U.S. military advisers were sent to help South Vietnam shortly after this invasion and by November 1963 their number had risen to 16,000. In November of that year President Diem of South Vietnam was overthrown and it is thought that the U.S.A. may have helped remove him as his regime was so corrupt. In August 1964 the Gulf of Tonkin incident occurred in which it was alleged that North Vietnamese gunboats had attacked U.S. vessels. President L. B. Johnson (in office since Kennedy's assassination in November 1963) had Congress authorize the 'Gulf of Tonkin Resolution'—a formal declaration of American support for South Vietnam in the war—although subsequent investigation showed that the Resolution had been drafted by the president *before* the incident took place in the Gulf of Tonkin! U.S. involvement in the Vietnam war rose dramatically; in April 1969 over half a million U.S. servicemen were involved and as early as 1965 North Vietnam was being heavily bombed.

South Korea, Thailand, the Philippines, Australia and New Zealand also sent contingents to help the South Vietnamese but that nation was divided (the Catholic minority ruled the Bhuddist majority) and corruption was rife so that the Viet Cong rebels survived in the countryside.

North Vietnamese regular army divisions were used in this war and their logistic supply routes ran south through Laos and Cambodia to the Mekong delta and Saigon areas. Cambodia and Laos were too weak to stop these infringements.

On 30 January 1968 the North Vietnamese, judging conditions ripe for a transition from guerrilla to open warfare, launched the 'Tet Offensive' and their troops were soon fighting in the suburbs of many South Vietnamese cities including Saigon and Hué. After two weeks however their offensive was broken and their losses in dead alone are estimated at 32,000 against 1,000 Americans and 2,000 South Vietnamese.

On 31 March 1968 there was a partial halt to the heavy U.S. bombing of the north and in May that year America and North Vietnam met in Paris for peace talks. They were joined on 31 October by South Vietnamese government and communist South Vietnamese 'National Liberation Front' delegates.

By December 1970 the 'Gulf of Tonkin Resolution' scandal was uncovered, the resolution repealed and the numbers of U.S. troops in Vietnam reduced. Richard Nixon (president since January 1969) continued these reductions to 184,000 in December 1971 and by mid-1972 U.S. involvement had almost ended.

In March 1972 the Paris talks were broken off by the U.S.A. and this was followed by a renewed North Vietnamese offensive with the U.S. retaliating by mining Haiphong and six other North Vietnamese harbours. The Paris negotiations were then renewed in July 1972 but in December Henry Kissinger reported to the president that there seemed to be no chance of success whereupon the United States renewed intensive bombing of North Vietnam for eleven days. This forced North Vietnam back to the negotiating table and peace was signed on 27 January 1973. Under its terms, North Vietnam was empowered to keep her troops in South Vietnam: U.S. troops were withdrawn.

The U.S. and South Vietnam had intervened in the war in Cambodia in April and June of 1970 and the Khmer Rouge evolved as the armed communist rebel group with Chinese support. Lon Nol's Cambodian government staggered on for five years but the Khmer Rouge ousted it in 1975. They then embarked on a totally ruthless campaign of population redistribution which is estimated to have caused over 2 million civilian deaths.

In Laos the pro-Soviet Pathet Lao overthrew the government in May 1975.

The situation in South Vietnam seemed reasonably stable but in 1975 the North Vietnamese renewed their offensive in the central highlands and quite suddenly the South Vietnamese army collapsed. The whole country fell to the North Vietnamese; Saigon being captured on 30 April 1975 and shortly afterwards being renamed 'Ho Chi Minh'.

Cambodia was the next seat of war. On 25 December 1978 the United Democratic Republic of Vietnam's army, supported by 4,000 Soviet advisers and backing the 'Kampuchean National United Front for National Salvation' (K.N.U.F.N.S.) invaded Cambodia, threw out the pro-Chinese Khmer Rouge and their bestial 're-education' policies and installed a pro-Soviet People's Revolutionary Council to rule the country. Prince Sihanouk was released from house arrest in China to go to the United Nations to plead for international action to stop the Vietnamese and K.N.U.F.N.S. invasion of Cambodia but he achieved nothing. Some elements of the Khmer Rouge fled into Thailand and there is a danger that the war will spread into that country. The Vietnamese attack on Cambodia led directly to the Chinese punitive attack on Vietnam in February and March 1979.

The casualties in the Second Indo-China war are estimated at:

	Killed	*Wounded*
United States	46,397	306,653
South Vietnamese Armed Forces	254,257	783,602
North Vietnamese Armed Forces and Viet Cong	925,000	2 to 3 million

The China-Vietnam Clash

In 1977 the Chinese People's Liberation Army (ground forces only) consisted of $2\frac{1}{2}$ million men in 111 divisions which were organized into 37 corps. In addition there were the following independent divisions: 8 infantry, 9 armoured, 3 anti-tank, 21 artillery, 5 cavalry, 11 railway construction and 20 border guards (10 on the Mongolian and 10 on the Soviet border). The Air Force has 30 divisions with 4,000 planes and there is a very small navy of about 160,000 men (including 30,000 marines), 1,700 surface vessels and 66 submarines dedicated to a coastal patrol role. China's surface-to-surface missiles include some with ranges of up to 5,500 km. Of the army 30 divisions form the Production and Construction Corps and are employed in industrial or agricultural projects. They are armed only with light, personal weapons.

There is also a huge, semi-trained militia of about 12 million men and women only part of which is armed.

On 17 February 1979, following the Vietnamese invasion of Cambodia and the overthrow of the pro-Chinese Khmer Rouge regime there, China invaded Vietnam in a limited punitive expedition employing about 30 divisions (200,000 men in all) at Lao Cai, Cao Bang, Lang Son (Friendship Pass) and Mon Cai on the coast.

Apart from the Tibetan campaign and subsequent clashes with Khamba guerrillas and Soviet border guards, the Chinese army lacks combat experience. The Vietnamese forces however, have been almost constantly at war since 1948 and from reports of the fighting it seems that the Chinese suffered extremely heavy losses and that their battle procedures were easily and repeatedly upset by the Vietnamese operating from well-dug-in positions. Only small advances were achieved (perhaps that was all that was desired) and an exchange of prisoners is now underway following the end of the fighting in mid-March.

Apparently only the commanders' tanks down to platoon level had radios fitted; communication below this level being by means of signal flags which must make operations in poor visibility or at night extremely hazardous.

In early May 1979, the Deputy Chief of Chinese Defence Staff, General Wu Xiuquan, announced that Chinese casualties in the 17-day war were 20,000 and claimed that Vietnam had lost 50,000.

China held 1,600 Vietnamese prisoners and Vietnam claims to have captured 240 Chinese.

The Indo-Pakistani Conflicts

In 1947 India achieved independence from Britain and was at once split into two main states. The mainly Hindu and Sikh central part became India, the mainly Moslem north western and north eastern parts became Pakistan. This partition had been at the express insistence of Mohammed Ali Jinnah and other Moslem leaders who refused to attempt to continue living in a mixed religious community. Each of the many states in the old British India was to be given the choice of joining the new India or Pakistan and generally they were permitted to do as their ruling bodies voted but there were important exceptions; Jammu and Kashmir being one and Hyderabad (Sind) another. In Hyderabad the legislative assembly voted 33 to 20 to join Pakistan but the Hindu ruler decided to join India and Indian troops soon confirmed his decision; in Jammu and Kashmir (with a population 80 per cent. Moslem) the Hindu ruler decided directly to join India and the state was soon under Indian control.

Indian troops also invaded the minor state of Junagadh on 9 November 1947 and secured it for their country. Even prior to Partition, religious feelings had been running high in the sub-continent and the uprooting of 12 million people, who had to move into the new states of their choice, caused endless misery which burst into bloody conflict all too often. It is estimated that over a million civilians died in the rioting and massacres which accompanied this event.

Partition of India had brought with it a splitting up of the 'British' Indian forces with the army being divided as follows:

	to India	to Pakistan
Infantry regiments	15	8
Armoured car regiments	12	6
Artillery regiments	18.5	8.5
Engineer regiments	61	34

The old infantry regiments going to India included: 2nd Punjab Regiment, The Madras Regiment, the Grenadiers, the Mahratta Light Infantry, the Rajputana Rifles, the Rajput Regiment, the Jat Regiment, the Sikh Regiment, Dogra Regiment, the Gahrwal Rifles, The Kumaon Regiment, the Assam Rifles, the Sikh Light Infantry, the Bihar Regiment and the Mahar Regiment. Cavalry regiments included Skinner's Horse, Gardner's Horse, Hodson's Horse, King George V's Own Light Cavalry and King Edward VII's Own Light Cavalry.

Pakistan took the 1st, 8th, 14th, 15th and 16th Punjab Regiments, the Baluch Regiment, the Frontier Force Regiment and the Frontier Force Rifles while cavalry units included Probyn's Horse, the 6th and 13th Lancers, King George V's Own Lancers and Prince Albert Victor's Own Cavalry.

Students of British military history will be glad to know that the best British regimental traditions are carefully maintained in regiments of both armies of the Indian sub continent.

The declaration of Kashmir's ruler for India, and its position, lying up against Pakistan's north eastern border was too much of a provocation for Pakistan. Firstly irregular Moslem tribesmen crossed into Kashmir and attacked police posts and in October 1947 India and Pakistan were at war in the province. The conflict remained localized in the mountains and by 1 January 1949 both sides agreed to a U.N. cease-fire which left India holding two thirds of Jammu and Kashmir, Pakistan holding the northern and eastern remainder which they term Azad Kashmir (Free Kashmir), the Indian held portion being called 'Ghulam Kashmir' (Slave Kashmir).

It was recommended by the U.N. commission that India should hold a plebiscite in Kashmir and abide by the decision of the people as to which state they wished to join; this plebiscite has still not been held.

While India chose to go her own way after partition, Pakistan sought international support; in 1954 she concluded a mutual defence treaty with the U.S.A. and in the September joined S.E.A.T.O. In 1955 she joined C.E.N.T.O. but left it in 1977. On the Pakistani political scene the military soon came to power when General Mohammed Ayub Khan was appointed prime minister by president Mirza in 1958. Ayub Khan then ousted Mirza in a coup on 27 October 1958.

Due to her treaty links, Pakistan had been able to replenish her armoury with modern weapons and enjoyed qualitative superiority over her Indian rival. This was to change however in a strange manner.

China had reasserted her control over Tibet in 1950 after defeating her internal Nationalist enemies under Chiang Kai-Shek who withdrew to Formosa (Taiwan). The Tibetans accepted Chinese rule in 1951 but in 1958 a full scale revolt against the Chinese broke out in Lhasa and quickly spread all over Tibet. The Chinese crushed the revolt and the Dalai Llama (Tibet's temporal and spiritual ruler) fled to India as did several thousand Khamba tribesmen who continued to raid the Chinese occupation troops across the borders from Nepal and India for some years. To maintain her Tibetan garrisons more easily, China built a road across the Aksai Chin area of Kashmir and thus came into conflict with India who claimed the territory as theirs. There were other border disputes with India in the North East Frontier Agency (N.E.F.A.) where the 'MacMahon line' was generally recognized as the frontier.

The tension grew between India and China in these widely separated disputed areas, both extremely remote and rugged with most terrain being over 25,000 feet in height. Pandit Nehru, India's prime minister, decided to adopt a 'forward policy' on both fronts even though the Indian army was not equipped for a prolonged operation in such high, remote terrain, had very few specialist mountain troops and even these were not wholly acclimatized to the combat altitude. On top of this the Indian brigade and divisional commanders, realising the impracticality of attempting to adopt an offensive role with the limited, ill-equipped available troops advised against it.

They were ignored and hostilities broke out (in very low key) in December 1961. The Chinese enjoyed massive numerical superiority in both contested regions and their troops were well equipped and acclimatized to the high altitude as they had been fighting the Khamba rebels for years. The action was mainly limited to platoon level outpost bickering but on 9 September 1962 Indian defence minister, Krishna Menon, decided on his own initiative to order the Indian army in the N.E.F.A. to push the Chinese from Thag La ridge, just east of Bhutan, in operation Leghorn. India had twenty-five infantry battalions scattered along the N.E.F.A. and while the Chinese had three divisions, these were concentrated, two being at Tawang (behind Thag La ridge) and one at Walong at the eastern end of N.E.F.A. The 7th Indian Brigade was ordered to carry out the task but the brigade commander refused and his divisional commander supported him.

Both officers were replaced and the desired attack was put in on 20 September. Chinese response was steady but effective; they poured through Thag La pass and through Tulung pass a few miles to the east and swept the Indians down through Sela and Bomdilla to Chaku on

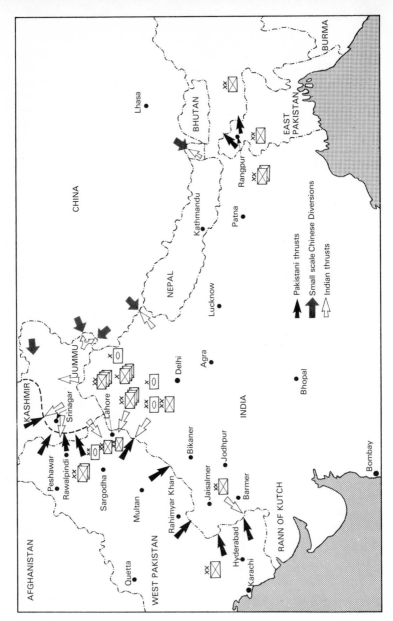

the road to Tezpur.

The defeat was complete and a ceasefire was agreed on 21 November 1962. Indian losses were 1,383 killed, 1,696 missing, 3,968 captured (90 per cent of these were in N.E.F.A., the rest in the Aksai Chin area). Chinese losses were 400 killed and an unknown number wounded. Some of the Indian regiments involved in the thick of the fighting were the Parachute Brigade, 4th Garhwal Rifles, 1st/8th Gurkhas, 1st/9th Gurkhas, Guards, 1st Sikhs, 9th Punjabis, Grenadiers and Assam Rifles.

This stinging defeat caused India to expand her army by six new mountain divisions as well as other units and Britain and U.S.A. quickly replenished her depleted arsenals with modern weapons and equipment, including the Vickers tank. Thus it came about that India's lack of modern armaments was remedied and she became a more dangerous foe for Pakistan.

The 1965 Indo-Pakistani War

There has never really been peace between these two states and border clashes have occurred periodically from 1947 on. Seeing India's growing military strength after the 1961 'war' with China, Pakistan began to woo that neighbouring giant as a counterweight to cancel out India's quantitative supremacy. By 1965 leading Pakistani generals and politicians thought it necessary to teach India a lesson by ejecting her from certain disputed areas in the Rann of Kutch—an extensive salt marsh and desert tract on the coast south east of Karachi. In April 1965 a short and effective campaign was mounted which achieved the capture of Biar Bet and Point 84 and the Pakistani army's morale rose considerably. It was however doubtful if their government had really weighed the likely reaction of India to this satisfying slap in the face.

India ordered general mobilization and Pakistan followed suit. The balance of forces was:

Divisions	India	Pakistan
Armoured	$1\frac{1}{2}$	$1\frac{1}{4}$
Mountain	9 (2 still forming)	—
Infantry	6	6 (1 in East Pakistan)
Men	825,000	230,000
Tanks	Centurions— 210	400 (M47 and M48)
	Shermans— 30	
	Stuarts— 80	
	AMX 13— 40	

| Militia and territorial army | 100,000 | 320,000 (including Azad Kashmir force, Frontier Corps, West Pakistan Rangers and East Pakistan Rifles (10,000)) |

Both armies were organized and trained on British lines.

In August 1965 about 3,000 Kashmiri 'Freedom Fighters' infiltrated into Indian-held Kashmir for sabotage purposes but most were quickly captured by the Indians. On 16 August an Indian battalion crossed the cease-fire line near Kargil in Kashmir and occupied three important mountain features; two more such attacks were mounted on 24 August at Tithwal (in West Kashmir) and another near Naushara (in south west Kashmir). The Pakistanis were active in the north west at Keran, Mirpur, Uri, Mendhar and Chamb. On 27 August an Indian brigade group attacked the 'Uri-Poonch Bulge' from the north and next day captured the Haji-Pir Pass, a traditional route for infiltrators from Pakistan.

The major actions in this war took place around Lahore, an area crossed from north east to south west by three major rivers—the Chenab, Ravi and Sutlej/Beas from north to south. It was also cut by three canals running south from the Chenab, through the Ravi and along the Sutlej—this was the Ichhoril canal—the Upper Chenab canal—lying between Chenab and Ravi—and a third canal running between and parallel to the Ravi and Sutlej/Beas. The intervening country was low lying, liable to flooding and covered in many parts by head-high sugar cane. It was thus an area unsuitable for armoured warfare.

Pakistan opened the action here on 1 September when one infantry and two armoured brigades crossed the border north of the Chenab, driving east on Chamb and brushing aside the two Indian battalions there. In the close and difficult country the advance was halted some miles short of Akhnur. The Indian response came on 6 September when five separate brigade attacks were launched towards the vulnerable Pakistani border city of Lahore on the front from Ferozepore to Amritsar.

The northernmost of these armoured supported columns was aimed at Jassar, the second from Amritsar on Lahore; the third was a few miles south and also aimed at Lahore; the fourth and fifth at Kasur. The Pakistanis had fortified the Ichhoril Canal (120 ft. wide by 15 ft. deep) and it presented a formidable tank obstacle even though only lightly-manned and the Indian advance was held along its length.

24

By 7 September the Pakistanis committed their armoured division in a counterattack in the Kasur area but, after bloody fighting, the assault was abandoned as it could make no headway against the Indian anti-tank defence. This action was known as the Battle of Asal Uttar. Indian efforts to breach the Ichhoril canal line were equally unsuccessful. On 8 September the Indians launched their armoured division and two infantry divisions from Jammu against Sialkot in two prongs but the hastily-reconstituted Pakistan armoured division was rushed up and stopped the advances about ten miles inside the frontier. As both tank forces outstripped their lorry-borne infantry on the rough terrain, there was a series of tank-to-tank battles lasting in all fifteen days and known as the Battle of Phillora (10-12 September) and the Battle of Chawinda (14-17 September). It seems that the British Centurion tank came out better than the American Patton due to its higher rate of fire and simpler procedures.

As soon as open warfare broke out both Britain and the U.S. had cut off supplies of arms and ammunition to both warring parties and the offensives began now to die out as stocks became exhausted. A U.N. ceasefire was agreed to on 23 September and in January 1966 Soviet premier Alexei Kosygin brought the two states together in Tashkent where they agreed to withdraw to positions held on 15 August 1965.

India claims to have gained 740 square miles of territory and Pakistan 1,600 square miles.

Casualties were declared by each side as follows:

	India	Pakistan
Killed	2,212	1,030
Wounded	7,636	2,171
Captured or missing	1,500	630

As most damaged tanks were recovered and repaired, the losses in this campaign are not known. Due to lack of movement, very few were captured.

Both air forces were used in the ground attack, reconnaissance and interdiction roles and Pakistan seems to have come out on top. Pakistan admits losing fourteen planes, India admits thirty-five.

Both sides made the mistake of using tanks in unsuitable terrain.

In March 1971 East Pakistan's Awami League leader, Mujibur Rahman, set up a provisional government independent of that in West

Pakistan. Rahman was arrested and widespread unrest broke out which was quietly supported from India. East Pakistani dissidents were trained and armed in India and formed the Mukti Bahini who then re-entered their own country and fought a guerrilla war against the West Pakistani authorities and army there. In November 1971 India invaded East Pakistan, ignoring a U.N. ceasefire call in December; by the end of the year the West Pakistani army in the new 'Bangladesh' collapsed and 60,000 were captured.

In West Pakistan Zulfikar Ali Bhutto (leader of the parliamentary majority) ousted the military leader General Agha Mohammed Yahya Khan (who had been in power since 1968) and released Mujiba Rahman who returned to Bangladesh to assume the leadership. Bhutto was overthrown by a military coup led by his chief of staff General Mohammed Zia ul-Haq on 5 July 1977 and executed in 1979.

Since August 1971 India and the U.S.S.R. have been linked by a treaty of friendship while Pakistan remains associated with China for arms supply.

In 1975 India annexed the tiny Himalayan kingdom of Sikkim, thus fuelling the fires of Pakistan's fears for her own integrity even further.

The Arab-Israeli Wars

Following World War II, with its horrific Nazi extermination of over 6 million Jews, there was a heavy exodus of surviving Jews from Europe to Palestine. Britain tried unsuccessfully to limit Jewish immigration but by mid 1947 the situation in Palestine was so explosive that she gave up trying to administer her mandate there and asked the U.N. to mediate between Jew and Arab. On 29 November 1947 the U.N. General Assembly adopted a resolution for the partition of Palestine into two states and next day fighting broke out between the Arab and Jewish communities there.

The Jewish para-military Haganah and Palmach (15,000 strong) were engaged with Palestinian Arabs aided by irregulars from neighbouring states including Syria, Lebanon, Jordan, Egypt, Iraq and Saudi Arabia. Despite these apparent odds, the Jews managed to strengthen their position by 14 May 1948 when a truce was declared and the British forces and administration left the country. Two Jewish terrorist groups also took part in the fighting—the Irgun Zevai Leummi (IZL) with 5,000 men and the Stern Gang (1,000) and there were 32,000 registered in the Heil Mishmar or Home Guard.

This phase of the war was spent consolidating Jewish hold on the areas they inhabited and in smuggling in weapons and equipment. The Arabs sought, mainly in vain, to cut off and starve out isolated Jewish settlements.

Israel had proclaimed its politically independent existence on 14 May 1948 and next day the very limited regular armies of Egypt, Syria, Iraq, Jordan and Lebanon attacked the new state. (Saudi Arabia sent some infantry to operate under Egyptian command.)

On 30 May 1948 the Israeli Defence Forces (IDF) were officially established and had 30,000 men under arms with anti-tank and anti-aircraft guns but no tanks, planes or field artillery.

In the south the Egyptians advanced to Gaza, Beersheba, Hebron and Bethlehem where they linked up with Jordan's Arab Legion around Jerusalem. An amphibious Egyptian force was also landed at Majdal on the Mediterranean coast.

New weapons now arrived in Israel including armoured cars, field guns and Messerschmitt fighters; they were rushed into action and halted the Egyptian advance. The Arab Legion pushed westwards from Jordan towards the coast at Tel Aviv and north west to join up with the Lebanese army coming south and the Syrians pushing south west through the Golan Heights.

On 28 May the Jewish quarter of Jerusalem surrendered to the Arab Legion after desperate IDF efforts to capture Latrun and break through from the west to relieve the garrison in the Holy City had failed.

In the north the Syrian assault on Deganyah was beaten off on 20 May and no further serious fighting occurred here but they did take Mishmar Hayarden north of Lake Kinnaret on 10 June.

A truce was called by U.N. Palestinian mediator Count Bernadotte on 11 June and lasted until 9 July. Fighting resumed until 18 July mainly in the south (where the Israelis broke through to their Negev settlements) and in the centre (where they captured Lydda airport and the surrounding area). In the North the Israelis captured Nazareth and made several smaller gains but failed to take Mishmer Hayarden from the Syrians. A second truce ran from 18 July to 15 October 1948 but was frequently violated by both sides; the first Israeli move was to burst through the Egyptian positions along the Majdal-Hebron road, to isolate the 'Faluja Pocket' and to clear the south of the Gaza strip in 'Operation Ten Plagues'. In the north Arab irregulars were expelled into Lebanon.

From 22 December 1948 to 7 January 1949 IDF Operation Horev cleared the major remaining Egyptian positions in the Negev and along the coastal strip. By now IDF planes had secured general command of the air which proved most valuable in this and future operations. The IDF crossed into Egypt at one point but international political pressure caused them to withdraw again. The Egyptians in the Faluja Pocket held out against all attacks and were permitted to withdraw with full honours of war on 24 February 1949.

Israel was now firmly established and her Arab neighbours signed armistices with her; the latest being Syria on 20 July 1949.

The 1956 Campaign (29 October–5 November)

An arms race had developed in the Middle East with Czechoslovakia supplying Egypt with weapons and with U.S.A. supporting Israel. Britain maintained the Jordanian army but on a much lower scale than that of the two other belligerent states. Egypt nationalized the Suez Canal in 1956 and closed it to Israeli shipping; she also formed a joint Arab military command together with Syria and Jordan.

Egyptian forces in Sinai were now given two tasks: 1—to act against Israel in the east; 2—to protect the Suez Canal (in the west) against expected action from Britain and France who had previously controlled the waterway.

The IDF launched a pre-emptive offensive in Sinai (Operation Kadesh) on 29 October with the aim of destroying terrorist (Fedayeen) bases in the Gaza strip, the Egyptian's army's logistic base in the peninsula and of opening the Gulf of Eilat to Israeli shipping. One of the first acts was the dropping of an IDF airborne battalion near Parkers' Memorial in the west centre of the Sinai peninsula to outflank Egyptian positions in the north east. The rest of this brigade raced via Kuntilla, Thamad and Nakhl to join up with their comrades and block the Mitla Pass on 30 October.

An IDF armoured brigade pushed through Rafa (at the base of the Gaza strip), attacked the Egyptian 3rd Division and by 1 November was at El Arish.

In the centre another IDF formation raced through Abu Aweigila and Quseima for the Khatmia Pass which they reached on 1 November. IDF planes seized air superiority and the Anglo-French assault on the Suez Canal and Egyptian airfields on 31 October completed the dislocation of the Egyptian army which collapsed.

The Gaza strip was cleared and the Gulf of Eilat opened; IDF losses were 171 killed, about 1,000 wounded and four captured. Egyptian personnel losses were 6,000 dead and wounded, 6,000 captured and vast quantities of stores and equipment were taken or destroyed.

Israel subsequently evacuated Sinai and the British and French left the canal zone but Egypt's military potential had been ruined for years.

Arab material losses were quickly replaced by the Soviets but the morale of the army took much longer to heal.

The Six Day War 5–10 June 1967

Following the 1956 war a U.N. force was stationed along the Sinai border to act as a buffer between Egypt and Israel, and at the Straits of Tiran to ensure free access to that waterway. The terrorists of the Palestine Liberation Organization (PLO), having been evicted from the Gaza strip, moved their operational bases into Syria and Jordan. Syria had moved into the Soviet camp and her forces were equipped with Soviet weapons. Egypt's President Nasser began to whip up anti-Jewish feeling in the Arab world but made a vital mistake for at this time he had about 60,000 Egyptian troops deployed in the Yemen fighting for the republicans there against the royalists. His available forces in Sinai were thus limited to about 100,000 men and 1,000 tanks. On 17 May he demanded that the U.N. withdraw their forces from Sinai and this was done; on 22 May he closed the Straits of Tiran to Israeli shipping and the IDF was ordered to prepare the now-familiar, crushing pre-emptive strike.

Air superiority was again the key factor and early on 5 June IDF planes mounted a series of low flying raids (to avoid detection by enemy radar) and completely destroyed the air forces of Egypt, Syria and Jordan for the loss of only 19 planes. At 8 a.m. that day IDF Southern Command (three armoured 'divisional' task forces) rushed into the Egyptian positions in Sinai in a near repeat of the 1956 advance. Again, the IDF by-passed enemy positions in order to race for and hold the three vital passes (Giddi, Mitla and Khatmia) to cut off enemy withdrawal and to block reinforcement and resupply. Having disposed of the Arab air forces the Israelis then put their planes into a ground support role and they took heavy toll of the retreating columns of Egyptian troops. Smaller IDF forces pushed south to take Sharm el Sheikh on the southern tip of Sinai on 7 June. The fighting in the Gaza strip was fierce but was over by 7 June by which time the passes had been secured and the Suez Canal reached in the north near El Qantara.

In the Jerusalem sector the IDF attacked Jordanian positions around the city and captured the place on 7 June. They then proceeded to clear all Jordanian troops from the Samarian triangle and the west bank of the Jordan.

The IDF had adopted a quiet role on the Golan Heights until forces were available from the other sectors and on 9 June they had been sufficiently reinforced to attack the Syrian army with the main thrust going in in the northern sector around Tel Azizyat. The fighting was hard but by 2.30 p.m. next day they had broken the Syrian defence and captured Quneitra on the road to Damascus. A U.N.-sponsored cease fire now came into force and the Six Day War ended. Losses for the IDF were 777 killed, 2,586 wounded and some prisoners; the Arabs had over 15,000 killed and wounded, 6,000 prisoners and had lost their air forces and hundreds of tanks, guns and large quantities of equipment. Israel refused to give up the territory she had taken and proceeded to integrate the Golan Heights, West Bank and Sinai into the rest of the state and to place settlements in the captured areas.

The Yom Kippur War 6–25 October 1973

In the period 1967–1973 Israel built the Bar-Lev line along the east bank of the Suez Canal and fortified their conquests in the Golan Heights.

Egypt conducted a war of attrition against the Israelis in Sinai and worked feverishly to rebuild and rearm her forces. This task was hampered by her breach with the Soviet Union in 1972 when 20,000 Russian military advisers were thrown out and all supplies to Egypt of Soviet arms and spare parts ceased. Syria managed to heal the breach however and Soviet aid was resumed.

In the two previous wars Israel had attacked first and had destroyed the Arab air forces to gain air superiority for subsequent operations. The Arabs decided that this time they would dictate the time and place of attack and would counter the undoubtedly superior Israeli air force by forcing it to act in a ground support role in areas saturated with Soviet surface to air missiles (S.A.M. 2, S.A.M. 6 and S.A.M.7).

The Israelis had now become so confident that their tanks alone could decide the outcome of ground conflicts that they had formed 'divisions' and brigades containing only tanks and lacking the conventional infantry and artillery support. They were to pay very heavily for this error.

The balance of forces at the outbreak of the war was:

	Divisions	Men	Tanks	Combat Planes	S.A.M. Batteries
Israel	11	270,000	1,700	500	60
Egypt	12	260,000	2,000	600	650
Syria	7	120,000	1,600	300	200
Iraq	3	30,000	400	60	?

Saudi Arabia and Morocco each contributed an infantry brigade.

The date chosen for the attack on Israel was 6 October—the Jewish feast of atonement. The Bar-Lev Line was only lightly garrisoned and was only designed as a trip-wire defence with two tank brigades in support but it had an extensive buffer zone (the Sinai) behind it whereas the Golan Heights were much closer to the Israeli heartland. When the simultaneous Egyptian and Syrian assaults came at 2 p.m. that day, it was soon clear to the IDF that they could afford to fight a holding action in Sinai while achieving a decision in the vital Golan area.

Syria attacked with three mechanized infantry divisions, two armoured divisions and two armoured brigades on Quneitra and Rafid and were initially opposed by two infantry battalions and two armoured brigades with eleven artillery batteries in support. The IDF planes, trying to stop these thrusts, suffered heavy losses from S.A.M. and from Z.S.U.-23-4 A.A. guns and by 7 p.m. 6 October the 'Barak' Israeli tank brigade had been destroyed, the defences pierced and Syrian armour began to roll towards the Sea of Galilee.

Israeli reserve formations were rushed forward to stem the flood, now only 7 km. from Galilee and, as the Syrians ran out of momentum, the defence strengthened, the Israelis held and on 8 October they were sufficiently reinforced (by three armoured divisions) to mount counter-attacks through Ein Gev and the Gamla Pass. Syrian S.A.M. supplies became exhausted and the IDF gradually gained the upper hand. By 10 October the Syrians had largely been pushed back to their start positions and the Israelis prepared to mount a counter-offensive.

About 8 km. north of Sasa the Syrians had built a strong defensive belt to which they now withdrew but their men were tired and much depleted by the fighting and their ammunition was running low.

On 11 October the Israelis closed up to this line where heavy fighting

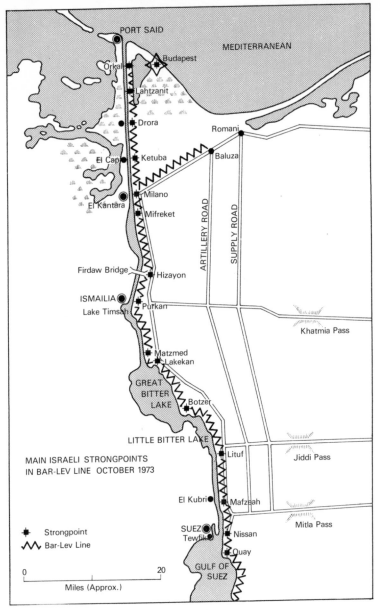

PORT SAID

MEDITERRANEAN

Orkal
Budapest

Lahtzanit

Drora

Romani

El Cap
Ketuba
Baluza

Milano

El Kantara

Mifreket

ARTILLERY ROAD

SUPPLY ROAD

Firdaw Bridge
Hizayon

ISMAILIA
Purkan

Lake Timsah

Khatmia Pass

Matzmed
Lakekan

GREAT
BITTER
LAKE

Botzer

LITTLE BITTER LAKE

Lituf
Jiddi Pass

MAIN ISRAELI STRONGPOINTS
IN BAR-LEV LINE OCTOBER 1973

El Kubri
Mafzeah

Mitla Pass

SUEZ
Tewfik
Nissan

Strongpoint
Quay

Bar-Lev Line

GULF OF
SUEZ

0   20

Miles (Approx.)

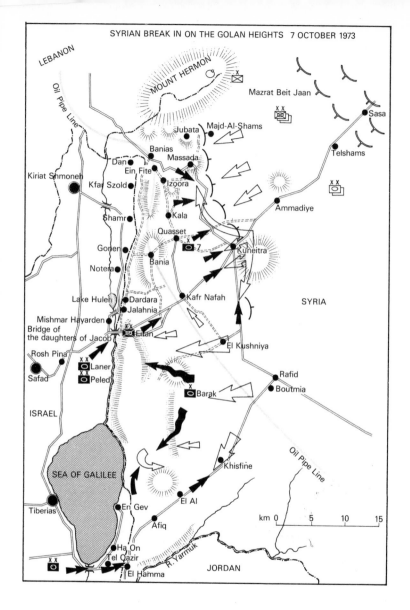

SYRIAN BREAK IN ON THE GOLAN HEIGHTS 7 OCTOBER 1973

LEBANON

Oil Pipe Line

MOUNT HERMON

Mazrat Beit Jaan

Sasa

Jubata

Majd-Al-Shams

Banias

Massada

Telshams

Dan

Ein Fite

Kiriat Shmoner

Kfar Szold

Izoora

Kala

Ammadiye

Shamr

Quasset

Gonen

Bania

Kuneitra

Notera

Lake Huleh

Dardara

Jalahnia

Kafr Nafah

SYRIA

Mishmar Hayarden

Bridge of
the daughters of Jacob

Eitan

Rosh Pina

El Kushniya

Safad

Laner

Peled

Rafid

Barak

Boutmia

ISRAEL

SEA OF GALILEE

Khisfine

Oil Pipe Line

Tiberias

En Gev

El Al

Afiq

km 0   5   10   15

Ha On

Tel Qazir

El Hamma

R. Yarmuk

JORDAN

33

went on for two days before stabilizing in the defensive belt until 22 October. The Syrians had lost 3,500 dead, 5,600 wounded, 400 captured and 1,000 tanks destroyed, damaged or captured.

The Suez Front
During the night of 5/6 October Egyptian frogmen swam the canal to plant explosive charges in the Bar-Lev sandbank line and to block up the mouths of pipelines designed to flood the canal with blazing oil in case of an assault. At 2 p.m. 16 October the Egyptian Second and Third Armies (two armoured, two mechanized and five infantry divisions plus artillery support from 2,000 guns and fifty S.A.M. batteries) attacked over the canal at three points—south of Qantara, north of Ismailia and south of the Bitter Lakes. About 1,700 tanks were available for this assault and they achieved immediate success. The Bar-Lev Line was washed away with water jets at selected spots to enable the assaulting amphibious tanks to get out of the canal and to push forward into Sinai. Infantry carrying the man-portable SAGGER A.T.G.W. poured across the 70 m. wide canal to form the vital defence screen against Israeli tanks and a dense umbrella of S.A.M. and Z.S.U. 23-4 was erected to act against the IDF air force. The Egyptian air force was held back at this stage so that it could act later in a ground support role in the advance through the three vital passes. The Egyptian plan worked. IDF planes suffered heavy losses against the S.A.M. and Z.S.U. 23-4 and their tanks were decimated by SAGGER fired in salvoes in the open, rolling terrain east of the canal.

While the Israelis mobilized and rushed reinforcements to both Sinai and Golan fronts, it was soon clear that the greatest threat was in the north so the Sinai troops were ordered to just hold on until forces could be released from the Syrian front to enable a counter offensive to be launched in the south.

From 6-14 October the Egyptians extended their bridgeheads in the north (Second Army) and south (Third Army) but did not join them up and this gap was to prove crucial later on. On 14 October the Second Army advanced from its S.A.M. cover to try to seize the vital passes but were repulsed with heavy losses after a fierce battle. A renewed attempt next day fared no better. By now the Golan front had stabilized and the Israelis began transferring forces to the southern front.

On 9 October an Israeli reconnaissance force had crossed the Great Bitter Lake in the gap between the two enemy armies and had found the western shores empty. The IDF seized this opportunity and began to send forces over the canal north of Duwer Soer to strike at the S.A.M. sites from the ground and thus weaken Egyptian air cover over their bridgeheads.

By now the vast majority of the Egyptian armies were on the east bank of the canal and they were unable quickly to transfer forces back to the western side to counter this Israeli raid.

A fierce battle developed at Chinese Farm (on the east bank) as the Egyptians sought to cut off the Israeli thrust on 15 October. They did slow it down but the build up of Israeli forces on the west bank continued and, as more and more S.A.M. sites were destroyed, the IDF air force was able to act more freely over the battlefield and the initiative passed into Israeli hands.

By 22 October the communications of the Egyptians on the east bank of the canal were severely disrupted and Israeli forces had pushed forward and fanned out towards Cairo, Ismailia and Suez.

A ceasefire was agreed upon at 0752 hours that day but it broke down next day because the Israelis wanted to push south to Suez and complete the encirclement of the Egyptian Third Army on the east bank of the canal.

They achieved their aim by 7 a.m. 25 October when a second ceasefire was agreed upon. The superpowers (U.S.A. and U.S.S.R.) had kept the opposing sides supplied with much-needed replacement weaponry and they now managed the ceasefire negotiations.

The fighting was over but this war had shown that the Egyptian and Syrian armies had learned their lessons from the past and had improved their war machines immensely. Israel finished the day in a strong tactical position but had to agree in subsequent negotiations to withdraw from the canal and to give up the three vital passes.

Estimated casualties in this latest Arab-Israeli war were as follows:

	Killed	Wounded	Captured or Missing	Tanks	Fighters	Ships
Israel	2,812	7,500	531	840	120	nil
Egypt	12,000	30,000	9,000	650	182	4
Syria	7,000	21,000	?	600	165	7
Iraq	125	260	18	80	21	nil

Cyprus

After many years of British rule, the Greek-Cypriot majority of the island's population (the minority were of Turkish extraction) began to agitate for independence in 1954. Head of the Greek-Cypriot community was Archbishop Makarios and he approved the setting up of a military wing of the independence movement which became known as EOKA with 'General' George Grivas (who died in January 1974) in command. From 1 April 1955 until 19 February 1959 EOKA mounted a guerrilla war on the British military garrison in the island and numbered at least one serviceman's wife among their kills. Britain exiled Makarios to Mauritius for some time but eventually gave up her control of most of the island following negotiations with Greece, Turkey and the Greek and Turkish Cypriot representatives in Zürich. Ultimate aim of EOKA had been 'Enosis' or political union with Greece but this was firmly vetoed by the Turkish Cypriots and after years of living peacefully together the two communities in the island became increasingly hostile to each other.

Archbishop Makarios (President of the new republic of Cyprus) proposed modifications to the Zürich Agreement and Greeks began to fight their Turkish neighbours on 22 December 1963. British, Greek, Turkish, and later U.N. troops restored an uneasy peace and on 22 March 1965 peace proposals were accepted by Britain and Cyprus but not by the Turkish minority.

The armed truce festered on and on 15 July 1974 there was a Greek-Cypriot coup against Makarios who left the island until 7 December that year, his place being taken by Glafcos Clerides, President of the Cypriot House of Representatives. The Turks, fearing that the coup would lead to Cyprus becoming a Greek province, invaded the island on 20 July and 14 August 1974 with 40,000 troops and secured the northern 40 per cent. of the country. There was a brief period of savage inter-communal fighting with wholesale massacres of men, women and children before all Turkish Cypriots were evacuated into the Turkish part of the island and the Greek Cypriots there were forced out into the south. The situation remains like this to this day. Britain retains two 'sovereign base areas' in the south of the island for national and NATO use (Akrotiri and Larnaca).

Sultanate of Oman

The Jebel Akhdar Campaign (1955–1958)

In December 1955 the Sultan of Oman used his limited armed force to put down a rebellion in the mountainous Jebel Akhdar region in the north of his country. Cause of the trouble had been a Saudi Arabian inspired attempt to cause their puppet—the recently elected Imam Ghalib bin Ali—to break free from the Omani sultans. Egypt and certain U.S. oil interests also supported the uprising. In a swift, small-scale operation the Imam was forced to abdicate but many of his dissident followers fled up to the fertile plateau on top of the Jebel and were able quite easily to block the very few and very narrow access routes to the Sultan's men. The deposed Imam's brother, Talib, fled into Saudi Arabia where he spent two years recruiting more forces and in May 1957 he returned to the Jebel Akhdar and Sharquiya areas to foment new rebellions against the ultra-conservative Sultan. The Sharquiya revolt fizzled out quickly but the Sultan's forces were ambushed as they tried to force the Jebel position and were almost wiped out. Only swift aid from Britain stopped the final defeat of the Sultan and the rebels withdrew up to the top of the Jebel again. For the next two years this stalemate continued while the Sultan's Armed Forces (S.A.F.) were reformed with British aid. They then comprised four regiments of infantry—Muscat, Northern Frontier, Desert and Jebel and were supported by a British artillery battery and a squadron of British armoured cars. S.A.F. now set out to isolate and capture the rebels on the Jebel. Firstly in 1957 the main rebel supply route from Saudi Arabia was cut when Tanuf village was captured and in November of that year the Muscat Regiment discovered an unguarded track up the north side of the plateau. A rapid assault plan was launched and in December Hijar village, half way up the plateau, was captured. The way to the top was still blocked by rebels on the Aqabat al Dhafar—a very strong position—and an assault from the now-unguarded south was decided upon.

On 27 January 1958, part of Northern Frontier Regiment, two squadrons of 22nd S.A.S. and one squadron of the Life Guards rushed rebel positions in Habit village and moved on to occupy rebel head-quarters in Sharaijah. With only light casualties on both sides the rebellion had been terminated.

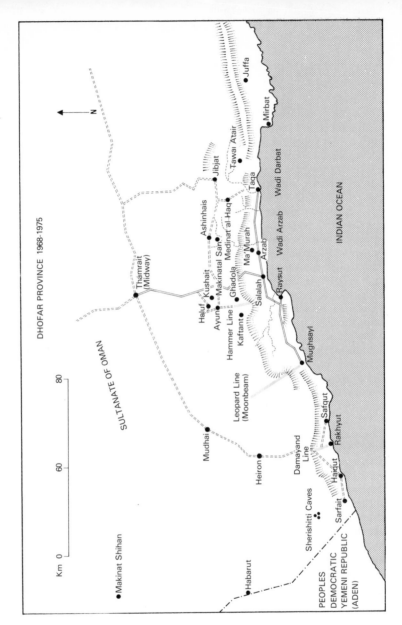

DHOFAR PROVINCE 1968-1975

SULTANATE OF OMAN

Km 0   60   80

← N

Makinat Shihan

Mudhai

Heiron

Leopard Line (Moonbeam)

Damavand Line

Thamrait (Midway)

Haluf
Ayun
Kushait
Makinatal San
Medinat al-Haq
Ghadola
Hammer Line
Kaffant

Ashinhais

Jibjat

Tawai Atair

Juffa

Mirbat

Taqa

Wadi Darbat

Ma'Murah
Arzab
Wadi Arzab

Raysut
Salalah

Mughsayl

Safqut

Rakhyut

Hajqut

Sarfait

Sherishitti Caves

Habarut

PEOPLES
DEMOCRATIC
YEMENI REPUBLIC
(ADEN)

INDIAN OCEAN

38

The Dhofar Campaign (1963-1976)

Trouble broke out in this southern province of Oman in 1963 when Saudi Arabian backed rebels sought to break away from the medieval rule of Sultan Said bin Taimur. Next year the Dhofar Liberation Front (D.L.F.) was formed and enjoyed wide support for their goal of independence within the province.

They mounted armed attacks on government and oil company targets and attempted to assassinate the Sultan. In 1968 the D.L.F. adopted Marxist Socialist doctrine and changed their name to Popular Front for the Liberation of the Occupied Arab Gulf (P.F.L.O.A.G.). Military operations were intensified successfully and aid was received from China who sent arms, equipment and military advisers.

The coastal town of Rakhyat fell to the rebels in 1969 and they soon controlled most of the inland part of the province. P.F.L.O.A.G. extended their raids into northern Oman and the United Arab Emirates but a turning point came on 11 June 1970 when their attack on the S.A.F. garrison at Izki (in central Oman) failed. This event caused the Sultan's son—Qaboos bin Said—to oust his father and take over the state. Educated in Sandhurst, he was well aware of the backward state of his country and sought to introduce progressive changes to avert revolution. He declared an amnesty for the rebels and introduced many reforms in government, education and health services. Many P.F.L.-O.A.G. rebels accepted the amnesty but the Marxist hardcore of the movement were not interested in peace; in September 1970 they ruthlessly purged their organization which caused a further 201 rebels to surrender to the government by March 1971. These reformed rebels were used as the backbone of the government sponsored Firqat (home guard) and the S.A.F. was expanded.

At this time S.A.F. controlled only the larger towns in Dhofar and their immediate environs. With air support Medinat al Haq and Tawi Atair in the eastern Jebel were occupied but garrisons were withdrawn again from June to September when the monsoon rains severely limited flying.

As much rebel aid entered Dhofar from Aden in the west, in November 1971 'Leopard Line'—a series of outposts running from Mughsayl on the coast north east into the Jebel—was set up with the aim of cutting these supply lines. Leopard Line was also evacuated during the monsoon. During 1972 Chinese aid for the rebels waned but the Soviets replaced them. On 19 July 1972 the rebels launched their last large-scale attack—an unsuccessful assault on the coastal town of Mirbat. They were repulsed and chased up into their mountain hideouts with heavy losses.

By October 1972 rebels had been driven out of all areas east of Jebel Samhan and the 'Hornbeam Line' was set up across their lines of supply from Mughsayl due north to Wadi Qaim. In this line the outposts were linked by barbed wire and minefields. The rebels suffered another setback in December 1972 when eighty of them, with quantities of weapons, were captured in Oman and Abu Dhabi. During the 1973 monsoon S.A.F. garrisons were maintained on the Hornbeam Line and at Jibjat and Medinat al Haq. That at Tawi Atair was withdrawn again. Apart from British troops, there were Jordanian engineers and an Iranian infantry brigade helping S.A.F. to fight the rebels who were now receiving help from the U.S.S.R., Libya, Cuba and Aden. By extending the road system, government aid and control was brought into increasing areas previously held by the rebels who in August 1974 changed their name to the Popular Front for the Liberation of Oman (P.F.L.O.).

On 2 December 1974 the Iranian brigade launched an unsuccessful attack on the rebel main base in caves at Sherishitti and Bait Handob and were then diverted to capture Rakhyut which they did on 5 January 1975. They then built the Damavand Line running north of that town. S.A.F. renewed the attack on Sherishitti in December 1974 and captured part of the complex together with much ammunition.

A rebel regimental headquarters together with much equipment was captured west of the Hornbeam Line on 21 February 1975 and in October of that year a new line of posts, wire and mines was built northwards from Sarfait on the coast. Later that month the Sherishitti caves were captured and the rebels lost their main operations base and began to slip away over the border into Aden. Dhalqut was occupied by S.A.F. on 1 December 1975 and the rebellion was practically over.

Since then there have been periodic outbreaks of artillery fire from within the People's Democratic Republic of Yemen (the old British colony of Aden) but Dhofar is pacified and under Omani control.

The Belgian Congo

In the wake of the 'Wind of Change', the Belgian Congo was granted independence, rather suddenly, on 30 June 1960 and was renamed The

Republic of Congo. The Congolese had not been well prepared to take over their own affairs and trouble lay ahead for the infant state. First president was Joseph Kasavubu and the prime minister was Patrice Lumumba. Katanga is a mineral-rich province of the Congo and its president, Moïshe Tschombe, seceded from the union on 11 July 1960, intent on keeping Katanga's riches for purely domestic consumption.

Kasavubu called for U.N. troops to assist in bringing the rebellion to an end but the response to his request was so slow that Patrice Lumumba, apparently on his own initiative, asked Russia to send forces into the country. For this he was deposed, jailed, removed to Katanga where he was murdered in January 1961. Tschombe engaged white mercenaries to lead his native troops and their exploits have brought them a fame and notoriety which lured hundreds to follow their example even as late as 1976 in the civil war in Angola where some of them are still in jail. It took three operations by U.N. troops to end the Katangan secession and Tschombe negotiated his return to the fold in January 1963; he became prime minister one year later. On 1 August 1964 the title of the state changed to the Democratic Republic of the Congo and on 27 October 1971 it was renamed Zaire. In November 1964 a revolt broke out in Kisangani province and many Belgian civilians were taken hostage and held by the rebels in Stanleyville. Belgian paratroops made a dramatic and successful dash into the chaotic city to save these hostages and bring them out. Tschombe was dismissed by Kasavubu in October 1965, but one month later Kasavubu himself was ousted by Lieutenant Colonel (now General) Mobutu. There have been white mercenaries operating in Africa since the Congo but it was here that their reputation was made.

The Biafran Secessionist War

Nigeria contains many 'sub-groupings' of widely differing ethnic backgrounds and while the British had maintained peace during their rule, when independence came these old divisions erupted again. In 1945, 1953 and 1966 there had been massacres of Ibo tribesmen living in the northern region by the Moslem Hausas, who inhabit the north. The mainly Catholic Ibos came from the Eastern Region with its capital at Enugu and after the latest outrages the 'immigrants' began to withdraw from the north and the west into their home area. Lieutenant Colonel 'Jack' Gowon (trained at Sandhurst) became Nigerian head of

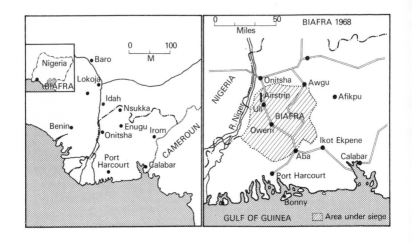

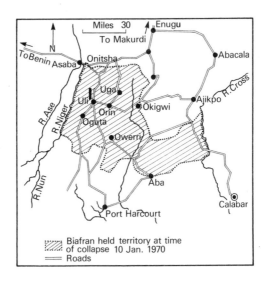

Biafran held territory at time
of collapse 10 Jan. 1970
Roads

state in place of General Ironsi, who was assassinated in 1966. The Ibos declared their secession from Nigeria on 30 May 1967 and an independent republic of 'Biafra' was set up with Lieutenant Colonel Odumegwu Ojukwu (formerly military governor of Nigeria's Eastern Region) as president. The Federal authorities then had 7,000 men, 50 armoured cars, 20 Dornier light planes and 6 Alouette helicopters; the Biafrans were able to muster 5,000 men, 2 B 26 planes and 6 Alouettes. Britain supported the Federal authorities but the Biafrans secured arms supplies from a variety of sources. During June 1967 there were sporadic clashes and on 14 July two Federal battalions took Nsukka. The Biafran 'Air Force' raided Lagos and the Federal army advanced on Enugu and Calabar. Bonny (in the Biafran oilfields) fell on 25 July and that same day the Biafran 120 ton ship *Ibadan* was sunk.

A Biafran counter-attack into the Western Region made great headway however, Yoruba western troops in the Federal forces mutinied and on 9 August 1967 Benin fell to be followed on the 13th by Okene. The Yorubas negotiated with the Ibos to form an alliance against the Hausas but in September and October the Federal army retook the mid-Western Region and entered Biafra, recapturing Enugu, Asaba and Calabar. On 22 March 1968 Onitsha fell; on 19 May Port Harcourt was captured and Biafra was cut off from the sea. Limited resupply was still possible by air into the Uli airstrip but Biafra's fate was now sealed.

This slow strangulation of the infant state continued with the Ibos defending fiercely every foot of territory.

The civilians suffered terrible hardships as the siege went on for the next two years but all to no avail. General Ojukwu fled from Biafra early in January 1970 leaving Major General Phillip Effiong, his chief of staff, to conduct the surrender. Effiong ordered a cease-fire on 12 January 1970 and formally accepted Nigerian Federal authority in Lagos on 15 January.

Angola, Mozambique and Rhodesia

The first shots in Mozambique's struggle for independence from Portugal were fired on 25 September 1964 and soon all Portuguese possessions in Africa were locked in deadly guerrilla wars with support for the terrorists coming from the usual Soviet, Czechoslovakian and Chinese sources as well as from Cuba in the latter stages. In Mozambique it was F.R.E.L.I.M.O. (Frente de Libertacao de Moçambique) which fought the Portuguese; in Angola it was U.N.I.T.A. By 1974 the Portuguese positions in her territories in Africa had become untenable and she withdrew; this precipitated the Portuguese revolution and the introduction of parliamentary democracy to that country. Aid for the guerrillas came not only in the form of weapons and equipment but also in training in the U.S.S.R. and other countries and the provision of bases in countries surrounding Angola and Mozambique.

Since Southern Rhodesia's Unilateral Declaration of Independence (U.D.I.) in 1965 there has been a growing terrorist campaign against that state, aided by the U.S.S.R.

Kenya and Aden

Kenya achieved independence from Britain on 12 December 1963 after suffering an emergency of some years in which a tribal terrorist group—the Mau Mau, based mainly on the Kikuyu tribe—sought unsuccessfully to gain control of the country. Mau Mau developed in the late 1940s and gradually became more active in terrorism until a state of emergency was declared in Kenya in October 1952 and the British army stepped in to help the civil police restore order.

That same month, Jomo 'Burning Spear' Kenyatta (president of the Kenyan African Union since 1947) was convicted of being head of Mau Mau and spent the next nine years in prison. By mid 1956 Mau Mau had been crushed and the fighting ended but the state of emergency continued until 1959. Casualties in this vicious civil war were Kikuyu— 11,500 dead (most of these were killed by Mau Mau in its attempts to gain control of the tribe); 95 Europeans, 29 Asians and 1,920 Africans died fighting Mau Mau. Jomo Kenyatta proceeded to become Kenya's prime minister in May 1963 and president in 1964.

After many peaceful years of British colonial rule Aden began to agitate for independence in the 1960s. Just prior to the British evacuation on 30 November 1976, the Adeni terrorist group, National Liberation Front, crushed its other guerrilla rival the Front for the Liberation of South Yemen (F.L.O.S.Y.) and the British-inspired South Arabian Federation of seventeen Sultanates around Aden collapsed. The old colony became the People's Democratic Republic of Yemen (P.D.R.Y.).

44

Private, Motor Rifles

2.   Senior Sergeant

3.   Woman Junior Sergeant

U.S.S.R.

4. Private, Motor Rifles

5. Senior Sergeant

6. Junior Sergean
Airborne Troop

Artillery Major

9. Private, Motor Rifles

8. Junior Tank Lieutenant

10. Warrant Officer, Medical Corps, U.S.S.R.

12. Lieutenant, Motor Rifle Bulgaria

11. Lance Corporal, Motor Rifles, Bulgaria

3. Engineer Major, Bulgaria

15. Lance Corporal, Motor Rifles, Czechoslovakia

14. Sergeant Major, Paratroops, Bulgaria

CZECHOSLOVAKIA

16. Corporal, Airborne Forces

18. Staff-Sergeant, Airborne Force

17. Major, Motor Rifles

. Sergeant, Czechoslovakia

21. Infantry Private, East Germany

20. Private, Guards Regiment,
East Germany

22. Tank Major, East Germany

24. Major General, Hungar

23. Corporal, Military Police,
Hungary

5. Corporal, Signals,
Hungary

26. Infantryman, Hungary

27. Private, Mountain Troops
Poland

28. Tank Crewman, Poland

29. Sergeant, Paratroops, Poland

30. Woman Musician, Rumania

. Corporal, Mountain Troops

33. Private, Motor Rifles

32. General

34. Lieutenant, Tank Troops
Rumania

36. Senior Warrant Office
Mountain Infantry,
Yugoslavia

35. Corporal, Yugoslavia

W.R.A.C. Sergeant,
Military Police

38.   Private, Light Infantry

39.   Gurkha Private

GREAT BRITAIN

40. Infantry Subaltern

41. Paratrooper

42. Infantrym

43. Infantryman

45. Infantry Corporal

44. Infantryman

46. Sergeant Major, Denmark

47. Infantryman, Denmark

48. Dutch Offic

9. Infantryman

50. Nurse (S.A.S.)

51. Paratrooper

FRANCE/ALGERIA

52. Algerian National Liberation Army (ALN)

53. French Légionnaire

54. Algerian National Liberatio Army (ALN)

5. Lance Corporal,
   Mountain Troops

56. Corporal, Airborne Troops

57. Staff Sergeant,
    Armoured Fighting Vehicles

ITALY

58. Private, Lagunari

59. Lance Corporal, Bersaglieri

60. Corporal, APC Infan

1. Lieutenant of Engineers

62. Corporal, African Forces

63. Trooper, Armoured Troops

64. Regimental Sergeant Major
Mountain Infantry,
Austria

65. Sergeant, Light Infantry,
Canada

66. Infantry Capta...
U.S.A.

7. Commanding General

68. Infantry Sergeant

69. Supreme Commander

70. Sergeant Farrier,
Switzerland

71. Adjutant, Infantry,
Belgium

72. Paratrooper, Spa

73. Infantry NCO, Sweden

74. Infantry Sergeant Major, Norway

75. Infantryman, Finland

76. Sergeant, Indian Army

77. Infantry NCO, Australia

78. Company Sergeant Majo
     Canada

9. Warrant Officer, North Korea

81. Infantryman, China

80. Infantryman, China

REPUBLIC OF KOREA/TURKEY

82. Infantry Lieutenant,
Republic of Korea

84. Infantryman, Turkey
UN Forces

83. Machine-Gunner, Republic of Korea

5. Gurkha Corporal,
UN Force

86. Mercenary Officer,
Katanga

87. Mercenary Soldier,
Katanga

NIGERIAN CIVIL WAR 1967–68

88. Biafran Major General

89. Nigerian Infantryman

90. Nigerian Infantry Sergeant

. Lieutenant Colonel,
Zambian Signals

93. Lance Corporal,
Commando Brigade,
Biafra

92. Regimental Sergeant Major,
Zambian Rifles

REPUBLIC OF SOUTH AFRICA

94. Major, Special Service Battalion

95. Corporal, Women's Service

96. Infantry Patrol Commande South West Africa (Namib

7. Signaller

98. Lance Corporal, Selous' Scouts

99. Private Rhodesian
African Rifles

RHODESIA

100. Major, Grey's Scouts, 19

101. National Guardsman,
Panama

102. Cavalry Sergeant, Brazil

103. Brazilian Infantryman

104. Soldier, Malayan Races
Liberation Army

106. Mau-Mau General, Kenya

105. EOKA Soldier, Cyprus

07. Paratroop Corporal

109. Officer, Territorial
Defence Corps

108. Tank Corps Major

110. Paratrooper

111. Major General

112. Infantryma

13. Christian Militiaman

115. Muslim Irregular

114. Christian Militiaman

116. Lieutenant Colonel, Engineers
Saudi Arabia

118. Sergeant, Tank Troops, Iran

117. Artillery Sergeant, Lebanon

19. Infantry Corporal, Syria

121. Major, Signals, Abu Dhabi

120. Guardsman, Muscat

IRAN/OMAN/MUSCAT

122. Iranian Infantryman

123. Second Lieutenant,
Trucial Oman Scouts

124. Corporal,
Sultan of Muscat
Armed Forces

25. Gurkha Corporal, Nepal

127. Major General, Pakistan

126. Major, Artillery, Nepal

128. Infantry Sergeant, Pakistan

130. Signaller, Indi

129. Lieutenant, Airborne Artillery,
India

31. Légionnaire

132. Colonial Paratrooper

133. Tirailleur Algérien

134. Viet Cong Guerrilla,
North Vietnam

136. Infantry Priva
North Vietnam

135. ARVN Ranger,
South Vietnam

37. Infantry Sergeant,
North Vietnam

138. Lieutenant Colonel,
Infantry, Mongolia

139. Staff Sergeant,
Military Police,
Taiwan

UNITED STATES ARMY IN VIETNAM

140. Specialist

141. Paratrooper

142. Sergeant,
U.S. Special Force

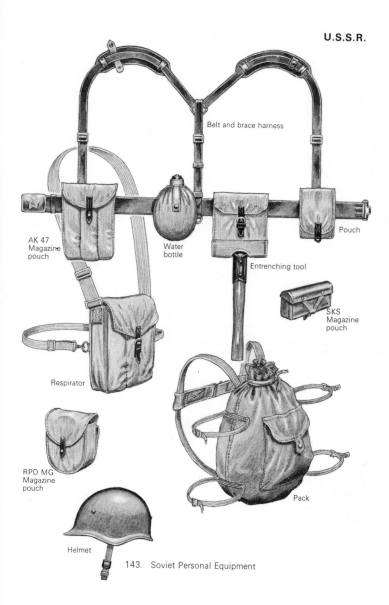

U.S.S.R.

Belt and brace harness

AK 47
Magazine
pouch

Water
bottle

Entrenching tool

Pouch

SKS
Magazine
pouch

Respirator

RPD MG
Magazine
pouch

Pack

Helmet

143. Soviet Personal Equipment

93

144. Armoured troops

145. Armoured troops

146. Airborne troops

   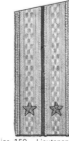 

147. Lance Corporal 148. Senior Sergeant 149. Sergeant Major 150. Lieutenant 151. Major

152. Armoured troops

153. Gunners

154. Motor Riflemen

155. Junior other ranks

156. Length of Service. Other ranks

144/156.   Soviet Insignia

157. APS (*Stetschkin*) 9 mm. pistol

158. SKS (Self Loading Carbine Simonow)

159. AK 47 (*Kalaschnikow*)

160. RPD (*Roschnoi Pulemet Detjarew*)

157/160. Soviet Infantry Weapons

U.S.S.R.

161. Officers' field service cap

162. Other ranks' side cap

163. Tropical hat

164. Fur cap

165. Military police helmet

166. Paratroopers' beret

167. Paratroopers' jump helmet

168. Tank crewmen's helmet

161/168.   Soviet Headdress

169. Polish
field cap

170. Polish
mountain troops

171. Hungarian
field cap

172. Czechoslovakian
field cap

169/172. Polish/Hungarian/Czechoslovakian Headdress

173. Yugoslav mountain trooper

174. Major,
Summer Combat Dress

175. Soldier,
Rubber NBC Suit

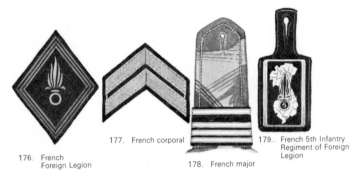

177. French corporal

176. French
Foreign Legion

178. French major

179.. French 5th Infantry
Regiment of Foreign
Legion

182. Polish cap badge

181. Bulgarian shoulder
board (sergeant major)

180. Bulgarian shoulder
board (junior
lieutenant)

183.
DDR
shoulder strap
(corporal)

184.
DDR
shoulder strap
(junior sergeant)

185. Hungarian
cap badge

188. Rumanian
mountain corps.

186. Yugoslavian
shoulder strap
(sergeant)

187. Yugoslavian
shoulder strap
(junior sergeant)

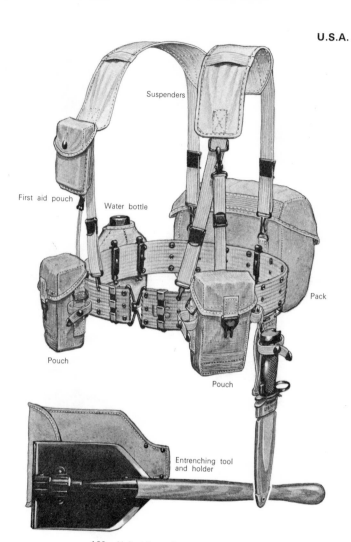

Suspenders

First aid pouch

Water bottle

Pack

Pouch

Pouch

Entrenching tool
and holder

189. United States Personal Equipment

U.S.A.

190. Private First Class

193. Captain's combat badge of rank

195. Combat dress

191. Sergeant Major

192. Specialist 5th Class

194. Fatigue dress name tag

196. Fatigue dress

197. Airborne and Special Forces

198. 1st Air Cavalry Division

190/198. United States Army Insignia

102

199. M 60 Machine-Gun

201. M 14
Self loading
rifle

200. M 16
Self loading
rifle

199/201. United States Infantry Weapons

U.S.A.

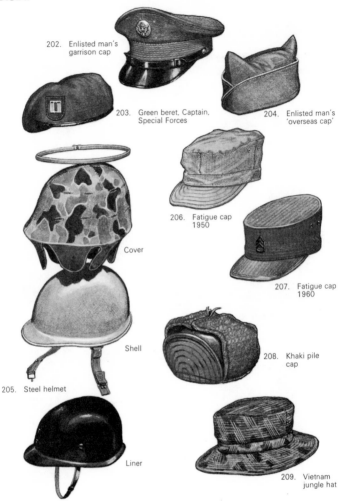

202. Enlisted man's garrison cap

203. Green beret, Captain, Special Forces

204. Enlisted man's 'overseas cap'

Cover

206. Fatigue cap 1950

207. Fatigue cap 1960

Shell

208. Khaki pile cap

205. Steel helmet

Liner

209. Vietnam jungle hat

202/209. United States Headdress

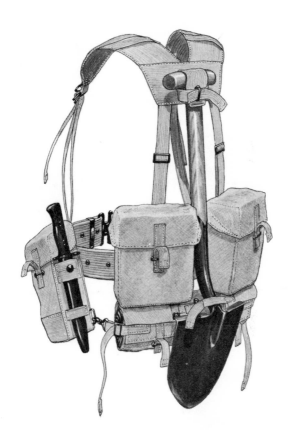

210. Web Equipment 1958 Pattern

GREAT BRITAIN

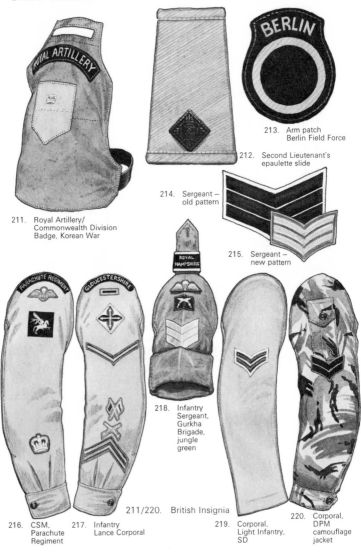

211. Royal Artillery/
Commonwealth Division
Badge, Korean War

212. Second Lieutenant's
epaulette slide

213. Arm patch
Berlin Field Force

214. Sergeant –
old pattern

215. Sergeant –
new pattern

218. Infantry
Sergeant,
Gurkha
Brigade,
jungle
green

211/220.   British Insignia

216. CSM,
Parachute
Regiment

217. Infantry
Lance Corporal

219. Corporal,
Light Infantry,
SD

220. Corporal,
DPM
camouflage
jacket

106

221. FN Machine-Gun

222. FN Self loading rifle

223. Individual Weapon (IW) (Bullpup)

224. Sterling Sub Machine-Gun

221/224. British Infantry Small Arms

225. Jungle hat

226. Gurkha hat

227. Infantry beret (Gloucestershire Regt)

228. SAS beret

229. Steel helmet with visor

230. DPM combat hat (1970)

231. Combat cap (1950)

232. Wessex Brigade (Gloucestershire Regt)

234. Cavalry beret (9th/12th Prince of Wales' Own Royal Lancers)

235. Para jump helmet

225/235. British Headdress

236. Bomb Disposal Officer

Glass-reinforced
plastic helmet with visor

Non-slip shoulder pad

Armoured vest

Shield

Riot baton

Leg shields

237. British Body Armour

WEST GERMANY

238. Oberfeldwebel, combat suit

239. Hauptfeldwebel's shoulder strap slide

240. Unterleutnant

241. 1st Luftlande — Division, arm patch

ITALY

242. Parachute Brigade, arm patch

243. Warrant Officer, shoulder strap

244. Major, shoulder strap

245. Sergeant Major Folgore (Airborne) Division

ISRAEL

246. Corporal

247. Staff Sergeant (combat only)

248. Lieutenant

238/248. Insignia, Various Nations

250. French MAT 9 mm.
Machine-Pistol
M-1949

249. French 7.5 mm.
M-1949/56 MAS

251. Israeli 9 mm.
UZI Sub
Machine-Gun

252. Israeli 5.56 mm.
GALIL Assault
Rifle

249/252. French and Israeli Weapons

254. Czechoslovakian 7.65 mm.
M-61 Skorpion
Machine-pistol

253. West German
7.62 mm.

255. Australian 9 mm.
F-3A1 Sub Machine-Gun

253/255. Various Small Arms

113

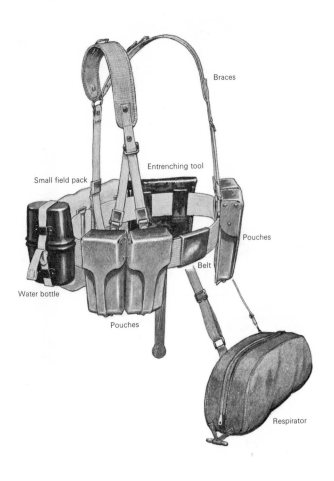

Braces

Entrenching tool

Small field pack

Pouches

Water bottle

Belt

Pouches

Respirator

256. West German Personal Equipment

257. Muleteer, Mountain Artillery

258. French Foreign Legion
junior ranks

259. French paratrooper's
combat hat

260. West German Mountain
Troops,
field cap

261. Malayan Races
Liberation Army

258/261.

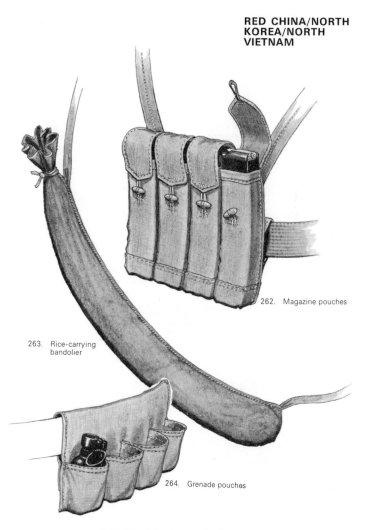

262. Magazine pouches

263. Rice-carrying bandolier

264. Grenade pouches

262/264. Asian Communist Equipment

265. British DMS boot

266. U.S. field boot

267. French patrol boot

268. West German
Mountain Troops
boot

269. South African
DMS boot

265/269. Boots

118

270. British jungle boot

271. Viet Cong jungle boot

272. U.S. Vietnam service

270/272. Boots

1. **U.S.S.R.: Private, Motor Rifles, Summer Field Dress, 1945-70.**
This is the uniform made famous in the great battles of World War II. The Gymnastjerka blouse was worn as fatigue and combat dress up until the new uniforms were introduced for the Soviet Army in the 1971-72 period. The small ammunition pouches are for the SKS rifle (see plate 158). Until quite recently the Russians wore foot cloths and not socks in their boots.

2. **U.S.S.R.: Senior Sergeant Lightweight Tropical Uniform, 1965-79.**
The Soviet army has a large area of operations in Central Asia in which the extremely hot summers certainly call for special clothing. Apparently shorts were considered to smack too much of colonialism to be adopted for the People's Army! The shoulder board ranks have been retained unaltered in the new uniforms. Jack boots and breeches were also worn with this form of dress until about 1960 as was a lightweight Gymnastjerka.

3. **U.S.S.R.: Woman Junior Sergeant, Summer Service Dress, 1945-70.**
During World War II women frequently fought and died alongside the men in the Red Army, but nowadays they are employed on clerical, administrative, culinary and signalling tasks as in most other armies. For parades the beret was dark blue and a single-breasted, khaki, four-button fronted jacket with brown gloves were worn. Summer field uniform was the khaki beret and shirt, no tie, Sam Browne belt, khaki shirt and jackboots.

4. **U.S.S.R.: Private, Motor Rifles, Winter Field Dress, 1945-70.**
Until 1971 Motor Rifles (Infantry) wore magenta facings on collar patches, shoulder boards and on piping and band of the peaked cap. After this date their facings changed to red. The fur cap seems to be worn with the earflaps firmly up regardless of the weather. His weapon is the ubiquitous AK47 (whose characteristics are given in plate 159) and his equipment pouches are different from those on the first figure because of the different magazines used.

5. **U.S.S.R.: Senior Sergeant, Summer Field Dress, 1945-70.**
The familiar Gymnastjerka is here decorated with the long service badge on the right breast (red banner over gold star and wreath, white,

triangular pendant with the number of years' service in black; silver wings) and two medal ribbons on the left breast; the white ribbon with two red stripes is the Order of the Red Banner, instituted in 1918 and awarded for outstanding courage or long service both on an individual and collective basis; the orange ribbon with three black stripes is the medal for Victory over Germany in the 1935-45 war. On the shoulder boards is the small regimental badge in matt bronze.

6. U.S.S.R.: Junior Sergeant, Airborne Troops, Summer Service Dress, 1970-79.
This jaunty, somewhat nautical costume was the 1970 replacement for the Gymnastjerka. Airborne troops, facings are shown on the beret, collar patches, shoulder boards and on the new arm patch. The facings of other corps of the Soviet Army are: tank troops, signals, engineers, artillery, transport, NBC and pipeline troops—black, medical—red, veterinary and administration—dark green.

7. U.S.S.R.: Major, Artillery, Summer Service Dress, 1972-79.
In the period 1970-72 considerable confusion reigned as to which facing colours were to be worn, artillerymen and others often appearing with red hat bands instead of their own colour. When the new uniforms had been fully introduced they received black hat bands with red piping. A new rank was also introduced at this time; this was the Praportschick or warrant officer. His shoulder boards were in the facing colour with two gold stars. With the introduction of the arm badges, interesting combinations could be seen on the uniforms of specialists attached to battalions. Transport corps drivers serving with infantry units for instance would wear black collar patches with transport badges but the motor rifles' red arm patch.

8. U.S.S.R.: Junior Lieutenant, Tank Crew, Summer Combat Dress post, 1972.
Members of tank crews wear black overalls, khaki shoulder boards and a small, yellow tank (of the same design as that on the arm patch) embroidered on the right breast. The crews of other armoured fighting vehicles wear the same helmet and overalls but no tank badge and wear their coloured regimental shoulder boards with gold CA if applicable.

9. U.S.S.R.: Private, Motor Rifles, Summer Suit, 1975.

With his 'skeleton order' NBC satchel and entrenching tool, this man carries an RPD light machine-gun of which details are given on plate 160.

10. U.S.S.R.: Warrant Officer, Medical Corps, Summer Parade Dress, 1972-80.

The Russian army wore dark green uniforms long before the Napoleonic era and in 1970-71 the colour was reintroduced for parade dress, khaki being retained for everyday wear. We see here the new warrant officer's rank stars on the colour-of-arm backing. Note that the medical corps' facings changed from dark green to red. The badges on the lower sleeve show years of service as follows: 1 thin chevron—1 year; 2—2 years; 3—3 years; 1 thick chevron—4 years; a star over a thick chevron—5 to 9 years; two stars over a chevron—over 10 years. The medical corps badge is a snake coiled over a goblet all in gold.

11. Bulgaria: Lance Corporal, Motor Rifles, Winter Combat Dress, 1968-79.

From 1945 to 1950 regiments in the Bulgarian Peoples' Army expressed their identity purely by facing colours (with gold or silver lace for officers) shown on collar patches and shoulder boards: infantry—red (and gold), paratroops blue piped red (and gold); field artillery black piped red (and gold); AA artillery black piped blue (and gold); self propelled artillery black piped red (with zig zag pattern on gold lace); tanks red piped yellow (and silver); cavalry red piped white (and silver); medical and veterinary—blue (and silver); engineers—black piped red (and silver); general staff officers—black edged red and silver; technical services—violet (and silver).

In 1968 badges were introduced for the various arms and they are remarkably similar to those of the Soviet forces except that the silver motor rifles badge has crossed rifles under the star. The collar badges of long service motor rifles' NCOs are red with black edging; those of conscripts brown with red edging. The weapon is the AK47 (see plate 159); the equipment Soviet pattern but the helmet is similar to the Wehrmacht coal scuttle.

12. Bulgaria: Lieutenant, Motor Rifles, Summer Combat Dress, 1968-79.

While soldiers wear a plain red star with brass edging on their caps, officers and senior NCOs wear an oval silver cockade with white-over-green over red centre bearing a red star.

All ranks wear the white-green-red shield on the side of the forage cap.

13. Bulgaria: Major, Engineers, Summer Walking Out Dress, 1968-79.

The engineers' facing colour (black) is shown on collar badges and shoulder boards as is the silver badge of crossed axes. For parade dress a brown leather Sam Browne belt would be added and the trousers and shoes would be replaced by breeches and jack boots.

14. Bulgaria: Sergeant Major, Paratroops, Summer Camouflage Uniform.

While most Bulgarian combat troops wear the field grey, paratroops have the camouflage suit shown here. He carries the short AK47 MPi with the collapsible butt.

15. Czechoslovakia: Lance Corporal, Motor Rifles Summer Combat Dress.

Throughout this book various patterns of camouflage clothing, all for use in roughly the same terrain, will be seen. It is interesting to speculate as to who has the right (or best) answer! After using the Soviet helmet for some time, the Czechs have produced their own version, rather similar to that worn by the German army from 1939-45. The badge of rank is well concealed—it is the small grey 'button' on the patch on the right breast. The weapon is the AK47 (see plate 159), the equipment Soviet pattern.

16. Czechoslovakia: Corporal, Airborne Forces, Summer Combat Dress, 1965-79.

Corporals wear two grey 'buttons', junior sergeants three, sergeants one silver star, staff sergeants two, company sergeant majors three (in a triangle), the three grades of warrant officer wear one, two and three stars in a horizontal line between silver bars top and bottom. Officers wear gold stars (1 to 4 up through captain; 1 to 3 between horizontal gold bars for major through colonel); gold stars with sequins between horizontal gold braid for major general, lieutenant general and colonel general. The light, plastic helmet was introduced for airborne forces in 1965.

17. Czechoslovakia: Major, Motor Rifles, Winter Dress.

The long parka is added over summer dress for winter use and a grey, Soviet-pattern pile cap would be worn in extreme cold. In service and parade dress rank badges are worn on the shoulders by all ranks and brass collar badges denote regiment. These are after the Soviet pattern except that AA artillery has its own badge—an airplane flying across an upturned gun barrel. Generals wear gold lime leaves embroidered on red backing on their collars.

18. Czechoslovakia: Staff-Sergeant, Airborne Forces, 1950-65.

This plate shows the old camouflage pattern replaced in 1965 by the subdued grey-green style.

19. Czechoslovakia: Sergeant, Summer Duty Wear.

The waist-length blouse is summer wear common to most Warsaw Pact States and is a comfortable, practical item.

20. East Germany: Private, Guards Regiment, Parade Dress, 1972.

This elite unit the 'NVA Wachregiment' as the cuff band proclaims— mounts guard daily in East Berlin at the Memorial to the Victims of Fascism on the famous Unter den Linden. Not only is the goose step unchanged from 1939 but every detail of the uniform, down to the pattern of the silver lace loops on cuffs and collar, are exactly as they were in the Wehrmacht. He carries the Soviet SKS rifle (see plate 158), retained for use with ceremonial troops because it lends itself to a good 'present arms'.

21. East Germany: Infantry Private, Summer Combat Dress, 1978.

The personal equipment is a replica of the black leather Wehrmacht items but in grey webbing with pouches modified to take AK47 magazines. These weapons are produced in East Germany, frequently with brown plastic butts and pistol grips. The helmet was designed for the Wehrmacht in 1944 but not introduced into service until about 1952.

22. East Germany: Major, Tank Troops, Walking Out Dress, 1972.

Once again, World War II buffs will recognize all items shown. The facings were pink for 'Panzers'; buff for infantry; black for engineers;

lemon yellow for signals; dark red for artillery; black for technical troops; blue for rear services. Badges of rank are also almost exactly as they were from 1939-45.

23. Hungary: Corporal of Military Police.
Hungarian and Finnish are languages which share almost nothing with any of the other languages which surround them. The F on the helmet equates to the Cyrillic P worn by the Soviet 'Regulators' or traffic police. The protective clothing obscures such uniform detail as facings and badges but the two stars on the helmet denote a corporal. Facings are worn on collar patches, piping and band to peaked cap, and on officers' shoulder boards; they are black for tanks, red for artillery and green for infantry, engineers, signals, medical, technical, transport and administration. Regimental badges in brass are worn on these collar patches; examples are; infantry—crossed rifles; tanks—a tank; field artillery—crossed gun barrels on three balls; AA artillery—as before but on a pair of wings; transport—a lorry within a cog wheel. He carries an AK47 with folded butt.

24. Hungary: Major General, Summer Walking Out Dress, 1970.
Hungary's extreme climate warrants special summer clothing like this smart lightweight white coat. The British army wore similar tunics in the tropics. The elaborate cap badge is the green-white-red national cockade surmounted by the red star. In about 1974 new parade and walking out uniforms were introduced for the army and all ranks were worn on the shoulder strap as follows: Lance corporal one bronze star; corporal two; sergeant three; staff sergeant a narrow gold bar under a star; company sergeant two stars and a bar; battalion sergeant three stars and a bar; junior warrant officer a star over a narrow and a wide gold bar; senior warrant officer as before but two stars. Junior lieutenant a star on a gold stripe; lieutenant a star; senior lieutenant two stars; captain three. Field officers have the lower part of the shoulder strap covered in gold lace with one, two and three stars (major through colonel), generals have all gold shoulder straps and one to three silver stars (major general, lieutenant general and colonel general).

25. Hungary: Corporal, Signals, 1945-71.
This NCO (recognized by the two white stars on his collar patches is in summer parade uniform with its peculiar brown leather gaiters. The signals collar badge is a circle enclosing a 'T' with six lightning flashes

radiating from it. Winter dress includes the Soviet-pattern grey pile cap (with red-white-green oval cockade and red star) and jack boots.

Junior ranks wear rank and regimental badges on their collar patches, officers wear their regimental badge under a gold button on their collar patches and wear the stars of their rank on their shoulders. In 1974 an arm badge was introduced for all ranks; to be worn on the upper left arm in service dress and in shirt sleeves; it was a khaki shield, outlined in white and bearing the white letters MN.

26. Hungary: Infantrymen, Summer Camouflage, pre-1970.
The helmet and RPD machine-gun (see plate 160) are Soviet and so is the personal equipment. This camouflage suit was replaced in 1970 by the subdued grey-green combination. The value to the Warsaw Pact of the Hungarian army has not been tested since the bloody Soviet repression of the Hungarian uprising in 1956.

27. Poland: Private, Mountain Troops, Winter Field Dress, 1945-79.
These specialist soldiers are deployed in the mountains in the South of Poland. Polish ponies are used for transport purposes; it is doubtful if they can carry as much as a good mule. The present Polish cap badge bears a strong resemblance to that worn by the army of the Duchy of Warsaw from 1807-1813.

28. Poland: Polish Tank Crewman, Winter Combat Dress, pre-1969.
In 1969 the Soviet-pattern cloth tankers' helmet was replaced by a Polish designed black plastic item with brown leather ear and neck piece. The black leather suit is relatively water resistant, has good fire-retardant properties and is readily available; thus combining many of the virtues demanded by tankers of the western world.

29. Poland: Sergeant, Paratroops, 1975.
The red beret, international symbol of the airborne forces, is decorated here with the Polish eagle and the badge of rank. Rank is also worn on the shoulders of the summer combat uniform. The helmet is similar to that introduced for tank crew personnel in 1969 but has no fittings for earphones. His weapon is an AK47 MPi with collapsible butt.

126

30. Rumania: Woman Musician, 1972.
As in many armies, women are employed in the non-combat sections of the Rumanian People's Army. Bands wear red facings and on their shoulder boards is a brass lyre.

31. Rumania: Corporal, Mountain Troops, 1973.
The collar patches show the facing colour—green. Facings for other corps are crimson for cavalry; black for tanks, artillery, technical troops, transport, engineers and signals; red for infantry and rear services; crimson for medical troops. On the shoulder straps are the rank badges (gold bars on the facing colour) and the corps badge—here a stylised sprig of fir. The weapon is the AK47 MPi with a collapsible butt.

32. Rumania: General, Summer Service Dress, 1972.
General officers have their own collar badges (gold oak leaves), hat badges and shoulder boards, and red piping to cuffs, red side stripes to trousers.

33. Rumania: Private, Motor Rifles, Summer Camouflage, 1975.
Here is yet another pattern of camouflage for the European summer flora! In 1974 the Rumanians replaced the Soviet helmet with their own pattern (shown here) which is very similar to that worn by the Rumanian army in 1939. The weapon is an AK47 (see plate 159).

34. Rumania: Lieutenant, Tank Troops, Summer Parade Dress 1974-79.
Here again is the new Rumanian helmet; for parade purposes an enamelled metal badge (the national cockade) is affixed to the front. The gold shoulder boards bear a silver tank, and are edged in the facing colour with a central stripe in the same colour. The pocket badge is awarded for attending a course at the war college.

35. Yugoslavia: Corporal, Summer Combat Dress, 1978.
The helmet has a distinct Wehrmacht flavour, the equipment is Soviet pattern but his 7.62 mm. machine-pistol is the Yugoslav-produced M-56, modelled on the German 9 mm. MP 40. (See half tone plate 172 for details.) The rank badges are all worn on the shoulder strap; one red chevron for lance corporal; one gold sergeant; two staff sergeant; three company sergeant; four junior warrant officer; one narrow over one wide—senior warrant officer.

There are four grades of lieutenant, the two junior being shown by small brass stars; the senior two by one and two large stars respectively; junior captain three stars; senior captain four. Field officers have gold edging to shoulder straps as well as the stars as follows: major—one; lieutenant colonel—two; colonel three. General officers have the gold edging and the stars above a gold laurel wreath enclosing crossed swords; major general—one star; lieutenant general—two; colonel general—three; army general—four; general—five.

36. Yugoslavia: Senior Warrant Officer, Mountain Infantry, Summer Parade Dress, 1972.

The cross strap of the Sam Browne is worn here in a novel but very practical way, supporting the pistol on the right hip. This pistol is a locally produced 7.62 mm. 'M-67' weapon with an eight round magazine; effective range 30 M.; muzzle velocity 420 m./sec. using the Tokarew cartridge. The brass collar badges are crossed rifles on a wreath. Other corps' badges are: artillery—crossed gun barrels; armour—a head-on view of a tank; ordnance—a cog wheel on which are a gun barrel crossed on a key behind a tank with a vertical adjustable spanner behind them; medical—a snake on a staff; veterinary—as before but with a letter v in the centre; NBC—crossed retorts; bands—a lyre; signals—crossed lightning flashes; engineers—an anchor behind a bridge with a wreath formed half of laurels (*left*) and half a cogwheel (*right*).

37. Great Britain: WRAC Sergeant attached to the Military Police in Northern Ireland, 1973.

Members of the Women's Royal Army Corps serve with a number of corps including Royal Signals, Intelligence Corps and Royal Army Ordnance Corps. In Northern Ireland they form a vital part of the search teams and as such are constantly exposed to attack. They are not armed and are deliberately distinguished by the bright red cap with Military Police badge (a Military Police collar badge is worn on the left breast). To protect them they wear the standard body armour vest which protects reasonably well against 9 mm. projectiles but is of very limited value against high powered rifles or the M 60 machine-gun.

38. Great Britain: Private, Light Infantry, Riot Order, Northern Ireland, 1972.

Since this figure was 'in action' a new, lighter combat helmet has been

128

introduced for the British army in the province. It is of glass reinforced plastic with improved ballistic protection over the steel helmet pictured here. It also sits much more securely and has built-in bump protection which the old helmet lacked. His 38 mm. riot gun can be used to fire tear gas grenades or baton rounds (rubber bullets). The batons can be either a single projectile or three smaller, thick discs designed to be used at very close range (about 10 m.) against crowds of rioters. The trousers are standard 1970 pattern DPM, the gaiters '37 pattern webbing. His hat badge is the silver, stringed bugle always associated with light infantry.

39.   Great Britain: Private, 6th Queen Elizabeth's Own Gurkha Rifles, Winter Combat Dress, Denmark, 1963.
Following the granting of independence to India in 1947, four regiments of Gurkhas were retained with the British Army; the 2nd King Edward VII's Own (The Sirmoor Rifles), the 6th, the 7th Duke of Edinburgh's Own and the 10th, Princess Mary's Own. At any one time three of them form the Gurkha Brigade which is normally stationed in Hong Kong and the fourth serves in the United Kingdom. They have not been employed in Northern Ireland. The cap badge includes the legendary Gurkha Kukri. He wears the 1960 Parka and the 'Cold Weather Warfare' boots with special thick soles and thermal insoles. His dark green gloves are regimental dress items, other units wearing khaki.

40.   Great Britain: Second Lieutenant, Devon and Dorsets, 1971.
To confuse snipers it is standard practice for officers as patrol leaders to carry the same weapons as the men, hence the SLR (see plate 222). He wears regimental cap badge (silver castle) and shoulder strap slip ons with one, four-pointed star over the regimental title all in black; 1958 pattern webbing and 1970 pattern DPM (Disruptive pattern material) trousers with puttees and DMS boots.

41.   Great Britain: Private, 3rd Battalion, The Parachute Regiment 1971.
With the famous red beret we see the Denison Smock (now being replaced by a DPM smock), lightweight olive green trousers, 1944 pattern webbing and puttees. On his shoulder brace a field dressing has been fixed on with 'jungle tape'. His weapon is the 84 mm. Carl Gustav, produced in Sweden, firing a hollow charge projectile with an

effective range against tanks of 400 m. The green arm patch denotes 3rd Battalion; the 1st wears red; the 2nd blue.

42. Great Britain: Private, 1st Battalion Royal Hampshires, Malaya, 1954.
The yellow hat badges are battalion and company recognition devices (here 'A' Company); he wears the Gurkha Brigade arm patch, modified '44 pattern web equipment with a belt made of parachute-drop harness, jungle boots and carries the Australian pattern sleeping bag. His weapon is the Australian 9 mm. Owen Gun with 24.7 cm. barrel, 33 round magazine, 700 rpm, effective range 75 m.

43. Great Britain: Private, 1st Battalion Gloucestershire Regiment, 1957.
This soldier is shown in battledress (which was worn from 1939 to 1962) and is in 'Internal Security (IS) Order' with helmet, shield and pick axe helve for crowd control. The helmet is painted in regimental gloss black and on the back is the regiment's back badge (awarded for the Battle of Alexandria). At the top of the sleeve is the U.S. Presidential Citation, awarded to this regiment and to 'C' Troop, 170th Independent Mortar Battery, Royal Artillery, for their heroic stand against overwhelming Chinese odds near Solma-ri on the Imjin river in Korea on 23, 24, and 25 April 1951. The diamond patch below is the Wessex Brigade badge, the cross of Athelstone.

44. Great Britain: Private, Black Watch, Hong Kong, 1972.
Instead of the beret worn by English regiments, this Scottish regiment wears the highland bonnet with khaki tourie and red hackle over the regimental badge.

He wears tropical olive drab shirt and trousers with the Hong Kong dragon sleeve patch and 1944 pattern web equipment which was found to be most useful for jungle use because it absorbs very little water and thus does not weigh much more wet than dry. His weapon is the Sterling SMG (see plate 224 for details).

45. Great Britain: Corporal, Queen's Own Regiment, Hong Kong.
The blue diamond on the jungle hat is a company recognition badge and he wears the temperate service khaki flannel shirt, favoured by some regiments for tropical wear. With the '44 pattern web equipment he

carries a U.S. M 16 A1 carbine, well suited for jungle use.

46.   Denmark: Sergeant Major, Service Dress, 1975.
Prior to 1969 the Danish army wore British-style khaki but the smart, rifle green and grey was introduced in that year. On the side of the cap is the army badge (three rampant lions on a crowned shield scattered with hearts—all in a laurel wreath) and on the collar the regimental badge (here the three rampant lions within a laurel wreath and under the cypher 'C4' of the Sjaellandske Livregiment). On the buttons is the infantry corps badge—crossed rifles over a shovel all under a crown. The crimson backing of his collar badges indicates regimental HQ: 1st Battalion wears red backing, 2nd white, 3rd yellow and 4th blue.

47.   Denmark: Infantryman in Combat Order, 1974.
The combat dress and webbing are Danish, the helmet and the M 1 7.62 mm. Garand rifle are U.S. pattern. The weapon weighs 4.37 kg. unloaded, is 1.105 m. long with a 61 cm. barrel, 300 m. effective range, gas operated, 24 rpm, 850 m./sec. muzzle velocity and an eight-round magazine. It is unusual that the trousers are worn loose at the bottoms.

48.   Netherlands: Lieutenant, Stoettroepen, Service Dress, 1974.
Rank is worn on the shoulder straps (up to about 1968 it was worn on the collar patches) and consists for officers of gold stars; for junior officers (1 to 3) stars (over a gold bar for field officers). Regimental identity is expressed by the hat and collar patches and the brass badges on them; Stoettroepen having a sword between antlers. On the left arm is the Netherlands lion holding a sword and a bunch of arrows over the scroll JE MAINTENDRAI. He wears parachutist's wings. In the Dutch army tank troops wear black berets, other troops wear khaki.

49.   France: Private, Line Infantry Algeria 1956-61.
In this bitter war Algeria gained her independence from France in the post war era of European colonial decline. The bush jacket can be worn inside or outside the trousers. The walking stick was a popular item with the men on long patrols in the rough country. The weapon is the MAS 36 (Manufacture d'Armes de Saint-Étienne) 7.5 mm. rifle.

50.   France: Nurse, attached to 'Sections Administratives Spécialisées (SAS), Algeria, 1958.

The SAS were an intelligence unit employed in 'hearts and minds' operations in close contact with the Algerians. She wears airborne pattern camouflage trousers and the French canvas and rubber patrol boots with a green scarf on the shoulder—the temporary field recognition badge of the column of French infantry and Algerian harkis that she is operating with. The 12-bore shotgun is for personal protection.

51.   France: Private, '3 Régiment de Parachutistes Coloniaux', Algeria, 1957.

This was one of the units of General Massu's airborne division which cleared the Algiers casbah of terrorists in the spring of 1957 with a thoroughness equalled only by the ruthlessness with which they completed the task. He wears French airborne camouflage suit and well polished jump boots, U.S. webbing and carries the French 9 mm. MAT (Manufacture d'Armes de Tulle) '49, blow back machine-pistol. It weighs 3.63 kg. empty (4.23 kg. with 32-round magazine), length 40.6 cm. with butt folded (66.1 cm. with it extended); barrel length 22.8 cm., effective range 100 m., rate of fire 600 rpm, muzzle velocity about 380 m./sec. The fighting knife does not double as a bayonet. The close haircut is typical of this élite, hard fighting unit.

52.   Algeria: ALN (National Liberation Army), 1960.

American clothing, equipment and weapons found their way into many hands after the war, including the ALN as shown here by the 1943 pattern jacket, the webbing and the Thompson .45 inch, blowback operated sub machine-gun. Magazines holding 20 or 30 rounds are available; the weapon fires 700 rpm, effective range 90 m., muzzle velocity 280 m./sec. making the weapon a very low grade threat. Algeria had been ruled by France for 150 years before achieving independence by force of arms in 1962 after seven years of bitter fighting. President de Gaulle conducted a referendum in France and Algeria which resulted in a majority for breaking the connection between the states and acted on this mandate. This made him extremely unpopular with certain sections of the French army who set up the OAS, a terrorist group dedicated to frustrating Algerian independence and to killing de Gaulle.

53.   France: Légionnaire, Compagnies Sahariennes Portées de la Légion Etrangère, 1959.

The Algerian Saharan sun has scorched the face of this latter day Beau

Geste. On his sleeve is the black and dark green badge of the infantry of the Foreign Legion and he wears the unmistakable képi here in a sand cover and with goggles as protection against sand storms. The wide scarf helps keep the sand from mouth and nose. He carries a U.S.-made 7.62 mm. M-1 Winchester, semi-automatic carbine; length 90.4 cm., barrel length 45.7 cm.; weight 2.37 kg. empty (2.7 kg. with full 15 round magazine); rate of fire 30 rpm.; effective range 150 m.; muzzle velocity 610 m./sec. There were four of these companies operating vigorously over the southern Sahara and the ALN were not successful in whipping up support in this region.

54. Algeria: National Liberation Army, 1960.
Once again a picture of international flavour with the British BD blouse, French infantry camouflage trousers and Wehrmacht MG 34. This blow back weapon was produced in Germany, Austria and Czechoslovakia during World War II; it was originally made by Mauser, had a calibre of 7.92 mm., length 1.219 m., barrel length 62.7 cm.; effective range 800 m., rate of fire 800-900 rpm., muzzle velocity not known. The weapon can be fed by belts of 50 or 250 rounds or it can use drum magazines holding 50 or 75 rounds. It weighs 12.1 kg. unloaded.

55. West Germany: Gefreiter (Lance Corporal), Mountain Troops, 1972.
The Federal German Armed Forces (Bundeswehr) were formed in 1956 and initially wore uniforms which seemed to have been designed by a rabid pacifist to make the wearers look ridiculous.

Dress in the German army has undergone many changes since then and the combat dress particularly is well designed and functional. All ranks wear the national flag on both sleeves, the mountain troops (one division of three brigades deployed along the country's southern border) wearing the same Edelweiss cap badge as was worn during World War II. The Alpenstock climbing rope and mountain boots with thick stockings, canvas gaiters and breeches enable the men to move well in the mountains.

56. West Germany: Corporal (Unteroffizier), Airborne Troops, 1976.
This NCO is wearing the red beret with silver plunging eagle cap badge with its oak wreath surround and the reddish-brown summer combat suit. The green loop across the bottom of the shoulder strap (on which

his badge of rank appears) indicates infantry. Other colours are pink—armour; black—engineers; red—artillery; lemon yellow—signals; blue —logistics; crimson—NBC; deep yellow—reconnaissance. He carries full marching order with sleeping bag on his pack, respirator in the green plastic satchel, 'NATO' helmet and MP 5 A 3, 9 mm., blow back machine-pistol with collapsed butt. The weapon is also used by the German Police and Border Guards. It weighs 2.45 kg., is 68 cm. long with butt extended; barrel length is 22.5 cm., effective range 100 m., rate of fire 650 rpm., muzzle velocity 400 m./sec. Magazines can hold 10, 15 or 30 shots. The weapon is made by Heckler and Koch.

57.   West Germany: Oberfeldwebel (Staff Sergeant), Armoured Fighting Vehicle Crewman, 1975.

Tank crewmen in the German army wear black berets with a bronze badge of a tank emerging from an oak wreath (this badge is often, unofficially, backed with pink silk—the tankers' facing colour). The crewmen of other armoured fighting vehicles (SP artillery, Armoured Recovery Vehicles, light reconnaissance vehicles, APCs) wear the red-brown beret with national cockade over crossed sabres shown here. All wear the one-piece 'Panzerkombination' or tank overall, with the jack boots known as 'Knobelbecher' (dice cups).

58.   Italy: Private, Lagunari, 1977.

The Lagunari are a type of marine force designed to operate in the shallow coastal waters around Venice and other river estuaries (hence the lifejacket). The beret badge shows a mural crown over an anchor over crossed rifles and the man wears a regimental cravat. The camouflaged kit is well known in Britain where much of it is imported for leisure wear! His canvas and rubber boots are specially designed for his amphibious role. He carries the Beretta 7.62 mm. BM-59 SLR. Length 1.095 mm. (1.235 m. with bayonet); weight 4.41 kg. (5.63 kg. with 20-round magazine); effective range 300 m., gas operated, 800 rpm.; muzzle velocity 840 m./sec.

59.   Italy: Lance Corporal, Bersaglieri, 1975.

Italian army uniforms have changed only very little since before World War II; as a reminder of their African colonial service, the Bersaglieri (famous as light infantry and for their 'run-past' on parades) wear a fez off parade or the bush hat with flowing, black cocks' feather plumes on formal occasions. Even on the Italian pattern steel helmet they wear this parade plume as the Alpini (mountain troops) wear a black pompom and eagle's feather on their steel helmets. On the collar of the camouflage jacket is the white star of Savoy. Rank badge (a black chevron) and divisional sign appear on a detachable brassard on the left arm. He carries the Italian produced BM-59 7.62 mm rifle.

60.   Italy: Corporal, APC Infantry, 1978.
The lightweight plastic helmet gives bump protection and communications facilities; uniform details as for previous figures. When not wearing specialist headgear like tank helmets, berets are worn in regimental colours as follows; Bersaglieri, armour and SP artillery—black; airborne—maroon; field artillery—khaki; Alpini wear traditionally their famous mountain hat with eagle's feather.

61.   Portugal: Lieutenant, 1st Engineer Regiment, Service Dress, 1960.
This severe, smart grey uniform is worn for parades. The cap badge has the national crest under a red cross and resting on flags over the regimental number (1) and the corps badge—a silver castle. The collar patches are in the corps colours and bear the castle, the buttons are matt gold. Badges of rank appear on the cuff. Other regimental badges (in brass) are: cavalry—crossed lances; infantry—crossed rifles; artillery —crossed gun barrels.

62.   Portugal: Corporal, African Force, 1964.
Angola, Mozambique and Guinea were considered by the Portuguese as part of Metropolitan Portugal but this constitution could not resist the anti-colonialist mood of Africa and by 1976 they had been granted independence after a prolonged guerrilla war heavily supported by the communist bloc. This native NCO's uniform reeks of the colonial past with its fez, shorts and puttees; rank appears on the shoulder straps. Sergeants have three gold chevrons point down, staff sergeants three point up; company sergeant majors four point up and regimental sergeant majors wear the silver national crest within a gold laurel wreath. Officers wear gold bars—1-3 for lieutenant to captain; the same system over a wider gold bar for major, colonel; brigadiers wear two, five-pointed silver stars, major generals three and lieutenant generals four. Generals have red collar patches with gold oak leaf embroidery.

63.   Portugal: Trooper, Armoured Troops, Angola, 1973.

The black beret bears the crossed lances and regimental number in brass but the tropical combat kit is suitably anonymous. French patrol boots were found to be useful in this environment and apart from issued weapons many soldiers carried their own fighting knives according to taste and pocket.

64.   Austria: Oberstabswachtmeister, Mountain Infantry, 1976.
The familiar Edelweiss cap badge of World War II Wehrmacht pattern is complemented by a Rucksack of similar design vintage. Rank is worn on the shoulder strap and is also indicated by the design of the hat cockade. A corporal wears two stars, junior sergeant three; sergeant a star over a silver bar; staff sergeant two stars and bar; company sergeant one star over a wide and a narrow bar; regimental sergeant major two stars and two bars; junior warrant officer three stars and two bars; senior warrant officer one silver star over a wide gold bar. The Alpenstock, climbing rope, breeches, stockings and boots are international mountaineering equipment; the Austrian 7.62 mm. SLR has integral bipod legs for greater stability when firing.

65.   Canada: Sergeant, Princess Patricia's Canadian Light Infantry, 1975.
The Canadian Brigade in Germany is now deployed in the South of Germany with the American army, having previously been stationed with the British army in the Soest area until about 1970. National identity is shown by the flag on both sleeves, ranks are as in the British army for soldiers but a new system of navy-style gold bars was introduced for officers at the time of the unification of Canada's defence forces in 1968. On the shoulder strap is worn the regimental title (here PPCLI) in light buff woven letters.

66.   U.S.A.: Captain, Infantry, Korea, 1953.
This helmet cover is an old sandbag and the boots are suede leather. Two types of hand grenade are attached to the flak jacket and the whole figure oozes fatigue.

67.   U.S.A.: General Ridgway, Korea, 1952.
After a distinguished career in World War II, General Ridgway took over command of the U.S. Eighth Army in the crisis of a withdrawal on 23 December 1950 when the U.N. forces were being pushed south from the Chinese border by half a million Chinese 'volunteers' fighting for

the North Koreans. On 11 April 1951, when General Douglas MacArthur was sacked by President Truman for disagreeing with the 'No attacks across the Yalu River' doctrine, General Ridgway assumed command of all U.N. forces in Korea. On the peak of his fur combat cap he wears the four stars of his rank over the parachutist's wings.

68.   U.S.A.: Infantry Sergeant First Class, Japan, 1953.
This man is probably in Japan on 'Rest and Recuperation' from service in The Korean War as evidenced by the 'Butcher's Apron' as the blue and white striped U.N. medal ribbon for that conflict is known in the British army. Here it is worn at the outer, lower end of the rows of ribbons. On his right chest he wears the U.S. Presidential Unit Citation—at the time America's highest collective award for bravery in the field. His collar badges bear the infantry crossed rifles and the blue badge half hidden under the lapel is the infantry combat badge. The bottle of PX Bourbon concealed behind his back would ensure a warm welcome anywhere in Tokyo.

69.   U.S.A.: General Alexander Haig, Supreme Commander Allied Powers in Europe, 1975.
In October 1975 the Federal German Army held a Corps exercise called 'Grosse Rochade' up against the Czechoslovakian border and General Haig, while visiting a German Fallschirmjäger battalion was presented with one of their maroon berets with its plunging eagle badge which he wore for the rest of his visit. As an old infantryman he wears the infantry combat badge on the left breast.

70.   Switzerland: Sergeant Farrier, Dragoons, 1973.
This mounted unit (Switzerland's last) was disbanded in 1973. Under the peculiar Swiss 'citizen army' system, the troopers provided their own horses and received an allowance for their fodder and upkeep. The horses were frequently transported by rail through the mountains to the desired area of operations. Despite having a relatively small army, the Swiss have a bewildering variety of badges to indicate regiment (the collar patches), regimental number (the shoulder strap slide), company within the regiment (the coloured band under the regimental number), specialist trades (the arm shield—here Farrier), rank (under the arm shield) and awards for achievements (over the left breast pocket—here marksman).

71. Belgium: Adjutant, Infantry, Service Dress, 1978.

The light khaki service dress is very similar in style to that of the British army and an Adjutant, as senior warrant officer, wears many officers' appointments such as the gold hat badge of the infantry of the line (repeated on the shoulder straps). The badge of the 3rd Parachute Battalion (on the right pocket) signifies that this man served with that unit in Korea as part of the U.N. forces. On the right sleeve is the elementary parachutist's badge.

72. Spain: Private, Spanish Parachute Brigade, Jump Gear.

This shows a fairly standard paratrooper's uniform, the unusual feature being the brigade badge (the Spanish eagle and the parachute) worn on the front of the parachute pack. The Spanish army uses its own 7.62 mm. SLR, the CETME (Centro de Estudios Técnicos de Materials Especiales) as seen in West Germany and many other states. Machine-pistols are the 9 mm. STAR blowback weapons with 10 or 30 round magazines, rate of fire 450 rpm, muzzle velocity 380 m./sec.

73. Sweden: Infantry NCO, 1960 Pattern Service Dress.

On the front of the cap is the national cockade and on the side the regimental badge (here a rampant Griffon for the Södermanland regiment. On the collar the crossed rifles of the infantry. Other corps badges worn on the collar are artillery—crossed gun barrels, cavalry—crossed sabres, engineers—a grenade. Generals wear three gold oak leaves on each collar patch. Badges of rank (worn on the left collar patch in combat (kit) are shown for junior NCOs by gold bars—lance corporal—1; corporal—2; corporal quartermaster—3; quartermaster—4; sergeant—one gold disc, staff sergeant—two; sergeant major—3; Officers wear five-pointed gold stars—second lieutenant—1; lieutenant—2; captain—3; major—1 star under a crown; lieutenant colonel—2 stars under a crown; colonel—3; senior colonel—4. Generals have golden shoulder straps with crossed batons under stars—major general—1; lieutenant general—2; general—3. All ranks through colonel wear the regimental number at the base of the shoulder strap.

74. Norway: Sergeant Major, Infantry, winter combat dress, 1970.

National identity is expressed by the hat cockade and the national flags on the upper arms. Although NCOs now wear their rank badges on the shoulder straps in combat kit, the badges themselves have not changed and are as for the British army for lance corporal, corporal, sergeant and officers up through captain. Staff sergeants have three stripes under a bar; field officers have silver edging to shoulder straps and from one to three silver stars for major through colonel. Major general through general have silver shoulder slides with from one to three larger stars. On service dress and battle dress officers wear their ranks on the collar. The weapon is the German 9 mm., blow back 'MP 40' of World War II vintage. It weighs 4.03 kg. (4.7 kg. with 32 round magazine), is 63 cm. long with butt folded (83.5 with it extended); barrel length is 25.1 cm., effective range 100 m.; rate of fire 500 rpm, muzzle velocity 390 m./sec.

75. Finland: Infantryman, Camouflaged Combat Suit, 1970.
The Finnish army still uses the old Wehrmacht World War II helmet and produces many of her own small arms, infantry weapons and ammunition. This man carries the M-44, 7.62 mm. Mosin-Nagant carbine with five round magazine—muzzle velocity 770 m./sec., barrel length 52 cm., effective range 300 m. In combat dress badges of rank are worn on an eight-sided tab on the right wrist, junior ranks wearing yellow chevrons (point up), officers wearing thick and thin gold bars. In service and working dress rank badges are worn on collar patches which are in the regimental colours as follows: infantry—green with white edging; field artillery—red with blue; coastal artillery—red with blue; AA artillery—red with white; logistics—blue with white; pioneers—crimson with white; veterinary—lemon yellow with blue; medical—grey with red; air force—blue with black; dragoons—deep yellow with blue; signals—dark crimson with yellow; anti-tank artillery—black with red edging.

76. Indian Army: Sergeant, 60th (Parachute) Field Ambulance, 1952.
The turban (here in crimson, regimental colour) uncut beard and steel bracelet on the right wrist (not visible in this plate) denote a Sikh soldier, much respected as a martial race. Badges of rank in the Indian and Pakistani armies have remained as they were under British rule except that the crown of British army ranks has been replaced by the three lions and the star and crescent respectively.

77. Australia: Corporal, 3rd Bn, Royal Regiment, 1953.
The famous bush hat of this 'Digger' is unmistakable in any environment. On the brassard is the U.S. Presidential citation over the Common-

wealth Division patch over his rank badges. The Australian army rank badges are as for the British army as are most of the corps badges. He wears both the British and U.N. Korean medal ribbons.

78. Canada: Company Sergeant Major, Royal (Can.) Army Service Corps, 1951.

Canadian battledress was slightly darker in colour than the British equivalent and was made of finer cloth. Corps badges and rank badges were as for the British army at this time except that Warrant Officers 1st class wore the Canadian crest on their forearms instead of the royal arms of the United Kingdom.

79. North Korea: Warrant Officer, Summer Dress, 1952.

The similarity with the Soviet Army of the period is striking as would be expected when it is remembered that from 1945 to 1952 the U.S.S.R. trained and equipped the North Korean army. For that reason the rank badge system was almost identical and the Soviet Gymnastjerka blouse can be recognized here. Small arms were of Soviet pattern as were artillery pieces and tanks.

80. China: Infantryman, Winter Combat Dress, Korea, 1950.

Although very few distinguishing marks were worn on this quilted cotton clothing, the Red Chinese army of this period had a system of rank and regimental badges somewhat similar to that of the Soviet army. Officers and Warrant officers wore shoulder boards on parade dress but in working and combat dress they wore their badges on the collar patches. He carries a hand grenade and a Chinese copy (known as the 'Type 50') of the Russian 7.62 mm. blowback sub-machine-gun PPsh M-41. The U.N. forces in Korea christened it the 'Burp Gun'. It weighed 3.64 kg. (5.4 kg. with 71 round drum magazine; its length was 83.8 cm., barrel length 26.5 cm.; effective range 100 m.; rate of fire 900 rpm; muzzle velocity 500 m./sec. Most Chinese weapons of this era were straight copies of Soviet equipments.

81. China: Infantryman, Summer Field Marching Order, Korea, 1951.

Partly to conceal their identity, many of the Chinese troops in Korea did not wear their regimental collar patches or their red star cap badges. Chinese equipment is characterized by simplicity and functionality.

The wooden pack frame allows the load to be rested at a moment's notice and forms a convenient section of a tent frame. The collar patches were red for soldiers of all corps except airforce and airborne forces (who wore light blue) and navy and public security (also part of the army) who wore black. The patches bore· yellow stripes and silver stars (to the front) to indicate rank and the corps badge at the rear (infantry had no corps badge). These badges were cavalry-crossed sabres; armoured troops—side profile of a tank; artillery—crossed gun barrels; pioneers—crossed pick axe and shovel; signals—a disc bearing a lightning flash, aerial mast and telephone; airborne—a winged parachute; transport—side profile of a lorry; medical—a round disc bearing an upright cross; administration—a round disc bearing a five-pointed star; railway construction—a stylised railway crossing; maintenance—crossed spanner and pliers. Rank badges were as follows; privates and lance corporals had plain red patches with one and two five-pointed silver stars respectively. Corporal, sergeant and senior sergeant had a yellow stripe along the centre of the patch and from one to three silver stars respectively. Officer cadets had red patches edged yellow; warrant officers—yellow patches with no stars. Junior officers had red patches with a single gold line along the centre; they wore from one to four silver stars from second lieutenant through senior captain. Field officers were as above but with two gold stripes and from one to four, larger, silver stars from major through lieutenant, junior and senior colonels. Generals' collar patches were edged gold and their silver stars were even larger—from one to four for major general through lieutenant, colonel and senior general. Marshals had one larger silver star under the Chinese crest; senior marshals had a pine frond wreath around the star.

During the cultural revolution (1967-69) all ranks in the Chinese army were abolished as were the badges and all personnel now wear plain red collar patches.

82.   Republic of Korea: 1st Lieutenant of Infantry, 1st Division, 1952.

The American influence in the uniform of this young army is unmistakable. The infantry collar badge is a crossed rifle and sabre; on helmet and shoulder straps are the two silver diamonds of his rank. A second lieutenant has one such diamond, a captain three. Major through colonel are shown by from one to three silver flowers each with nine-pointed petals; brigadier general to general wear five-pointed silver stars, from one to four in number. Warrant officers have a golden diamond on the shoulder strap, NCOs wear their ranks on the upper arm or, on certain forms of dress, on yellow edged, light green rectangles on the left breast. Ranks are shown by yellow chevrons (point down) and for senior NCOs these are worn over horizontal yellow bars. Lance corporal—one chevron, corporal—two; sergeant—three, staff sergeant —three over one bar, sergeant first class—three over two bars; master sergeant—three over three bars, first sergeant—as before all under a star.

83.   Republic of Korea: Machine-Gunner, Winter Combat Clothing, 1953.

Those who took part in this war know how bitter the winters could be, thus the cocooned appearance. In warmer, more peaceful times, in service dress, the Korean army wears the national crest within a five-petalled silver flower all within a laurel wreath on the peaked cap, the badge of rank on the side hat. Collar badges show the corps badge and these are on a circular disc for other ranks as in the U.S. Army. Examples are: artillery—crossed gun barrels; tanks—the front profile of a tank on crossed sabres; medical corps—a winged staff with entwined snakes; transport—a ship's wheel enclosing a wing; NBC—crossed retorts on a shield; women's army corps—a female head; bands—a lyre. These are all in brass; silver badges are—military police—crossed pistols under a star; quartermaster—a key with wings in a laurel wreath. Other badges are engineers—a castle gate in silver enclosing a gold star; signals—crossed signal flags over a silver torch; ordnance—a gold grenade on three interlocking silver rings.

84.   Turkey: Private, Infantry Battalion, Korea, 1952.

The Turks wrought a great fighting reputation for themselves in the war although their identity was only shown by helmet badges and arm patches, their clothing being supplied entirely by the Americans. Badges of rank for soldiers were worn on the upper arms in chevrons (point down); second class private—one red chevron; first class private —two; lance corporal—one yellow chevron with, in its centre a yellow circle enclosing a yellow star and crescent; staff sergeant—four and sergeant major—five. Officers wore gold, five-pointed stars on the shoulder strap, one to three up through captain. Field officers had at the base of the shoulder strap a gold oak wreath closing at the top with the star and crescent and then one to three stars major through colonel. Generals were as for field officers but the wreath was underlaid with silver crossed sabres on a red ground.

85. U.N. Force: Corporal, 5th Gurkha Rifles, 1966.
Nowadays it is the custom that all U.N. troops wear sky blue berets, but in 1964 troops wore their own headdress. At the time of partitition of British India into India and Pakistan in 1947, the 2nd, 6th, 7th and 10th Gurkha Rifles transferred to the British army and the 1st, 3rd, 4th, 5th, 8th, 9th and 11th Regiments continued to serve with the Indian army. This NCO wears British 1937 pattern web equipment and is every inch as smart a soldier as we have come to expect in the British Army. He carried the well known .303 inch (7.7 mm.) Lee-Enfield No. 1 Mark 3 British rifle; weight 3.9 kg. (4.45 with bayonet), length 1.132 m. (1.567 m. with bayonet); barrel length 64 cm.; effective range 400 m.; ten round magazine, 20 rpm; muzzle velocity 745 m./sec.

86. Katanga: Major Mike Hoare, 1964.
During Katanga's brief independence it was white mercenaries like this Britisher who trained and led the province's armed forces by methods as dramatic as they were often unconventional. 'Mad Mike' Hoare led No. 5 Commando and the dark green beret is doubtless related to that of the Royal Marine Commandos. The hat and shoulder badges have a strong Belgian flavour.

87. Katanga: Mercenary Soldier, No. 5 Commando, 1964.
The fluid situation in the Congo attracted many soldiers of fortune for a great variety of reasons. As can be seen, the equipment (and weapons) came from equally diverse sources.

88. Biafra: Major General.
In its brief existence the Biafran army was continually fighting and had little time or effort to expend on the niceties of dress such as uniformity. Men wore what they could get and frequently went without much of what would be regarded as basic essentials. The General wears U.S. style camouflage with British gorget patches and cane and the Biafran army emblem on the upper sleeve. The rank badges were generally as in the British army but we see here two, six-pointed black stars under the Biafran crest in yellow (a spread eagle on an elephant's tusk over three interlocking 'horse shoes').

89. Nigeria: Infantryman.

143

British, American and Soviet equipment was used by both sides if available; this casualty has a label pinned to him describing wound and treatment given so that should he fall unconscious, the next medic will know what to do.

90. Nigeria: Infantry Sergeant.
The helmet is American and bears a private decoration. These were fairly common during this war and included phrases like 'Jungle Bunny' and 'Killer'. He wears British 1958 pattern web equipment and carries a British Sterling SMG (see black and white plate 224 for details). Rank badges in the Nigerian army were almost identical to those in the British army.

91. Zambia: Lieutenant Colonel, Signals, 1972.
After achieving independence in 1966, Northern Rhodesia became Zambia and at once began the task of 'Zambianising' its government and armed services. By 1972 only half a dozen European officers were left and in the next year they were all replaced by natives. This officer wears signals badges on collar and hat as in the British army except that the crown is replaced here by the Zambian fish eagle (as it is on the rank badges on the shoulder straps). The dark blue lanyard on the right shoulder is also as worn in the Royal Signals; the black hat plume and pugree stripe are regimental distinctions.

92. Zambia: Regimental Sergeant Major, Rifles, 1972.
As a battalion of the 'King's African Rifles' this regiment had worn shorts under British rule but these were replaced by long trousers after independence. The brass, British coat of arms on the right wrist seems to have been retained as the RSM's badge for a little longer however, as was the highly polished pace stick.

93. Biafra: Lance Corporal, 4th Commando Brigade, 1967.
White mercenaries were also active in this war; the brigade commander here being a German named Steiner who had previously served in the Foreign Legion. Under the Biafran sun badge is the skull and bones of the 4th Commando Brigade, one of the army's best fighting units.

94. South Africa: Major, 1 SDB (Special Service Battalion), 1972.
This unit is part of the armoured corps, hence the black beret. South African forces have been involved in several 'hot pursuits' of guerrillas

across their northwest border through South West Africa (Namibia) and into Angola. Rank badges are roughly similar to the British army system but without the crowns.

95. South Africa: Corporal, Women's Service.
The rank chevrons have a distinct Wehrmacht flavour. This corps is employed in administrative, signalling and civil defence tasks.

96. South West Africa (Namibia): Infantry Patrol Commander, 1978.
Here comfort has amended the issue uniform quite heavily and for security reasons he wears no rank badges. Namibia had elections in 1978 and now has a government which—like that of Zimbabwe-Rhodesia—is recognized by practically no one.

South Africa and Rhodesia both actively recruit blacks into the security forces as indeed they must if they are to survive. He carries the N.A.T.O. SLR (see plate 222 for details).

97. Rhodesia: Signaller, 1976.
As can be seen from the rain cape and the mud, this figure is operating in the rainy season. Apart from the usual supporting arms and services, the Rhodesian army contains the following infantry regiments—Rhodesian African Rifles (a black regiment); Rhodesian Light Infantry, Rhodesian Regiment and 'C' Squadron Rhodesian Special Air Service Regiment. Armour is represented by the Rhodesian Armoured Cars Regiment (The Selous' Scouts) and mounted infantry (dragoons?) by the 250-strong Grey's Scouts. Badges of rank are exactly as in the British army except that the crown is replaced by the lion holding an elephant's tusk and the RSM's coat of arms badge is that of Rhodesia.

98. Rhodesia: NCO, Selous' Scouts, 1978.
The camouflage pattern of this unit is very similar to that of the Denison smock worn by British airborne forces in World War II. On his hat front is a black chevron—lance corporal. The badge of this regiment (which has an SAS-type role) is the head of a sable over the motto ASESABI LUTHO the Sindebele for WE FEAR NOUGHT. He carries a N.A.T.O. SLR and wears locally produced webbing and South African boots.

99. Rhodesia: Private, African Rifles, 1976.

The neck flap on the caps is to keep water from running down the men's backs in bush fighting. This regiment distinguished itself in the Burma campaign in World War II by routing the Japanese at Tanlwe Chaung and has recently been increased to two battalions.

100. Rhodesia: Major, Grey's Scouts, 1978.
Students of saddlery will recognize quite the simplest snaffle bridle with no nose band—a far cry from the traditional military double-bitted bridle. The saddle seems to be modelled on the American army McClellan saddle of 1874 which itself was derived from the wooden saddles used by the Turks in the Middle Ages. The rider is U.S. citizen L. H. 'Mike' Williams with the following military career: 1942 enlisted in U.S. Army and served with 88th Division in Italy; commissioned in 1948; 1952 in Korea commanding 7th Bn 3rd Partisan Infantry Regiment and later in 77th Special Forces Group, 101st Airborne Division; discharged 1960. 1964 saw him in 'Mad Mike' Hoare's mercenaries in Katanga (Congo); 'deported' by CIA. Joined Rhodesian army in 1976 as a captain; in November 1978 he was in America running for Congress in Florida.

101. Panama: National Guardsman, 1969.
The maroon beret and shoulder strap slides, together with the hairstyle, point unmistakably to an airborne unit. Rank badges are somewhat similar to the U.S. system.

102. Brazil: Sergeant, Brazilian Cavalry, 1972.
Like Argentina and Chile, Brazil still employs horsed cavalry in certain parts of the country where the terrain severely limits vehicular movement. Under the stripes can be seen the cavalry badge—crossed lances. Other corps badges are infantry—crossed rifles on a hand grenade; artillery—a grenade; engineers—a tower; armour—head-on view of a tank. Badges of rank for soldiers are similar to the U.S. system and are worn on the upper arm in service and working dress, on the collar in shirt sleeve order. Officers wear five-pointed gold stars on the shoulder, one to three through captain; field officers repeating this scheme but adding a large gold and silver star burst enclosing the green and yellow cockade and five silver stars on a blue ground of the national crest at the base of the shoulder strap.

103. Brazil: Private, Infantry, 1972.

Brazilian army webbing is very similar to the U.S. pattern items but they use the FN N.A.T.O. 7.62 mm. SLR and the Danish Madsen (11.43 mm. as opposed to the Danish 9 mm. model) machine-pistol and called the INA-953 in Brazil. It weighs 3.15 kg. (3.74 with 32 round magazine) is 53 cm. long (78 cm. with folding butt extended), has a 20 cm. barrel, 500-550 rpm rate of fire, effective range 100 m., blow-back operation, muzzle velocity 280 m./sec.

104. Malaya: Soldier, Malayan Races Liberation Army, 1953.
This organization failed in its attempt to subvert Malaya to Communism immediately following World War II. It was mainly Chinese-recruited and this may be a factor pointing towards its lack of popularity with the indigenous population of the state. He carries the U.S. M-1 Carbine, webbing made up of British 1937 pattern items and modified parachute drop harness. At his left hip is a local machete (panga).

105. Cyprus: EOKA Soldier, 'Andarte' Group, 1956.
He carries the Wehrmacht 1944 pattern Sturmgewehr, copied (in concept) from the AK 47. It is a gas operated, 7.9 mm. semi-automatic weapon, 95 cm. long; barrel length 41 cm., weighing 4.62 kg. with 30 round magazine; rate of fire 500 rpm, effective range (bursts) 300 m., muzzle velocity 650 m./sec.

106. Kenya: Mau-Mau General, 1952.
This figure, with home-made rifle and panga is based on personal observation by Mike Chappell. On the shoulders are five red, yellow and green 'pips' indicating rank.

The Mau-Mau preyed mainly on their own tribe—the Kikuyu—who suffered most during the emergency which preceded Kenyan Independence. One of Mau-Mau's leaders (Jomo 'Burning Spear' Kenyatta) later became Kenya's first president.

107. Israel: Paratroop Corporal, Six Day War (5th-10th June), 1967.
Israeli army soldiers' ranks are worn on the upper arms as follows: Turai—Rishon—one bar; Rav-Turai—two; Samal—three; Samal Rishon —three with a superimposed bronze fig leaf. Warrant officers wear bronze badges on the cuff; Rav-Samal—a fig leaf within a six-pointed star all within a laurel wreath; Rav-Samal-Rishon—as above but the central badge is a sword and olive branch instead of a fig leaf. Officers'

ranks are worn on the shoulder in bronze; Mamak (officer cadet)—a silver bar; Segen Mishneh—one bronze bar; Segen—two; Seren—three; Rav-Seren—a fig leaf; Sgan-Aluf—two; Aluf-Mishneh—three; Tat-Aluf—crossed sword and olive branch; Aluf—as before under a fig leaf; Rav-Aluf—as before but two fig leaves. This man carries the Israeli-produced UZI (see figure 251), here with collapsible butt.

108. Israel: Tank Corps Major, 1967.
Regimental identity is shown by the cap badge (on red backing for combat units): armour—side profile of a tank; artillery—a gun; engineers—a vertical sword behind a tower all on a twelve-pointed star; infantry—a sword and olive branch; signals—a winged vertical sword between lightning flashes; medical—serpent and staff under the star of David; ordnance—sword, flaming grenade and cog wheel; supply—sword, horse-drawn chariot, crossed ears of barley; bands—a lyre; all badges are above a scroll and within a wreath.

109. Israel: 1st Lieutenant (Segen), Territorial Defence Corps, attached to the NAHAL organization.
The Nahal organization have responsibility for the agricultural settlements hence the sickle and sword arm badge. They also carry out their own first-line self defence. Israeli women soldiers are not employed in combat roles but do undergo arms training.

110. Egypt: Paratrooper, 1973.
Helmet and AK47 are Russian (see figure 159 for technical details); the camouflage is designed for the desert environment. Badges of rank of soldiers are worn on the upper arms and follow the British scheme except that a five-pointed star is used instead of a crown and the CSM wears an eagle over four white chevrons; a warrant officer wears the Egyptian eagle on both cuffs. Officers wear their five-pointed gold stars on the shoulder, the system is as for the British army—with the eagle replacing the crown—except when dealing with general officers.

111. Egypt: Major General, 1977.
Service dress is very much as for the British army, but the shoulder boards are green for general officers, the rank badges thereon being crossed sabre and baton, star and eagle in ascending order. Brigadiers have the eagle over sabre and baton; lieutenant general eagle, two stars

(side by side) and crossed sabre and baton; general—as before but three stars in triangular formation.

112. Egypt: Infantryman, 1967.
This man carries the Soviet RPD light machine-gun with drum magazine (see plate 160 for technical details) and the Soviet NBC satchel with respirator. In service dress regimental brass badges are worn on the collar (and facing colour is worn as backing to rank badges) as follows: infantry—a charging soldier within a wreath (blue); armour—a winged horse rising out of a tank between two vertical lances (green); artillery—a flaming grenade (black); engineers—three wagon wheels splashing through water (khaki); signals—two lightning flashes over two wings in a wreath (khaki); paratroopers—not known (crimson); medical—serpent and staff within a wreath (khaki); ordnance—a trophy of arms (khaki); supply—an eight-pointed star (khaki); maintenance—a cog wheel within a wreath (khaki).

113 and 114. Lebanon: Christian Militiamen.
Following the Lebanese civil war and the intervention of the Syrian Arab Peacekeeping Force in the struggle, the Christian minority in Lebanon have withdrawn into the west and south of the country and obtain much support from the Israelis. The Christian Militia has recently been in action against the newly reconstituted Lebanese Army and refuse to allow the UNIFIL (U.N. Interim Force in Lebanon) troops access to the areas they control. They are also violently opposed to the PLO who operate in Arab-controlled areas of the country. The weapon is the AK47—see plate 159 for technical details.

115. Lebanon: Muslim Irregular.
In the chaos of modern Lebanon arms from East and West find their way into opposing hands; here the U.S. M-16 carbine (see plate 200 for technical details) is used by the Arab equivalent of the Christian Militia.

116. Saudi Arabia: Lieutenant Colonel, Engineers, 1976.
There is great similarity between the corps badges of the Saudi and the Egyptian army (both worn on the collar); the main difference being that Saudi badges are surmounted by a crown which is replaced by a star and crescent for the Egyptian equivalents. The same applies to rank badges except that soldiers' chevrons are worn point up instead of point down and Saudi's wear a crown instead of the Egyptian eagle.

117. Lebanon: 1st Sergeant, Artillery, 1960.

In March 1975 a vicious civil war, based on religious lines—Christian upper-classes versus Muslims—broke out in the Lebanon. In the following turmoil the Lebanese army dissolved. It has recently been reformed at about battalion strength but is composed almost entirely of Arabs. Soldiers wear chevrons as for the British army with the star replacing the crown; officers also follow the British system with gold, five-pointed stars—one to three through captain, the senior captain wears a star in a wreath and field officers repeat the system but their stars are all over a star in a wreath and all bear a cedar tree in the centre. Brigadiers have crossed sword and baton over the star within a wreath.

Regimental colours are worn on the collar patches; armour—light grey; artillery—red; engineers, signals and logistic troops—black; infantry—blue; medical—crimson; transport—dark green.

The weapon is the U.S. M-3A1 11.43 mm. (.45 inch) General Motors machine-pistol, it weighs 3.71 kg. (4.6 with 30 round magazine; length 57.7 cm. (75.6 with butt extended); 20.3 cm. barrel; rate of fire 350-450 rpm, effective range 90 m.; muzzle velocity 280 m./sec.

118. Iran: Sergeant, Tank Troops, 1979.

Iran bought arms and advice from East and West with its oil riches; Britain supplied Chieftain tanks, America sold anti-tank missiles and the small arms are the G3 as used by West Germany (see plate 253 for technical details). Soldiers' rank badges follow the U.S. army system from Private 1st Class (one chevron) through 1st Class Sergeant (three chevrons over two arcs). Next come the technician specialists— 'Hofomars'—who wear one, two or three gold bars edged black on each shoulder. Officers wear five-pointed gold stars on the shoulder, second lieutenant through captain—one to three respectively; field officers wear larger, eight-pointed silver stars bearing in the centre the lion and sword—major—one; lieutenant colonel—two; colonel—three; general officers wear the imperial crown in gold over the large silver stars thus—brigadier—one crown over the star; major general—the crown over two stars; lieutenant general—the crown over three stars in triangular formation; general—the crown over four stars in a square. Regimental badges are worn in brass on the collar; cavalry—crossed sabres; armour—crossed sabres behind the front profile of a tank; artillery—crossed gun barrels; engineers—a tower within a triangle; signals—crossed lightning flashes; infantry—a flaming grenade;

medical two snakes entwined around a goblet; transport—head-on profile of a lorry; technical—crossed lightning flashes on a cog wheel; bands—a lyre.

119.   Syria: Corporal, Infantry, 1973.

The camouflage suit is based on current British army DPM with the green dye removed. Helmet, webbing and AK47 are Soviet supplied (see plate 159 for technical details). While lance corporals and corporals wear their chevrons point down; the senior NCOs wear them point up as follows: sergeant—two; staff sergeant—three; master sergeant—three over a white, five-pointed star; first sergeant—three over two stars. Officers wear gold, five-pointed stars on the shoulder, second-lieutenant through Captain—one to three respectively; major—an eagle; lieutenant colonel—an eagle over a star; colonel—an eagle over two stars side-by-side; brigadier—an eagle over three stars in a triangle; major general—crossed sabres under the eagle; lieutenant general—crossed sabres under two eagles; general—three eagles over crossed sabres. In service dress regimental collar patches (in the facing colour) with brass badges are worn; examples are: armour—light grey with an advancing tank within a wreath; artillery—dark blue with crossed gun barrels within a wreath; infantry—dark green with crossed rifles in a wreath; cavalry (colour unknown)—crossed lances within a wreath; engineers—light brown; signals—dark brown; medical—crimson; military police—red piped black with an upright sword behind a shield and under a scroll.

120.   Sultanate of Muscat: Private, Baluch Guards Battalion, 1972.

Many of Oman's soldiers are enlisted from the Pakistani province of Baluchistan; indeed it was only in 1970 that Omani natives were recruited for their country's own armed forces and the Baluch element has now dropped to about 40 per cent. The Sultan of Muscat's forces are armed with British small arms (see plates 221–24 for technical details). Badges of rank are very similar to the British system except that officers wear gold, five-pointed stars and silver Omani crowns.

121.   Abu Dhabi: Major, Signals, Defence Force, 1976.

The cap and belt plate badge are the eagle within a circular scroll, the collar badge is the eagle, and on the shoulder appears the shoulder title (ADDF in Arabic script) under the rank badge of the eagle. The arm flash is the signals squadron badge. The brick-red shirt is designed to blend in with the sands of the Liwa area where the army operates. Rank badges follow the British pattern with the eagle replacing the crown.

122.　Iran: Infantryman, 1978.
The U.S. style helmet, uniform and webbing are seen here with the West German G3 7.62 mm. SLR (see plate 253 for technical details). An Iranian brigade fought against Communist-inspired insurgents in the Omani province of Dhofar in 1972-75 and helped to bring that campaign to a successful conclusion.

123.　Oman: Second Lieutenant, Scouts, 1971.
The British army has traditionally supplied many volunteers to serve in the armies of the Gulf States and in fact the Trucial Oman Scouts was raised by the R.A.F. Regiment in 1946 as the Trucial Oman Levies. Rank badges are as in the British army; the cap badge is crossed daggers over a scroll but only officers wear the silver daggers on the shirt collars.

124.　Muscat: Corporal, Sultan's Armed Forces, 1974.
This plate shows desert operations dress with the shmag tied tightly around the head and plimsolls providing light and adequate footwear.

125.　Nepal: Corporal, Devi Dutt Regiment, Parade Dress, 1972.
The yellow hat badge and tourie denote the regiment, the red diamond on the arm is the brigade badge. The system of rank badges is similar to that in the British army and British small arms are used (see plates 221–24 for technical details). For daily wear the Gurkhas wear their famous bush hat, shirt and jersey instead of the Chinese-style tunic seen here.

126.　Nepal: Major, Artillery, Service Dress, 1974.
Prior to 1971 the Nepalese army wore British SD with gold buttons and gold and silver rank badges, but this oriental costume with black buttons and badges, replaced it in that year. Regimental shoulder titles (in Nepali script) are worn under the rank badges; for all combatant officers these commence at the base with crossed kukris and proceed in seniority as follows: 2nd lieutenant—the Kukris alone: 1st Lieutenant— a moon; captain—a sun; major—a sun over a moon; lieutenant colonel —two suns; colonel—two suns over a moon. General officers wear the

kukris within a laurel wreath; brigadier—just the wreathed kukris; major general—a moon over the kukris; lieutenant general—a sun over the kukris; general—a sun over a moon over the kukris.

127. Pakistan: Major General, 1976.
Rank badges are as in the British army except that the crown is replaced by the star and crescent; the Denison smock camouflage pattern (worn by British airborne forces) has been adopted here.

128. Pakistan: Sergeant, Infantry, Battle Order, 1971.
In this year East Pakistan (with much support from India) rose against West Pakistan and seized independence to become Bangladesh. The Pakistani army in East Pakistan lost 60,000 prisoners. The SMG is a later mark of the famous 9 mm. blowback STEN. The gun has here two 32-round magazines taped together to enable quick changes to be made in action without interrupting seriously the firing rate. It weighs 2.99 kg (empty), is 76.2 cm. long with a 19.6 cm. barrel, effective range 75 m., rate of fire 540 rpm, muzzle velocity 400 m./sec.

129. India: Lieutenant, Airborne Artillery, 1971.
The Denison Smock, red beret, 1937 pattern web equipment and Webley and Scott, six-round revolver are all very British as is the cap badge which is identical to that of the Royal Artillery except that the crown is replaced by a five-pointed star. The revolver uses .455 in. cartridges, weighs 1.08 kg. empty, has a 15.2 cm. barrel, effective range 45 m.; muzzle velocity 183 m./sec.

130. India: Indian Signaller, Kashmir, 1965.
The signaller carries the British 'A 41' manpack set with associated satchels and aerial rod case in addition to his own small pack and pistol. Mountains limit communications by radio quite severely.

131. France: Private, 13 Demi-Brigade, Legion Étranger, 1954.
The white kepi cover, epaulettes, aiguillette and waist sash are parade items.

132. France: Colonial Paratrooper, 1952.
The helmet provides a handy place to keep cigarettes and matches; the weapon is the M1 .30 calibre carbine with folding butt. This is a gas operated weapon with 45.7 cm. barrel, 150 m. effective range, 90.4 cm.

long with butt extended, rate of fire 30 rpm; muzzle velocity—610 m./
sec., 15-round magazine.

133.   France: Tirailleur Algérien, 1953.
This regiment later formed the basis of Algeria's army. He carries the
MAS-36 rifle. His light blue arm patch has double green edging and
green crescent over a green '7'.

134.   North Vietnam: Viet Cong Guerrilla, 1967.
The Viet Cong in the Vietnam War were supposed to be exclusively
recruited from the South Vietnamese population but particularly after
the Tet offensive of 1968, in which the Viet Cong were practically
destroyed, their ranks were filled with North Vietnamese 'volunteers'.
On the hat is the wearer's name; he carries a black bandolier full of rice,
an AK 47 (see plate 159) together with magazine and grenade pouches.

135.   South Vietnam: ARVN Ranger, 1972.
Another, large scale assault by Viet Cong and North Vietnamese forces
was launched on South Vietnam from Laos and Cambodia in 1972. The
Army of the Republic of Vietnam (ARVN) was by now U.S. trained and
equipped but due to the national emergency (which had lasted from
1958) many of the soldiers involved in the fighting seem to have been
scarcely more than schoolboys. He carries a US M-16 carbine (see
plate 200). Although heavily influenced by their American allies in
many things, the South Vietnamese evolved their own system of rank
badges (after discarding those inherited from the French in 1955).
NCOs (and soldiers) wear a small round silver badge enclosing a vertical
flaming sword; rank badges consist of chevrons worn on the left arm
(point downwards) or (in smaller size) over the left breast pocket in
combat dress. Private 1st Class—one yellow; corporal—two; chief
corporal—one silver over two gold; sergeant—one silver; 1st sergeant
—two; chief sergeant—three silver chevrons. Officers' rank badges
were similar to those worn by the Japanese army and were worn on
black shoulder boards (with a central gold stripe) in service dress; both
collars and on the hat in fatigues and combat dress. Junior officers wore
from one to three gold plum blossoms on plain gold braid; field officers
had silver plum blossoms on embossed gold braid and generals wore
from one to three five-pointed silver stars on embroidered gold lace.
Officers' gold hat badges showed the national eagle with a striped
shield on the chest all on a shield over a scroll (bearing VIÉTNAM

CÔNGHÒA) under a sunburst and flanked by two stylised eagles.

Regimental badges seem not to have been worn although formation patches were worn on the upper left sleeve. Airborne forces wore the maroon beret with silver parachute and gold wings. Rangers wore a hat badge consisting of a yellow shield bearing a black warriors head on a white, five-pointed star.

136.   North Vietnam: Infantry Private, Cambodia [Kampuchia], 1979.

Since the collapse of the South Vietnamese regime in 1976, the North Vietnamese have occupied Laos and Cambodia, destroying in the process the 'Khmer Rouge' regime of the latter country. This drive against the Khmer Rouge led to the Chinese retaliatory invasion of North Vietnam in March 1979 and to the fighting extending to the borders of Thailand by June of the same year. His weapon is the AK 47 of Soviet supply (see plate 159). This army wears red collar patches (in service and working dress) showing rank and regiment in a system very similar to that of the Red Chinese army except that officers wear their silver stars over one bar (for juniors) and two (for field officers). Generals have from one to four gold stars and their collar patches are edged gold.

137.   North Vietnam: Infantry Sergeant, 1979.

As in the Red Chinese army the infantry have no corps badge on their collar patches. Other corps badges (worn to the rear of the silver rank stars) are: armour—a tank in three-quarter profile; artillery—crossed gun barrels; pioneers—crossed pick and shovel over a half cog wheel; signals—a circle with a lightning flash over radio waves; transport—a steering wheel resting on waves; technical services—crossed rifles on a cog wheel; medical—a red cross on a silver, round disc. The fire-power of the Soviet weapons, coupled with over twenty years of constant battle experience, enabled the North Vietnamese to cause the Chinese very heavy casualties in their '79 invasion.

138.   Mongolia: Lieutenant Colonel, Infantry, 1974.

In political terms, Mongolia leans more towards Moscow than Peking at present and the uniform shown here could be mistaken for that of the Soviet army as could the Combat dress. Just after World War II, the Mongolian officers wore a system of symbolic knots on their shoulder boards but these have now been replaced by Soviet pattern stars.

139.   Nationalist China: Military Police Staff Sergeant, 1978.
In contrast to the Red Chinese army, the Taiwanese forces have become very Americanized in general appearance. Corps badges are worn on the collar in this form of dress and on round brass discs for soldiers. The MP's badge (crossed pistols beneath an open book and under a flower blossom) appears on the belt plate and the red, white and blue chest badge, bearing a golden unicorn, is an emblem also peculiar only to the MP's. Badges of rank are worn on the arm (as here) or on the collar in fatigues and are similar to the U.S. army system. Weapons and equipment are American.

140.   U.S. Army in Vietnam: Specialist, 5th Class, 1965.
We see here the summer walking out uniform with regimental collar badges.

141.   U.S. Army in Vietnam: Airborne Trooper, 1970.
Standard U.S. equipment complete with jungle boots; the bottle in the helmet band is probably insect repellant. He wears the famous 101st Airborne's 'Screaming Eagles' formation sign.

142.   U.S. Army in Vietnam: Sergeant, 1st Class, 7th Special Forces Group, 1963.
The 'Green Berets' have a fighting reputation second to none and this N.C.O. has obviously 'been around'. On the shoulder straps are worn small enamelled badges which are traditionally linked to individual battalions of the fighting arms and equate to British regimental cap, collar, and button badges.

Black and White Plate Descriptions

143.   Soviet Personal Equipment.
Top to bottom: Basic 'skeleton order' of brown leather, the left pouch holds magazines for the AK 47; water bottle and entrenching tool are at the rear and grenades are carried in the right pouch. The Soviet respirator is still of the old-fashioned type with a long tube connecting the rubber head mask to the filter unit which remains in the haversack. To the right is the small leather pouch used by men armed with the SKS

rifle. Below left is the round-bottomed pouch for the drum magazines of the RPD MG. The pack is fitted with four strap loops to hold the folded greatcoat or raincape. The Soviet helmet is remarkably similar to the U.S. item in profile.

144/156.   Soviet Insignia.

In 1971 new uniforms began to be issued and they included arm badges (worn on the upper left arm) which expressed regimental and corps identity. *Top row:* **144.** armoured troops—black and yellow with red star. **145.** brass collar badge, armoured troops, this badge remained unchanged by the 1971 uniform reforms. **146.** airborne forces—light blue and yellow with red star.

Second row: shoulder boards for field uniform, Khaki with red embellishments. **147.** lance corporal. **148.** senior sergeant. **149.** sergeant major. **150.** lieutenant (one red stripe). **151.** major (two red stripes).

Third row: collar patches. **152.** armoured troops (parade, pre-1970; everyday and parade since then)—gold and black. **153.** artillery (daily wear, pre-1970) gold and black. **154.** motor rifles (field) matt bronze on khaki. **155.** Cyrillic gold letters worn since 1971 on parade and service shoulder boards by junior other ranks; they stand for 'Soviet Army'. **156.** length of service badges for other ranks; worn on the lower left sleeve; they are gold on red and here denote 5 to 9 years' service.

157/160.   Soviet Infantry Weapons.

157. APS (*Stetschkin*) 9 mm. pistol with the wooden holster shown here being used as a detachable butt. The weapon weighs 0.76 kg. unloaded; 1.78 kg. with butt. Barrel length 12.6 cm.; weapon length 22 cm. length with butt 54 cm. Effective range—up to 100 m., rate of fire—725 rpm.; the magazine holds 20 rounds. This weapon can fire single shots or bursts and is thus often called a machine-pistol.

Left to right: **158.** SKS (Self Loading Carbine (*Simonow*) 7.62 mm. rifle. This is a World War II vintage weapon no longer used by combat units of the Warsaw Pact Forces but often seen in the Third World. It has been built under licence in China (Type 56), Egypt (Raschid) and Yugoslavia (M-59 and M59/66). Its bayonet is permanently attached and folds down under the barrel. Length 1.022 m. (or 1.25 m. with bayonet fixed), barrel length .52 m.; effective range 400 m. Gas operated with piston; 30 rpm.; 10 shot magazine with the M-43 cartridge. **159.** AK 47 (*Kalaschnikow*). Perhaps the best known and certainly the most numerous infantry carbine in the world. Originally designed and produced during World War II, it has been copied by many states including China (Type 56), Czechoslovakia (M-58), Finland (M/60, M/62), East Germany (MPiKM), North Korea (Type 58, Type 68), Poland (PMK-DGN), Rumania and Hungary. It is a gas operated weapon operating on single shot or burst at 600 rpm.; 7.62 mm. calibre, barrel length .413 m. overall length .87 m. (1.070 with bayonet fixed); 30 shot magazine using the M-43 round; weight 3.8 kg. unloaded; effective range 400 m. Versions with collapsible butts have been produced. **160.** RPD (*Roschnoi Pulemet Detjarew*) 7.62 mm. LMG. Once again, a World War II weapon with drum magazine holding a belt of 100 M-43 cartridges. An improved version is the Soviet RPDM and it has been copied in China (Type 56 and Type 56-1) and in Korea (Type 62). Barrel length .52 m.; overall length 1.035 m.; effective range 800 m.; weight with bipods 7.08 kg. (8.8 kg. with full magazine); rate of fire—variable 650-750 rpm.

161/168.   Soviet Headdress.
Top to bottom: **161.** officers' khaki field service cap with khaki plastic cockade. **162.** Khaki side cap for other ranks with red and gold star badge. **163.** Khaki tropical hat with red and gold star. **164.** Winter grey fur cap 'USCHANKA' with red and gold star. **165.** Military police helmet, red and white—often bears cyrillic 'P' (R) for 'Regulators' as traffic police are called. **166.** light blue paratroopers' beret with new style OR's red and gold badge. **167.** Paratroopers' brown leather jump helmet. **168.** Tank crewmen's padded helmet with earphones.

169/172.   Warsaw Pact Headdress.
Top to bottom: **169.** Square-topped Polish army Czapka in olive drab with silver eagle badge—worn in fatigue dress. **170.** Polish mountain troops headdress—Edelweiss brooch to eagle feather plume. **171.** Hungarian field cap with khaki (plastic?) cockade. **172.** Czechoslovakian camouflage field cap' with khaki (plastic?) badge bearing a rampant lion.

173.   Yugoslav Mountain Trooper.
The white camouflage and snow goggles are international for these specialist troops; his weapon is the Yugoslav produced M-56 machine-pistol using the 7.62 mm. P (Tokarew) cartridge. Weight 3.06 kg. (3.6 kg. with full magazine of 32 rounds); barrel length .25 m.; overall length .64 m. (.87 m. with butt extended; 1.04 m. with butt extended

and bayonet fixed); effective range 100 m. It is a blow-back weapon with a firing speed of 600 rpm.

174/175. Poland.
Left: **174.** Major, summer camouflaged combat suit with the square-topped czapka and 9 mm. PM (Pistolet Makarowa) Soviet pistol with 8 round magazine; effective range 50 m.; weight .73 kg. (.81 kg. with full magazine); barrel length 9.8 cm., overall length 16 cm. With a muzzle velocity of about 330 m./sec., this is a relatively low-powered weapon. On the shoulder straps are the two silver bars under a star which signifies a major.

Right: **175.** Warsaw Pact, grey rubber NBC suit. The great problem with NBC clothing is the strains it places on the wearer, particularly in hot weather.

176/188. French and Warsaw Pact Insignia.
Top row: **176.** French Arm badge, Foreign Legion (dark green on dark blue). **177.** French corporal's chevrons (red on dark blue). **178.** French major's rank bars on camouflage jacket—brass bars on dark blue. **179.** French regimental device (pocket badge) of the 5th Infantry Regiment of the Foreign Legion (the Legion grenade on the map of Indo-China). *Second row:* **180.** Bulgarian combat dress shoulder boards —junior lieutenant (khaki, red stripe, silver star)—**181.** sergeant major (khaki, red edging and braid). **182.** Polish army woven cap badge. **183.** German Democratic Republic shoulder straps—Stabsgefreiter (corporal)—**184.** Unterfeldwebel (junior sergeant). *Bottom row:* **185.** Hungarian cockade (gold star and surround, red over white over green oval). **186.** Yugoslavian shoulder straps sergeant (two red chevrons)—**187.** junior lieutenant (gold star). **188.** Rumanian mountain troops silver shoulder badge.

189. United States Personal Equipment.
Khaki webbing and blackened metal fittings, widely used in the Middle and Far East. The small pouch on the right brace is for the field dressing; the two front pouches for ammunition and the small pack at the rear holds washing and eating equipment as well as rations. The folding entrenching tool can be worn as convenient around the belt, clipped through the many holes provided.

190/198. United States Army Insignia.

(Rank badges—gold on dark blue)—**190**. Private First Class. **191**. Sergeant Major. **192**. Specialist 5th Class. **193**. Captain's combat badge of rank (matt black on olive drab). **194**. Fatigue dress name tag (worn on right breast)—white with black letters. U.S. Army badges for (**195**) combat and (**196**) fatigue dress (black on olive drab); old pattern (gold on dark blue). Black on olive drab combat and fatigue arm patches. **197**. Airborne and special forces. **198**. 1st Air Cavalry Division.

199/201.　United States Infantry Weapons. 199. M60 7.62 mm. light machine-gun. Produced by Bridge Tool & Die Manufacturing Coy Inc. Overall length 1.105 mm., barrel length .65 m., effective range 600 m., gas operated action, 550-600 rpm, belt fed using the N.A.T.O. round giving up to 840 m./sec. muzzle velocity, weight 10.46 kg. Later versions include the M 60E1; the heavy MG version is called the M 122 (with range up to 1,100 m.), the helicopter version is the M 60C and the version produced in Taiwan is termed the M 60D. The IRA have recently been supplied with these weapons from America. **200**. M 16A1 Armalite SLR. Made by Colt, this weapon has a calibre of 5.56 mm., it weighs 2.95 kg. (3.18 kg. with bipod added). There are two magazines—20 or 30 round; rate of fire 700-800 rpm; effective range 300 m.; barrel length .508 m.; overall length .99 m.; muzzle velocity 990 m./sec. **201**. M 14 7.62 mm. Springfield SLR. This gas-operated weapon weighs 3.94 kg. with an overall length of 1.117 m.; barrel length .558 m.; effective range 300 m.; rate of fire 750 rpm; 20 round magazine; muzzle velocity up to 840 m./sec.

202/209.　United States Army Headdress.
202. Enlisted man's dark green, peaked garrison cap. **203**. Dark green beret of a captain, Special Forces (crimson patch, silver bars). **204**. Enlisted man's 'overseas cap'. **205**. Steel helmet with plastic liner, steel shell, camouflage cover and circular band for twigs, etc. Fatigue caps (**206**—1950; **207**—1960 style with senior sergeant's matt black rank chevrons). **208**. Winter khaki pile cap. **209**. Vietnam jungle camouflage hat.

210.　British 1958 pattern Web Equipment.
Olive drab webbing (requiring no cleaning or blancoing); the bayonet holder behind the pouch does away with a separate bayonet frog; below the two 'kidney pouches' is the cape carrier. The rigid shovel is being replaced by a much smaller folding entrenching tool.

211/220. British Insignia.

211. Royal Artillery Korean War brassard (red letters on dark blue) with light blue Commonwealth Division badge. 212. Second lieutenant's epaulette slide (black star). 213. Berlin Field Force arm patch, red on black. 214. Old pattern sergeant's chevrons (here red on white for wear by certain regiments in tropical khaki drill). 215. New pattern white on khaki for service dress. 216. Battle Dress sleeve of a company sergeant major, Parachute Regiment, 1955; lettering and Pegasus light blue on crimson; this man is a despatcher. 217. Lance corporal, marksman, signaller, 1st Bn Gloucestershire Regiment, 1957, with five years' service, lettering white on red; presidential citation royal blue edged gold (for Imjin River, Korea), yellow, red and blue Wessex brigade diamond patch. 218. Sleeve of Jungle Green jacket worn by sergeant, 1st Bn Royal Hampshires, 1954. Yellow lettering on black, light blue and white parachute wings, white on dark green Gurkha Brigade patch, white chevrons. 219. SD sleeve of corporal, Light Infantry, 1960; dark green chevrons on buff. 220. sleeve of DPM camouflage jacket; black chevrons on khaki.

221/224. British Infantry Small Arms.

221. L-7A2 7.62 mm. FN General Purpose Machine-Gun, Belgian designed N.A.T.O. weapon, 1.255 m. long; barrel length .569 m.; effective range 600 m.; a gas-operated weapon with variable rate of fire 700-1000 rpm; belt fed (500 or 200 round belts) using the N.A.T.O. round with up to 840 m./sec. muzzle velocity. Weight 10.84 kg. with bipod. 222. L-1A1 FN 7.62 mm. SLR. This gas operated weapon uses the same N.A.T.O. cartridge as the GPMG; length 1.09 m.; barrel length .533 m.; weight 4.32 kg. unloaded; 20 round magazine; effective range 300 m. 223. 4.85 mm. Individual Weapon (IW). This new weapon (known as Bullpup) is currently (1979) undergoing trials. The layout of the rifle will be familiar to those who remember the experimental British weapon produced in about 1946. It is a gas-operated, magazine-fed gun weighing 4.12 kg. with 20 round magazine (.398 kg.). Barrel length 51.85 cm.; overall length 77 cm.; 4 grooves in the barrel with up to 4.5 kg. trigger pull; muzzle velocity 900 m./sec., 4.42 Joules recoil energy; 700-850 rpm. It is made by the Royal Small Arms Factory, Enfield, Middlesex. The 4 x 4 SUSAT optical sight is a standard fitting. The weapon is all steel except the forestock which is nylon. It can be used on right or left shoulder with equal ease. 224. L-2A3, 9 mm. Sterling Sub Machine-Gun. This replaced the Sten of World

War II and later fame; a blowback weapon with 19.6 cm. barrel (48 cm. length with butt folded; 71 cm. with butt extended) a bayonet can be fixed. It weighs 2.72 kg. (3.74 kg. with bayonet and 34 round magazine). Effective range 75 m.; rate of fire 550 m./sec. Muzzle velocity up to 360 m./sec.

225/235. British Headdress.
225. Jungle hat (olive drab) also issued in light khaki for desert use. **226.** Gurkha hat (6th Gurkha Rifles); these are always two hats sewn together. **227.** Dark blue beret. 1st Bn Gloucestershire Regiment 1950-1979. This regiment wears a small sphinx within a wreath at the back of its headdress to commemorate the Battle of Alexandria (21 March 1801) when they fought back to back to beat off French attacks. **228.** Beige beret of Special Air Service Regiment with the dark blue patch and woven badge known as the 'Winged Dagger'. (The dagger was intended by its originator to be the 'Sword of Excalibur'.) **229.** Steel helmet with IS visor. **230.** 1970 pattern DPM combat cap. **231.** 1950 pattern olive drab combat cap. Three regimental side hats: **232.** Wessex Brigade—Gloucestershires (note back badge) dark blue and red. **233.** Royal Artillery red and dark blue. **234.** 9th/12th Prince of Wales' Own Royal Lancers, red and yellow. **235.** Parachutist's 'Bowler' jump helmet.

236. British Ammunition Technician in Explosive Ordnance Disposal Suit.
This bulky suit was developed to protect our ammunition technical officers (ATOs) from the blast effects of IRA bombs. It consists of several layers of Kevlar—a fibre originally used in the U.S. Space programme and having excellent ballistic protective properties—with extra glass-reinforced plastic shields to chest and pelvis. The helmet has an extremely heavy visor and a built-in radio communications set. As one ATO said to me 'It enables you to be buried in one piece!'

237. British Body Armour.
The situation in Northern Ireland has spurred development of protective clothing including the items shown here: a new, glass-reinforced plastic helmet (lighter than the steel item but with improved ballistic and shock protection); armoured vest (using Kevlar and having non-slip shoulder pads so that the rifle can be used with accuracy); leg shields of glass-reinforced plastic and various models of shields. The

riot baton is a slight refinement on Neanderthal Man's club.

238/248. Insignia, Various Nations.
Federal Germany—238. Oberfeldwebel, combat suit. **239.** Hauptfeld-webel's fatigue and combat shoulder strap slide. The colour of the cloth loop at the base gives the arm of service (infantry—green, tanks—pink, artillery—red, logistic services—blue, signals—lemon yellow, reconnaissance—deep yellow, engineers—black, NBC—crimson). **240.** Unterleutnant. **241.** Arm patch 1st Luftlande-Division light blue with black and white edge and white badge. The three brigades of the division have different coloured badge edgings as follows: 1st—white, 2nd—red, 3rd—yellow. **Italy—242.** Arm patch parachute brigade—red and yellow; shoulder strap rank badges: **243.** warrant officer—three gold stripes on red. **244.** right major—yellow frame and star. **245.** Arm patch (red and yellow) and yellow rank chevrons of a sergeant major, Folgore Division. **Israel—246.** Corporal's white sleeve chevrons. **247.** staff sergeant's chevrons with bronze olive leaf on the red backing used only by 'teeth arm' (fighting) units. **248.** Lieutenant's bronze bars on red backing.

249/252. French and Israeli Weapons.
249. French 7.5 mm. M-1949/56 MAS (Manufacture d'Armes de Saint-Étienne). A gas-operated, self-loading rifle, effective range 300 m.; weight 4.24 kg. empty (4.47 kg. loaded with a magazine of ten M-1929 rounds); barrel length .526 m.; overall length 1.102 m.; rate of fire 20 rpm; muzzle velocity approximately 800 m./sec. **250.** French MAT (Manufacture d'Armes de Tulle) 9 mm. Machine-Pistol M-1949. A blowback weapon weighing 3.63 kg. empty (4.23 kg. with 32-round magazine); barrel length 22.8 cm.; overall length 40.6 cm. (66.1 with extended butt); rate of fire 600 rpm; effective range 100 m.; muzzle velocity about 400 m./sec. **251.** Israeli 9 mm. UZI Sub Machine-Gun. A highly successful, Israeli-developed weapon also used by the Federal German army (there called the MP2A1-UZ1); the Belgian, Dutch, Peruvian, Portuguese and Thai forces. Apart from the wooden butt, there is a version with collapsible steel butt. It is a blowback weapon, effective range 100 m.; weight 3.51 kg. empty; barrel length 26 cm.; overall length 63.5 cm. (43.2 cm. with butt collapsed); rate of fire 550 rpm; muzzle velocity 400 m./sec. using Parabellum rounds. There are three magazines with 25, 32 or 40 rounds. **252.** Israeli 5.56 mm. GALIL Assault Rifle. Like the UZ1 this gas-operated rifle with collap-

sible butt is produced by Israeli Military Industries. Weight 3.9 kg. (4.6 kg. or 4.9 kg. with 35 or 50 round magazine); barrel length 46 cm.; overall length 98 cm. (74 cm. with butt folded); muzzle velocity 990 m./sec.; effective range 300 m.; rate of fire 650 rpm. The magazines hold 35 or 50 rounds.

253/255. Various Small Arms.

253. West German Gewehr G3A3 7.62 mm. Based on the Spanish CETME (Centro de Estudios Técnicos de Materials Especiales); this blowback rifle uses the standard N.A.T.O. cartridge in a 20-round magazine. It weighs 4.25 kg. (4.7 kg. fully loaded); length 1.02 m.; barrel length 45 cm.; effective range 300 m.; rate of fire 550 rpm; muzzle velocity 840 m./sec. **254.** Czechoslovakian 7.65 mm. M-61 Skorpion machine-pistol. This tiny, blowback weapon weighs 1.31 kg. (unloaded); barrel length 11.4 cm.; overall length 27.1 cm. (52.2 with butt extended); effective range 75 m.; rate of fire 700 rpm; 10 or 20 round magazines are available; the 7.65 mm. short Browning cartridge gives a muzzle velocity of approximately 290 m./sec. **255.** Australian 9 mm. F-1A1 sub machine-gun. This Australian-developed blowback weapon is similar to the British Sterling and is made by the Lithgow Small Arms Factory. Weight 3.26 kg. (4.47 kg. with bayonet and full 34-round magazine); barrel length 20.3 cm.; overall length 71.4 cm. (92.7 cm. with bayonet); effective range 75 m.; rate of fire 600 rpm; muzzle velocity 400 m./sec.

256. West German Personal Equipment. (Kampfaüsrüstung).
Students of World War II will doubtless recognise the old Wehrmacht leather equipment pattern, the principle has been retained although webbing is now used for belt, packs and straps; plastic coated webbing for ammunition pouches and for the zip-closed respirator haversack. The equipment has many metal-to-metal fittings and is noisy for night patrol work.

257. West German Muleteer of the Mountain Division Artillery.
The Italian-designed 105 mm. Pack Howitzer breaks down into four mule loads so that artillery support can be provided in mountainous terrain at times when helicopters (the alternative solution to artillery mobility in these areas) may well be grounded by bad weather. The Germans import mules from Sardinia as they carry these heavy loads better than domestic mules. The Austrian mountain artillery use a mix of mules and native Haflinger ponies (the latter for national prestige

reasons although they cannot carry the loads that a mule can).

258/261. Miscellaneous Headdress.
258. French Foreign Legion junior ranks' képi. **259.** French para-trooper's combat cap. **260.** West German Mountain Troops grey field cap with Edelweiss badge—exactly as for World War II. **261.** Malayan Races Liberation Army khaki cap with red star.

262/264. Asian Communist Equipment.
262. Magazine pouches for AK 47 magazines. **263.** Rice-carrying bandolier. **264.** Grenade pouches. Red China, North Korea and North Vietnam use these items.

265/269. Boots.
265. British DMS (Direct Moulded Sole) boot with the short puttee. **266.** Black U.S. field boot with composition sole. **267.** French canvas and rubber patrol boot. **268.** West German mountain troops boot. **269.** South African brown leather DMS boot—used by several African armies.

270/271. Boots.
270. British olive green canvas and rubber jungle boot. Footwear does not last long in the jungle and this boot was specially designed as a cheap, throw-away item. Commercial hockey boots have also proved their worth in this environment. **271.** Viet Cong Jungle Sandal soled with old rubber tyres. **272.** U.S. Vietnam nylon and leather topped boot with steel-reinforced DMS.